WINGSPAN
INSIDE THE MEN'S MOVEMENT

WINGSPAN™
INSIDE THE MEN'S MOVEMENT

EDITED BY
CHRISTOPHER HARDING
EDITOR OF

WINGSPAN™
JOURNAL OF THE MALE SPIRIT

ST. MARTIN'S PRESS
NEW YORK

To Peter, Nick, Luke, and Mark

You may never really understand what the men's movement means, but
you certainly know what it means to be loving brothers.

PRINTED ON RECYCLED PAPER

WINGSPAN INSIDE THE MEN'S MOVEMENT.
Copyright © 1992 by Wingspan: Journal of the Male Spirit™. All rights reserved. Printed in the United
States of America. No part of this book may be used or reproduced in any manner whatsoever without
written permission except in the case of brief quotations embodied in critical articles or reviews. For information, address St. Martin's Press, 175 Fifth Avenue, New York, NY 10010.

Editor: Jared Kieling
Production Editor: Eric C. Meyer
Copyedited by: Adam Goldberger
Design by: Robert Bull Design

LIBRARY OF CONGRESS CATALOGING-IN-PUBLICATION DATA

Harding, Christopher
    Wingspan: inside the men's movement / Christopher Harding.
        p.   cm.
    ISBN 0-312-07886-2
    1. Men—United Sates. 2. Masculinity (Psychology)—United
States I. Title
HQ1090.3.H37   1992
305.31—dc20   92-2781
                                               CIP

Wingspan: Journal of the Male Spirit™ is a trademark of Wingspan, a non-profit corporation.

First Edition: September 1992

10 9 8 7 6 5 4 3 2 1

Books are available in quantity for promotional or premium use. Write to Director of Special
Sales, St. Martin's Press, 175 Fifth Avenue, New York, NY 10010, for information on discounts and terms, or call toll-free (800) 221-7945. In New York, call (212) 674-5151 (ext. 645).

CONTENTS

What is Wingspan™?   ix
Acknowledgments   x
What's All This About a Men's Movement?   xi

PART I: ISSUES THAT CONCERN MEN   I

"Am I a Real Man?"   2
Call of the Wild—Asa Baber   4
   The appeal of Iron John and New Warrior Training to a veteran
   of divorce and the Vietnam War.
Longing for the Great Father—George Taylor   13
   Even with the best of human fathers, men long for contact with
   *   someone greater.*
Rainbows: A Poem by Hank Blackwell   16
Chain Saws to Toenail Clippers: Logger Turns Father—Mark Judelson 18
   A new father and former lumberjack faces the ordeal of snipping
   *   his son's toenails.*
Mentoring for Masculine Leadership—Joseph Palmour   22
   Fathers need mentors' assistance in raising their sons.
What a Man Becomes: An Essay on the Best of Friends—Edgar Allen Beem 30
   On different kinds of male friends.
Touching the Masculine Soul—Barry Cooney   36
   American males' reluctance to hug other men.
Mirrors on the Wall—John Guarnaschelli   39
   What sports photos say about men over the years.
Hung Like a Hamster: The Heavy Weight of a Small Penis—Greg Perry 41
   Lack of size can loom large in a man's life.
Notes on Three Erections—Michael Ventura   43
   Links between the men's movement, creativity, and sexuality.
Men and Intimacy—Douglas Gillette   52
   Men want intimacy; but are understandably wary.

Work and Gender —Michael Meade   60
    Interviewed by John Lang and Anthony Signorelli
    Women in the workplace challenge men's security.

"Male" is Not a Four-Letter Word—Jack Kammer   63
    According to men's rights activists, male bashing is rampant
    in the United States.

State of the Gender—Charles Varon   72
    Fellow males, take heed!

PART II: IN SEARCH OF MALE COMMUNITY   **75**

Support Groups, Councils, and Retreats   76
Dancing in the Cracks between Worlds—Tom Daly   80
    Daly recalls the wonder of boyhood, the isolation of traditional
    manhood, and the rediscovery of magic in the formation of
    a men's council.

Box H—Doug Hufnagel   84
    Not having "the slightest idea of what a men's group was," Hufnagel
    puts an ad in a Maine paper to try to start one.

My Conversation With Ernie—George Mathews   87
    Mathews unsuccessfully tries to invite a suspicious man to
    a men's dance.

Dance—Paul Reitman   90
    Nervous Reitman attends a men's dance for the first time.

The Force of Unseen Hands—John Taylor   92
    A comparison of fraternity initiation and men's rite initiation.

Men's Group: A Poem by James Oshinsky   94
What Happens at a Mythopoetic Men's Weekend?—Shepherd Bliss   95
    Veteran "group animator" Bliss describes the retreats he leads.

Finding the Door into the Forest—William R. Finger   100
    A classic Robert Bly, Michael Meade, James Hillman,
    and John Stokes five-day rustic retreat.

Creating Our Own Event—Eric Pierson   109
    Small-town men from Wisconsin improvise their own weekend
    retreat, but call it an "advance."

Men's Secret Societies—1890s to 1990s—Chris Harding   115
    Parallels between American fraternal organizations such as
    the Masons and Elks and men's groups of today.

PART III: LEARNING FROM MYTHOLOGY   **119**

What Oedipus, Narcissus, and Superman Can Teach Us   120
Why Use Myths and Fairy Tales? —George Taylor   122
    Ten points on why men should use stories and myth to mature.

The Dark Man's Sooty Brother—Robert Bly   127
  A Grimm Brothers' Story Retold
Male Naïveté and the Loss of the Kingdom—Robert Bly   130
  Appreciating the Grimm Brothers' tale
  of "The Dark Man's Sooty Brother."
Still Questing for the Holy Grail—Robert Cornett   137
  A blueprint for a workshop using Arthurian legend.
Renewing of the Flesh: Michael Meade on Storytelling   143
    Michael Meade interviewed by John Lang and Anthony Signorelli
  A master storyteller shares his secrets.

PART IV: LIVING THE MALE ARCHETYPES   **149**

Patterns from the Collective Unconscious   150
In Quest of Archetypal Masculinity—Aaron R. Kipnis   152
  Understanding archetypes as models for manhood.
Raj at The Bluffs: A Poem by Eric Kolvig   156
A Walk with the King—Gabriel Heilig   157
  One man's efforts to get in touch with the King archetype.
The Blessings of the Green Man—Aaron R. Kipnis   161
  Building ecological awareness through exploration
  of the Green Man.
For My Brothers: A Poem by Walton Stanley   166
Of Wild Men and Warriors—Christopher X. Burant   167
  Burant distinguishes between these two much talked about
  forms of male energy.
Spiritual Warrior—Joseph Jastrab   177
  Some men do battle without weapons.
Warrior Images—Gregory J. Scammell   184
  Memories of a Vietnam War veteran.
The Trickster Archetype: Potential and Pathology—Robert Moore   189
  This immature form of the Magician archetype brings welcome
  disruptions.
Roger Kose: Visual Poems of the Dreamtime—Tom de Mers   194
  An appreciation of and gallery of photographs by Roger Kose.

PART V: CEREMONIES: BODY AND SOUL WORK   **199**

Sacred Ceremony or "Goofy Circus"?   200
Ritual in Men's Groups—Bill Kauth   202
  Practical suggestions for simple rituals in men's support groups.
The Voice of the Drum—George A. Parks   206
  One man's passion for drumming with an overview
  of different kinds of drums.

Descent into Drum Time with the Sons of Orpheus—Bruce Silverman   213
    Inside San Francisco's all-men's weekly drumming group.
Every Man's Story, Every Man's Truth—Joseph Jastrab   218
    How to conduct a talking staff council.
Boxing: A Path with Heart—Ken Albright   223
    A physically oriented workshop with emotional release.

PART VI: CHALLENGES   **229**

Friendly Fire   230
The Mythopoetic Men's Movement: A Political Critique—Harry Brod   232
    Observations from the profeminist point of view.
Rapacious Normality: The War Between the Sexes—Sam Keen   237
    An unsparing attack on the old warrior mentality.
Masculinity and Sense of Community: An interview
    with James Hillman—Forrest Craver   242
    What kind of preparation does a man need for involvement
    in public life?

PART VII: RESOURCES   **249**

Now What?   250
Selected Men's Centers and Councils   253
Men's Movement Publications   256
Bibliographies   260
Book and Tape Sources   260
Other Resources   261
Photo Credits   264
About the Editor   265

What is Wingspan?

—————◯—————

MYTHOPOETIC MEN'S activity is here to stay as a deep, historical shift in world culture. Growing to keep pace with rapidly expanding interests, *Wingspan: Journal of the Male Spirit*, an international quarterly, has emerged as the movement's most comprehensive and widest circulation publication. This 16-page tabloid-sized newspaper is currently issued in editions of over 150,000 copies and has always been distributed free to anyone who requests a "subscription." Since 1986, *Wingspan* has been representing the scope of men's work through provocative leadership interviews, workshop profiles, discussions of myth, and poetry as well as timely reviews of men's books, films, and tapes.

The name *Wingspan* was chosen by Joseph Jastrab, who gave this explanation: "For many native people, the soaring eagle embodies the state of grace that is achieved through the completion of initiatory tests. These great birds have a spiritual perspective that helps us to see ourselves beyond the horizon of the familiar. Our original intention for *Wingspan* was that it serve to report on the personal and planetary initiatives taking place on the horizon of men's inner work these days.

There was an energetic connection to the image of a bird's wingspan that attracted me as well. As you spread your wings, your heart opens and becomes vulnerable and seen. So the name of the journal honors the hearts of men willing to leap into the horizon and return with a story of their journey."

Most of *Wingspan*'s financial support comes from the generosity of its readers, and most of its staff works on a volunteer basis. Nearly 1,000 men and women around the world receive *Wingspan* in bundled units of 50 copies and distribute them free to men's groups, churches, therapists' offices, prisons, libraries, personal growth centers, health food stores, universities, independent book stores, restaurants, and a host of other locations, even in Laundromats.

Anyone interested in receiving a sample copy or becoming a distributor of *Wingspan* is invited to write: *Wingspan*, P.O. Box 23550, Brightmoor Station, Detroit, MI, 48223.

ACKNOWLEDGMENTS

—————————⬤—————————

THIS BOOK is the result of a project that lay fallow for several years and then came together in a relatively short period of time. Many fellow writers would envy my having an editor of the stature and good humor of Jared Kieling, who swooped down with an invitation to bring this gathering of men's writings into print. His unfailing courtesy and his personal enthusiasm for men's work made a complex and daunting project much easier.

My former partners in the *Wingspan* enterprise, publisher Robert Frenier and marketing director Forrest Craver, were invaluable in negotiating contracts and chasing down permissions from elusive authors. I feel a sincere and deep gratitude to all those who contributed their words or pictures to this book, asking for little or nothing in return. I am proud to be able to showcase your achievements in this book and in *Wingspan*. To those men who offered pieces for which there was ultimately not enough room, my apologies and my appreciation.

To George Fanning and the Blue Devil Jet, thanks for friendship and top-notch limo service. To Joseph Jastrab, who first introduced me to men's work in 1984, you continue to be an inspiration.

The biggest debt of gratitude goes not to a man, but to a woman. Ruth Munden did much more than word-process the manuscript. Her organizational abilities and forethought made the process of fitting this book together much easier and smoother than it would have been if I had been left to my own devices. But most importantly, her sense of fun and ready laughter brightened our hours working together immeasurably.

—CHRISTOPHER HARDING

x

WHAT'S ALL THIS
ABOUT A MEN'S MOVEMENT?

—————●—————

AT THE conclusion of Opening the Heart for Men, a retreat held on a rural hillside in central Massachusetts, participants were asked to summarize their feelings about the weekend. When his turn came, one man took a deep breath, threw back his shoulders, and announced simply, "I glory in my manhood."

Most men these days could not make the same declaration with a straight face or with much conviction. Many women, on hearing such a statement, might shake their heads, thinking that being a Y-chromosome bearer is something to be a little ashamed of rather than boasted about.

Sadly, many, perhaps most, men lack pride in their masculinity. No matter how tough, cool, or jovial they may seem on the outside, inwardly many guys feel a little sheepish: spiritually and emotionally inferior to women, physically and financially inferior to other men. However pleased a man may be about himself as an "individual," he often senses there is something vaguely wrong with being proud of being a *man*. Any gleam of male pride these days is likely to be dismissed as ungrounded and unhealthy, and may even be equated with "typical male chauvinism" or "machismo."

Some champions of women ceaselessly remind men that they are to blame for all the woes of the world. It is men who wage war. It is men who cut down the rain forests and destroy the ozone layer. It is men who profit off the misery of starving babies in Third World economies. Wholesale male bashing is a politically correct activity practiced freely by those who wouldn't dream of making similar sweeping criticisms about Jews, blacks, or women. George F. Will in a *Newsweek* column on men summarized the predominant dim view of men when he wrote without irony, "Nature blundered badly in designing males . . . because of neurochemical stuff like testosterone, males are not naturally suited to civilization."

This smear campaign that most of us don't even stop to question takes a terrible toll on men's self-esteem. Like fish swimming in polluted water, the majority of men never notice how their environment is poisoning them. A Colorado newspaper column entitled "Masculinity Is Not a Disease" reported how male students at Berkeley were signing up for assertiveness-training courses because the political atmosphere at the university made them so profoundly ashamed of their gender. These men had clearly overdosed on the pernicious message with which our culture bombards us from all sides—namely, that men are wayward, unloving, naturally defective creatures.

Counter to this prevailing sentiment and arising partly in response to it, the growing men's movement is largely about men discovering the simple truth that being male is "an honorable estate." In essence, the men's movement involves men gathering in large groups and small to consider what it means to be a man today. The group may be as intimate as five guys who meet in a particular booth at their favorite diner for breakfast every Monday, or as populous as a thousand men who assemble in a civic auditorium for a day of poetry recitals and analysis of myths.

These gatherings provide positively charged environments that a man can visit as often as he needs to be inspired and empowered. Even a single weekend retreat can open his eyes to the deep passions and the heroic altruism that he never suspected lay beneath the inexpressive fronts of his fellow workers and neighbors. Regular attendance at support groups or council meetings can reinforce and deepen these insights, providing him frequent opportunities to readjust his attunement and to continue unlearning negative stereotypes about fellow males.

All over the country—all over the world, in fact—men are flocking together in whatever settings and organizational formats seem most congenial in their region. In this roll-up-your-sleeves, do-it-yourself movement, men get to exercise their genius for invention. Men's groups vary dramatically and marvelously in size, structure, tone, purpose, orientation, sophistication, longevity, and sense of humor. Most men celebrate the movement's diversity and their region's unique character, resisting calls for homogenization, umbrella organizations, and national agendas. They would rather merrily dance to their local piper than fall into a lockstep march behind the banner of any army, no matter how noble.

It's not easy to convey in a few words what really drives our men's movement. Unlike the women's movement, which is largely outwardly directed, aimed at changing laws, societal structures, and other people's way of thinking, the men's movement is inwardly directed. It is generally much less concerned with new dogmas and presuming to "correct" other people's thought patterns and behavior than it is with encouraging men to find and follow their individual path, that personal myth or mission that will give meaning and form to their lives. Much of the movement is so revolutionary and wonderful that it is difficult to explain succinctly or to really understand without actually experiencing it. But it is not all "Out with the old, in with the new." Much of it harkens back to the best that has characterized typically male behavior for centuries.

While the focus of men's work is not directly on societal change, the movement certainly has far-reaching benefits for individual couples, families, and society in general. For example, men's retreats provide opportunities and safe container-spaces for the catharsis of pent-up anger and rage that might otherwise be expressed dysfunctionally at home.

FOUR MAIN BRANCHES OF THE MEN'S MOVEMENT

It is often remarked that it might be more accurate to refer to the men's movements rather than a single men's movement because there seem to be so many diverse, even opposing contingents claiming to be the "real" men's movement—or the "real men's" movement. At the outset it is useful to distinguish, in theory at least, four major branches, remembering that in practice and in individual instances, distinctions are not easy to make.

A. The Mythopoetic Branch is a freewheeling exploration of male spirituality and male psychology (especially from a Jungian perspective). It encourages men to delve into their psyches by reintroducing them to literature, mythology, and art. Adherents are primarily heterosexual, midlife men.

- By far the biggest and fastest-growing segment of the movement.
- Often identified by the press and in the public's mind as "the" men's movement.
- Some retreats have a pronounced neoprimitive quality. Widespread borrowing from Native American traditions includes exploration of such forms as the medicine wheel, the sweat lodge (or sweat cave), talking staff/stick council, and the giveaway ceremony.
- *Most popular activities:* small weekly or biweekly support group meetings (5–10 men); citywide, drop-in monthly council meetings featuring drumming, rituals, and presentations (30–300 men); weekend or weeklong rustic retreats (20–150 men); one- or two-day lectures (100–1500 men).
- *Publications: Wingspan, Men's Council Journal, Inroads.*
- *Most widely recognized authors-presenters:* Shepherd Bliss, Robert Bly, Douglas Gillette, James Hillman, Robert Johnson, Michael Meade, Eugene Monick, Robert Moore.
- *Strongholds*: Midwest, especially Minnesota, and Colorado; greater Washington, D.C.

- *Critics Say:* Self-indulgent, ignoring pressing problems of the world while play-acting meaningless rituals; disrespectful of Native American traditions.

B. The Profeminist/Gay-affirmative Branch encourages men to renounce sexist, homophobic, and racist behavior and thought. It is supportive of men to the extent they are willing to change and adopt this branch's political philosophy. It vigorously lobbies for women's rights, gay rights, and other minority causes. It celebrates gay and bisexual love.

- Best established, grew up alongside the women's movement.
- Known in the 1970s as "men's liberation."
- Virtual monopoly on the content of university men's studies courses and academic journals.
- Membership declining because critical attitude toward men alienates many potential supporters and newer branches offer more positive alternatives.
- *Most popular activities:* Protest marches (BrotherStorm, Brother Peace; Take Back the Night) (50–200); concerts and entertainments with a satirical political slant (50–100); annual conference on men and masculinity (500 men and women).
- *Publications: Changing Men, R.F.D.*
- *Most widely recognized authors-presenters:* Robert Brannon, Harry Brod, John Stoltenberg.
- *Strongholds:* New England; Madison, Wisconsin; much of California.
- *Critics say:* Populated by men who were hurt by males as children and now are getting back at white males by championing women; heterophobic gays and bisexuals far outnumber straight men in their ranks.

C. Men's Rights/ Fathers' Rights groups are largely focused on changing laws and the public's perception of men. Fathers' rights groups lobby for changes regarding child custody, child support awards, rights of unmarried fathers, and abortion issues. Men's rights advocates, who tend to be very militant, rail against male-only draft laws, abrogation of men's rights in laws designed to protect women from violence, and male bashing in the media.

- Fathers' rights groups tend to be populated by financially strapped "walking wounded" victims of divorce courts. There is a considerable turnover in membership because men tend to stop coming to meetings once their personal legal situation is resolved or they begin a new relationship.
- Men's rights attracts only a handful of men, but they tend to be very media savvy and command attention to a degree disproportionate to their numbers.

- *Most popular activities:* Father's Day events involving kids; legal strategy sessions; media campaigns.
- *Publications: Transitions, The Liberator.*
- *Most widely recognized authors-presenters:* Frances Baumli, Mel Feit, John Gordon, Warren Farrell.
- *Strongholds:* New York City, Texas.
- *Critics say:* Woman haters pure and simple; men hurt by females as children or through divorce now getting back at women by championing men.

D. Addiction/Recovery groups evolved out of twelve-step programs like Alcoholics Anonymous. Newcomers resonate with terms like "woundedness," "toxic masculinity," and "inner child." Confronting grief over unhappy relationship with father is a big issue.

- Second only to mythopoetic branch in size, and there is an ever-increasing exchange of ideas and practices between these two branches.
- *Most popular activities:* "Men in Recovery" gatherings; lectures and workshops.
- *Publications: Man!, Quest.*
- *Most widely recognized authors/presenters:* Marvin Allen, Jed Diamond, John Lee.
- *Strongholds:* Southwest.
- *Critics say:* Premised on negative ideas that men are wounded, poisoned by their testosterone, and need to be "fixed" by therapists.

Lance Morrow, in a profile of Robert Bly for *Time* magazine, reports that "by Bly's calculation there are at least seven different men's movements: 1) a sort of right-wing men's movement that is, in fact, frequently antifeminist; 2) feminist men; 3) men's rights advocates who think, for example, that men get a raw deal in divorce; 4) the Marxist men's movement; 5) the gay men's movement; 6) the black men's movement, extremely important in Bly's view because of the devastation to black males in American society; and 7) men in search of spiritual growth, the Bly wing of the idea, dealing with mentors and 'mythopoetics.' The mythopoetic characters, Bly points out, are dividing into two groups: those concentrating on recovery, and those, like Bly, who are interested in men's psyches as explored by art, mythology and poetry."

Men drawn to the mythopoetic men's movement tend to be older than the men who were involved with men's liberation a generation earlier. Studies of men's liberation participants put the median age between 18 and 35, while mythopoetic men tend to be in the 35 to 50 range. Men's libbers tended to have wives or close female friends involved in the women's movement. Mythopoetic men count among their number a substantial number of divorced men who, suddenly without their sole emotional outlet, discover that in many ways men can understand other men better than a woman can, no matter how sympathetic she is.

Many feminists simultaneously take credit for and dismiss the men's movement as simply an outgrowth of and reaction against the women's movement. While the profeminist, gay-affirmative men's groups and the fathers' rights/men's rights organization certainly respond either positively or negatively to issues raised by women's advocates, the mythopoetic majority are apples that coexist peaceably enough with women's-issue oranges but have their focus principally on other matters.

However the contingents are defined, there is generally a cordial relationship among the groups. On a few issues, like questioning the value of circumcision, there is some agreement among all branches. At most large gatherings, there are likely to be men who range over the whole spectrum of opinion. Some organizations such as the Twin Cities Men's Center pride themselves on being a forum for all aspects of the movement, scheduling meetings of divorced men, gay men, and mythopoetic men on different nights of the week. Their publications (in this case *Men Talk*) reflect that diversity of opinion. A given edition might contain one article supporting a feminist position and another questioning it.

MEDIA DISTORTIONS

Various commentators (most of whom have little or no firsthand experience of the men's movement) have disputed whether there really is such a thing because to them the term "movement" necessarily implies a segment of the general population with a clear political agenda, engaged in concerted motion in one direction. Some people have denied the *existence* of a men's movement when what they should be saying is that perhaps the word "movement" is a *misnomer*.

Semantics aside, there can be no question that there has been a deep and widespread cultural shift taking place in our society. It's easy to document that there is a lot of activity going on. In every state and province of North America, there are men's support groups and councils with new ones forming all the time. They vary greatly in focus, size, history, and purpose. In California, a state with the reputation of being in the vanguard of trends, it's not so surprising that among the scores of support groups there are ones for men with disabilities and others for bisexual Asian men. But men's activity is going strong in some little towns in the heartland and the Smoky Mountains as well as in big coastal cities, from the Sawtooth Mountains Gathering of Men in Idaho and Hawaii Men's Gathering at Kalani Honua to the Little Rock Men's Council in Arkansas.

Any reporter who presumes to cover this subject should first be forced to write a hundred times on the blackboard: The men's movement is not a cult and Robert Bly is not its guru. An isolated photograph or an article written by someone who bolted halfway through a workshop can make the proceedings at any event seem a tad bizarre. Imitating animals, invoking ancestors, or wearing masks can seem strange if we judge these activities from within the context of our everyday lives. But the purpose of these exercises is to try to get in touch with parts of our bodies and minds that have been cramped and sealed off from our day-to-day consciousness. Unlike the strictly regimented thinking and behavior in true cults, the men's movement celebrates individual discovery and personal process, rather than orthodoxy. Though there's a lot of soul searching and discussion about male spirituality, no one has even suggested establishing any universal doctrines or creeds.

Though reporters repeatedly make the mistake of labeling Robert Bly a guru, he is far from being a self-styled spiritual leader like the Reverend Sun Myung Moon. True, there are "Blydolators," star-struck, grandfather-hungry fans who hang on his words and actually go up to him at intermission for a few personal words and what amounts to a blessing. Bly usually affably accedes to their requests, but  he has repeatedly declared, "I hate being a pop figure," and he advises men to work out their father issues with their real fathers and grandfathers rather than to attempt the process with surrogates like himself.

Also indicating that Bly is no Jim Jones is the sometimes very vocal negative response of large segments of his men's audiences to his pronouncements about the nature of war and the corrupt motives behind the U.S. campaign against Saddam Hussein. Veterans especially have expressed sharp disapproval; they see Bly's and fellow presenter Michael Meade's area of expertise as poetry and myth and feel that these two men's personal feelings about international politics are "not what we paid to hear about."

Bill Moyers's television interview with Robert Bly, "A Gathering of Men," and the chart-topping sales history of *Iron John* have led some media observers to the erroneous conclusion that the movement is a recent phenomenon, the trickle-down result of Bly's media success. Quite the reverse, Bly's words and personality brought to the surface issues that have been concerning men for the last couple of decades. When one studies the scope of men's activity and remembers that the Twin Cities Men's Center in Bly's home state of Minnesota has been in existence for 15 years, one realizes that this is a grass-roots phenomenon.

Much of the recent media coverage of the movement has suggested that men are now

rejecting "the John Wayne mentality" and learning "that it is okay for men to cry." While this reductive description might have characterized the men's liberation movement of the 1970s, it is too narrow and inaccurate to describe what is going on in the 1990s. Certainly there are those who have been crippled by exaggerated macho expectations and are liberating themselves from those constraints—by feeling freer to express emotions. But there are also those among us who are disappointed with the so-called Alan Alda sensitive male. How poorly we have examined stereotypes about men may become a little more apparent when we stop to think that John Wayne's real name was Marion Morrison, that he never served a day in the real military, and that he wore makeup when he went to work. On the other hand, sensitive Alan Alda is best known for his role of the womanizing practical joker Hawkeye Pierce on "M *A * S *H."

For many men who sensed themselves to be different from the images of men presented in the media, the men's movement is a godsend. Men who felt isolated, thinking they were the only ones on earth with such sensibilities, are overjoyed to discover like-minded men. The real average Joe does not sit around puffing on his pipe reading leather-bound volumes in a den decorated with duck decoys the way greeting cards picture him. He may never have been to a Saturday night poker game with the boys—an activity that's more a figment of TV than a fixture in men's lives; on Saturday night, he is too busy tucking in kids whom he may only get to see on the weekends. And certainly he doesn't feel himself to be the ruthless planet-raper social critics make him out to be, even if he remains manfully silent and lets the slurs against his gender go unchallenged.

ABOUT THIS BOOK

Most of the essays that follow were either commissioned especially for this book or come from the last 15 years of the new men's press. The book naturally reflects two kinds of articles that appear in such publications: 1) reports on and descriptions of the status of men and various aspects of the movement and 2) personal accounts of what it felt like to participate in events.

Part of the impetus for compiling this book came from the desire to correct impressions created by the media. Many commentators remain stuck in an either-or dichotomy: if you're pro-men, you must be anti-women, and vice versa. Fortunately, those involved in gender reconciliation are getting out the message that the best parts of the women's movement and the best parts of the men's movement are not incompatible.

In recent years there have been best-sellers about men, but like *Men Who Hate Women and the Women Who Love Them*, most of them pandered shamelessly to women's insecurities and martyr complexes by perpetuating negative stereotypes of men. In stark contrast, the one you hold in your hands is unabashedly positive about men, and frankly evangelical about the men's movement, especially the mythopoetic branch. This gathering of essays, personal accounts, and poems challenges readers to perceive the hurtfulness and unfairness of stereotypes about men and rediscover the perceptiveness, wit, compassion, and beauty of males. Those readers with the lowest opinion of men will get the biggest surprises about the depth of men's grief, passion, and hunger for a full life.

At the outset, we might sound a lament for the fact that the vocabulary we have for talking about men has been denigrated and distorted. The term "male bonding," popularized by Lionel Tiger in his 1969 anthropological study *Men in Groups*, is now—thanks in no small part to the depiction of the relationship between yuppies Michael Steadman and Elliott Weston, characters on the former ABC show "thirtysomething,"—used derisively, with condescending or sniggering overtones. Likewise, a "patriarch" used to be a high compliment reserved for the likes of Old Testament figures like Abraham or heads of TV clans like "Bonanza"'s Ben Cartwright; now "patriarchy" is an all-purpose, male bashing term, equivalent to "evil empire." Even the tongue-tripping word "mythopoetic" is an uncomfortable one to be saddled with. Mocking versions of the word like "mumbopoetic" and "mythopathetic" point to the fact that even some movement insiders consider the term unwieldy.

Shepherd Bliss seems to be have been the first person to apply this last adjective to a wing of the men's movement. In an article called "Beyond Machismo: The New Men's Movement" in the November-December 1986 issue of the *Yoga Journal*, he chose "mythopoetic," a rather obscure literary term, to describe the movement because he was dissatisfied with the phrase "New Age men's movement" that was coming into fashion. Bliss, a scholar of mythology who studied under Mircea Eliade, used the term correctly to mean "creating or making myth." Yet often "mythopoetic" is misunderstood to mean "myth 'n' poetry."

The term "mythopoetic" also has an elitist ring that alienates men who haven't been to college, and many men who have. This reaction is unfortunate since a basic tenet of the movement is that all males have much in common and that common denominators, not differences, should be our focus. Despite the generally perceived inadequacy of the term, no one has been able to come up with a generally accepted replacement—though some have suggested "men's soul movement" and "men's renewal movement."

This book aims higher than simply to rebut criticisms of the male sex in general and of the mythopoetic men's movement in particular. Rather than coming out of a purely reactive stance, it frankly and proactively recruits men to adopt this new-old way of living in a male body and to rekindle the vitality that is lacking in so many lives. The writing of dozens of different men here attests to the universality of certain doubts, fears, and feelings of emptiness and futility as well as to the easily realized possibility of transcending those negative emotions and finding previously unimagined fulfillment in newly discerned identities as friends, lovers, artists, and citizens of the planet.

This book sounds the call to high adventure, latent even in the most ordinary setting. It points the way for those men who feel something scared, yet excited stirring inside, responding to that call they only half understand. Like the quarterly newspaper *Wingspan: Journal of the Male Spirit*, where many of the following pieces first appeared, this book is meant above all to whet the appetite. Reading other men's thoughts, and considering in private how those ideas relate to one's own experiences, are merely first steps that must lead to physically venturing into new encounters with men and nature. Perusing leads to sharing from the heart, helping and accepting help, growing and fostering growth, and acting as a man with all the responsibilities and opportunities that role implies.

This book is intended to sharpen men's hunger for soul growth and adventure. It then outlines practical, proven ways of satisfying that hunger and provides the resources and contacts to get started.

Women will find this book full of surprises. Its candid firsthand accounts about what specifically goes on at men's gatherings may confirm certain suspicions, but are more likely to uncover a range of emotion and behavior that men rarely permit themselves to exhibit in the presence of females. When they learn the scope of men's work, women often remark that they had no idea that men could feel as deeply as they do. Many a man pens poetry in secret, even if the subject of his ode is not his spouse but his BMW. This book will go a long way in explaining the issues that every man struggles with, but it will be particularly valuable to women in relation-

WHAT'S ALL THIS
ABOUT A MEN'S
MOVEMENT?

ships with men who disappear mysteriously for weekends (especially at solstices and equinoxes) or who make cryptic allusions to their kiva. Such knowledge, coupled with sympathy and goodwill, can enable a woman to support her man in his quest for wholeness; such understanding and support will be richly repaid in a vastly improved relationship.

Before exploring the men's movement per se, Part I of this book looks at issues that concern all men, including being a father, being a son, finding a mentor, making friends, becoming intimate with women, and coming to terms with body image, work, and society's image of men. In Part II, men recount their first, often fumbled, attempts to create a safe male community. Part III demonstrates how folk tales, legends, and myths continue to serve as useful guides to mature masculinity, while Part IV introduces some basic concepts of Jungian psychology and demystifies the archetypes of the Wild Man, the King, the Warrior, and the Trickster.

Rituals like drumming and the talking staff council are the focus of Part V, while criticisms of the mythopoetic movement make up Part VI. The book concludes with a comprehensive, up-to-date resource guide, listing men's centers, publications, counseling services, and book and tape outlets all over North America. Scattered throughout the book are specialized bibliographies on such topics as male-female relationships and sexual abuse. There are even top ten video rental suggestions for home film festivals on subjects like mentoring and buddies.

Wingspan™ *Inside the Men's Movement* musters striking pictures and words to give readers an in-depth, plain-English introduction to what will doubtless be one of the most significant social forces of the 1990s. May the stories men tell here inspire and challenge many others to spread their wings and so unfold the glory of their own manhood. 🖋

I

ISSUES THAT CONCERN MEN

"Am I a real Man?"

WHAT ISSUES preoccupy men? What topics do men discuss at men's gatherings that they very often have no other place in their lives to examine?

Men are concerned about being good providers, good fathers, good sons, good husbands, good lovers, good friends, good leaders, and good workers. But many of these questions boil down to "Am I a real man?"

Our society is largely driven by the simple but insidious mechanism of withholding from its male drones a sense of secure masculinity. In order to keep a man working and competing and achieving, he is kept in doubt about whether he is a real man. In order to keep him acquiring and consuming, he is offered products and services to keep this uncertainty at bay. Yet no matter how much money he earns, how striking his build, what the size of his penis, or what make of car he drives, the average guy is left with the uneasy suspicion that perhaps he isn't all the man he could be or should be. Many men would rather die than admit this gnawing fear, but silence doesn't limit the scope of the problem. In fact, silence makes the pressure more intense.

The benefits to society of this withholding are great. It keeps men producing, creating, building, and pioneering, in endless efforts to prove themselves. It's no news that men take credit for the vast majority of inventions, artworks, and organizations in world history, but the cost to the individual man is high. Men die eight to nine years earlier than women. Males are much more likely than females to keep working when health problems flare up. Little boys are taught early, "You gotta play hurt" and "No pain, no gain."

The focus of societal reform in the last two decades has been on what women need, deserve, want, and demand. The needs and deserts of men have been largely ignored because if men are considered at all, they are assumed to be in a position of power. In reality, many men feel trapped and powerless. They may earn money, but they abdicate to their wife or ex-wife responsibility for deciding how to spend it. They don't have the hope for change that women do, or expect that their situation will get (or even merits) a sympathetic hearing. Manliness is equated with silence and the uncomplaining taking of one's lumps.

I've a poster, and it says "Lost Dog" at the top. Underneath it says, "Three legs, blind in left eye, missing right ear, tail broken, recently castrated . . . answers to the name of Lucky." Many people who are attacking the patriarchy imagine that men are "lucky." They imagine these "lucky" men have power. But this poster is closer to the situation of men now.
—Robert Bly
in an interview with the *Bloomsbury Review*, January-February 1991

In a society more concerned about the rights of women reporters to be present in a pro football locker room than with nude male players' rights to shower and dress in privacy, it is hard to argue for the fact that men need safe all-male spaces in which to form and consolidate their masculine identities. Many men are afraid they will be dismissed as hopelessly chauvinistic or old-fashioned or worse—"in the closet"—if they resist the opening of every all-male organization to both men and women. Even if they could articulate the pressing need for bonding space, the plea would likely sound too airy and unmasculine to be taken seriously. Yet if healthy, constructive environments are denied them, young men will create unhealthy, destructive ones such as gangs. There is no question that some all-male organizations have their shadow side. Adding women to the mix, however, is not always the solution.

Men have a profound innate need to be affirmed in their masculinity by other males. Some men feel they do all the proving of their virility they need to by sleeping with a string of women or by fathering a child. These are among the affirmations a woman can give a man that other men cannot. Perhaps even more important, but less easy to pinpoint, are those ways in which a man can be affirmed by another in his masculinity, ways in which no woman can validate him no matter how earnestly she might wish to.

We are told that men in centuries past got a comfortable sense of masculinity from their fathers and their mentors. Today middle-aged men report that the number-one issue drawing them into the men's movement is the sense that here at last is a place to voice and grieve their unsatisfactory or nonexistent relationships with their fathers. There's a lot of talk about physical and/or emotionally absent dads, but sons are also beginning to ask themselves, Was my father really absent, or did he and I unconsciously conspire to ignore each other?

The first section of this book, its symbol the maze, concentrates on the concerns that men carry with them into the movement. If more men had truly satisfactory relationships with their fathers, mentors, friends, and lovers, perhaps there would be no need for a men's movement. ✍

CALL OF THE WILD

[Originally appeared in *Playboy* magazine.]

BY ASA BABER

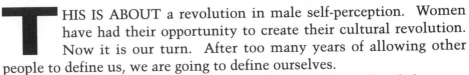

Asa Baber has been called the "unsung crusader of the American male." As the Men columnist for *Playboy* magazine for the last nine years, he has a huge audience of men. Though many dismiss *Playboy* as slick, outmoded, and hedonistic, he writes courageously in its pages about painful issues like divorce, separation from children, and survivor guilt. An ex-marine, proud father, and active leader of the men's movement, he makes a perfect bridge between "ordinary" Middle America and the still-new men's movement. 🖋

THIS IS ABOUT a revolution in male self-perception. Women have had their opportunity to create their cultural revolution. Now it is our turn. After too many years of allowing other people to define us, we are going to define ourselves.

Just for openers, do you remember when you first realized that men had their own problems in this culture? Was there a moment when you saw that sexism was as frequently targeted against men as against women?

When did you recognize that the formation of a solid male identity was not always easy to achieve in this society, that there were as many obstacles to growth and maturity *and equality* for men as there were for women?

And, finally, how long have you yearned to turn this feminized and prejudiced culture on its ear and assert your own identity and work as a man?

Stick around; the next revolution is happening. Men—the average guy, not the GQ dandy, not the teacher's pet—are taking back the culture. It is a great time to be alive.

The seeds of my own revolution were planted early. The year was 1973. The place was Honolulu. At the time, I was losing custody of my two sons, Jim and Brendan, ages eight and five.

The sexism against men that I found in divorce court and its attendant provinces was overwhelming. In law offices, in courtrooms, in counseling sessions with the so-called experts who staffed the system, in classroom meetings with teachers and administrators, I was learning that the sexist bias against men in child-custody matters was intense and all-encompassing. The male in the divorce process was considered an irrelevant appendage to the nuclear family.

I fought hard for it, but I knew in my heart that I didn't have much of a chance of winning custody of Jim and Brendan. In those days, something like 95 percent of contested child custody cases were resolved in favor of the mother. (The figures are a little better today, but the system is still stacked against the father's rights.)

I had been a good father, a very involved father, a man who had spent at least as much time with his children as their mother had. But I lost custody of my sons, and the weight of that decision shattered me. I was losing the two most important people in my life, young sons who had taught me how to love, how to nurture, how to pare down my aggressive ego and place other human beings ahead of myself.

After the divorce, I went through several years of feeling unmanly and useless. Cut off from my sons—communication between us often obstructed, visitation frequently under threat of change and postponement—I had no pride in myself as a male.

All of these difficulties and failures were important things for me to experience, however. Without any preconceived plan, I started writing about the subject of men and the sexist prejudices they endure. At first, I wrote for myself to explain things to myself. And then I got lucky. *Playboy* published an article of mine in December 1978 titled "Who Gets Screwed in a Divorce? I Do!" In that article, I talked about the difficult problems that men face in divorce and child-custody cases. I discussed the need for divorce reform. I also considered a larger subject (and one that is central to the next revolution): How can we find identity and pride in self-worth *as men*?

It was a simple but important question, and not many people were asking it publicly in those days. "Men must begin making a case for themselves," I wrote. "Manhood is an honorable condition . . . . It seems clear that men need help today perceiving themselves as men, and such help can come only from themselves." I outlined certain qualities that American males have in abundance but do not always advertise, including qualities such as courage, generosity, sensitivity, intellect, wit, and humor. "Men have a job to do redefining our roles and reaching out for health and identity," I wrote.

My 1978 prediction about male resourcefulness turned out to be accurate. It took us a while, but here at the beginning of the nineties, we are redefining our roles as men. That is what the next revolution is about: the establishment of a tough *and* loving male identity that cannot be obliterated by the sexism and prejudice under which we live.

We are aiming for the very best qualities of manhood. In pursuit of this goal, groups of men across the country are starting to meet on evenings and weekends to attend workshops, to think and explore and write and examine their roles as men. True, their efforts are occasionally awkward and improvisational and, yes, there are times when their methods could easily be mocked and misunderstood. But that does not discourage them. "For this is the journey that men make," wrote James Michener in *The Fires of Spring*. "To find themselves. If they fail in this it doesn't matter what else they find."

This is Daddy's bedtime secret for today. Man is born broken. He lives by mending. The grace of God is glue.
—Eugene O'Neill, *Great God Brown*

BABER
CALL
OF THE WILD

5

In April 1982, I published my first Men column, "Role Models." In it, I talked about the way men learn and work and grow: "Men are by nature collegiate. We are convivial scavengers, patching our personalities together with chewing gum and baling wire. We collect traits from a million different sources."

The sources we are using to patch together our male revolution are likewise numerous and eclectic. They include the writings of Carl Jung, the poems, stories, and interviews of Robert Bly, Bruno Bettelheim's theories about the uses of enchantment, fragments of fairy tales from the Brothers Grimm, the work of Joseph Campbell, medieval legends about King Arthur's court, the perceptions and story-telling of the contemporary mythologist

Michael Meade, the novels of D. H. Lawrence, the writings of William James, American Indian practices and rituals, segments of classical Greek myths, the writings and lectures of John Bradshaw on the origins and functions of shame in our culture, the insights of Jungian psychoanalyst Robert Moore, and a host of other influences and properties.

Let's take a quick look at two men from the roster just listed: Joseph Campbell and Robert Bly.

A fundamental source of our next revolution is the work of the late scholar Joseph Campbell. His writings including such books as *The Hero with a Thousand Faces* and *Myths to Live By*, and his interviews with

Bill Moyers on PBS (published under the title *The Power of Myth*), have shown men how to take myths and stories from different ages and different cultures and make them useful in their own lives.

Myths are "*models* for understanding your own life," Campbell says. "Anybody going on a journey, inward or outward, to find values, will be on a journey that has been described many times in the myths of mankind."

It is this idea of the journey inward, every man an explorer and hero as he faces his inner self, that suits us as men today. Our fathers and their fathers before them faced great hazards and overcame them with courage and persistence. And although their journeys were generally outward bound, not inner directed, the heroes of those ancient myths serve as examples as we confront our own difficulties and scrutinize the dynamics of our own male identity. Granted, it takes some grandiosity for the contemporary American male to see himself as an explorer embarking on a difficult expedition, but he is just that.

Under the fire of contemporary feminist scolding and sexism, the average man has been forced to question his identity and sexuality, and he has usually done so in isolation. But if he examines the myths of the past, he will learn that he is not as sequestered as he thought, that other men have traveled into treacherous territory before, experienced certain risks, and come out of the labyrinth alive and well.

Take the tale of Aeneas. Wandering the world after the fall of Troy, Aeneas ventures into the underworld in search of his father, Anchises. Aeneas fords the dreadful river Styx, braves his way past Cerberus, the monstrous three-headed watchdog of Hades, and finally manages to converse with the ghost of Anchises, who teaches Aeneas things he needs to know to continue his journey. Like most sons encountering a long-absent father, Aeneas tries to embrace his father, but his efforts are in vain; his father is a spirit and physically unavailable. However, Aeneas leaves Hades with his father's advice clear in his mind, bolstered by this visit into the unknown.

Most men can identify with the journey of Aeneas (which is recounted in Virgil's *Aeneid*). First, we understand the demands of the physical risks that Aeneas ran. Our lives, too, begin with boyhood quarrels and athletic competition that continue into vigorous adulthood (yes, boys are raised differently than girls). Second, we identify with Aeneas's loneliness, because our lives are frequently unsupported and isolated, in our homes as well as in the culture. Third, we understand the story of a man's going on a hazardous search for his father's spirit. We have all been there. Our fathers baffle us, intrigue us, haunt us. We never get away from them, and yet we are often fearful of confronting them, even after they have left us. The quest of Aeneas is our quest.

The search for our father is at the heart of male identity and you will

Joseph Campbell (1904–1987) was America's most prominent mythologist, a man whom Sam Keen called "our greatest teller of timeless myths." A world traveler, he taught at Sarah Lawrence College for thirty-eight years. He reached millions more people through his books The Hero With a Thousand Faces *(1949, 1973) and the tetralogy* The Masks of the Gods *(1959–1968) and his popular PBS series with Bill Moyers, "The Power of Myth."*

find no more emotional or difficult subject on the male agenda. We know we will travel where Aeneas has traveled. He is our brother, our contemporary, and he reminds us of how direct our link is to our forefathers.

No discussion of men and the next revolution can take place without consideration of Robert Bly, a major resource for men today. A highly respected poet, writer, and lecturer, Bly is the foremost popularizer of the mythic approach to the male journey. In a recent issue of *New Age* magazine, he is saying much the same thing that he said there nine years ago in a pioneering interview with Keith Thompson. The subject centers on contemporary men and their struggles toward masculinity.

In that 1982 interview, Bly begins by citing the men of the past three decades who mark some kind of break in historical traditions of masculinity: "The waste and anguish of the Vietnam War made men (of the sixties and seventies) question what an adult male really is . . . . As men begin to look at women and at their concerns, some men began to see their own feminine side and pay attention to it. That process continues to this day, and I would say that most young males are now involved in it to some extent."

Bly then sounds a note of caution. "The step of the male bringing forth his feminine consciousness is an important one—and yet I have the sense that there is something wrong. The male in the past twenty

SEVEN INITIATION MOVIES

1. **Dragonslayer** (1981) Young sorcerer's apprentice must hunt down a dragon in its lair.
2. **Fraternity Row** (1977) Sentimentalized picture of college fraternity life, brought down to earth by a hazing death.
3. **The Graduate** (1967) Naive Dustin Hoffman falls for Mrs. Robinson, then for her daughter.
4. **Hope and Glory** (1987) Young boy lives through the London air-raids.
5. **Lord of the Flies** (1963) Gripping tale of schoolboys, stranded on an island, regressing to savagery.
6. **A Man Called Horse** (1970) An English aristocrat undergoes grueling Indian Sun Vow ordeal to be accepted into the tribe.
7. **Tea and Sympathy** (1956) Broadway stars recreate their roles in this toned down version of the play about a sensitive lad at prep school who proves he's not homosexual by sleeping with the headmaster's wife.

years has become more thoughtful, more gentle. But by this process, he has not become more free. He's a nice boy who now pleases not only his mother but also the young woman he is living with.

"I see the phenomenon," Bly continues, "of what I would call the 'soft male' all over the country today . . . . But something's wrong. Many of these men are unhappy. There's not much energy in them. They are life-preserving but not exactly *life-giving*."

For me, Bly presents a precise summation of what has happened to many men over the past three decades—when the feminist revolution has taken over the culture and told us how terrible we were as men and how much we needed to change. To be *macho* in any manner has been unfashionable. And yet, every man has an element of the *macho* in his genetic structure. To deny it and suppress it can be deadly to men (and to the culture). Such denial can leave us depressed, without energy or passion or identity.

As men, we have special gifts. One of those is the ability to be in touch with the Cro-Magnon man who lives somewhere deep inside our hearts and minds and calls to us. It is vital to remember that this man is not a savage. In no way is he an uncontrolled killer or evil oppressor. He is primordial but not barbaric, aboriginal but not vicious. He represents what is best in the spirit of manhood. Indomitable and invincible and wild, ready to protect and defend and compete, his instinct and perceptions necessary to ensure the survival of the human race, this primitive man at the center of our psyches must be allowed room to live and breathe and express himself. If this rudimentary part of us dies, male identity dies.

Bly, borrowing a term from "Iron John," a tale written by the Grimm Brothers in 1820, calls this primitive man "the wildman." It is not a bad name for him.

In "Iron John," a young man on a difficult journey sees a large, hairy creature—the wildman—at the bottom of a pond that the young man is emptying, bucket by bucket. This discovery is frightening and intriguing. "What I'm proposing," says Bly, "is that every modern male has, lying at the bottom of his psyche, a large, primitive man covered with hair down to his feet. Making contact with this wildman . . . is the process that still hasn't taken place in contemporary culture . . . . Freud, Jung, and Wilhelm Reich are three men who had the courage to go down into the pond and accept what's there . . . . The job of modern males is to follow them down."

Accepting what is dark down there—what he calls "the shadow"—is another task that Bly assigns to any man who would discover his true male self and become an initiated male. Under Bly's urging, men are beginning to explore this shadow side of their personalities. Anger, aggression, grief, feelings of abandonment and rejection, rage, confu-

It is nothing like the women's movement, and probably never will be. Each man seems to be struggling with it quietly—at twenty-five or thirty-five, or before it is too late, at forty-five or fifty-five. . . . American men are at the edge of a momentous change in their very identity as men, going beyond the change catalyzed by the women's movement. It is a deceptively quiet movement, a shifting in direction, a saying "no" to old patterns, a searching for new values, a struggling with basic questions that each man seems to be dealing with alone.

—Betty Friedan,
The Second Stage (1981)

BABER
CALL
OF THE WILD

9

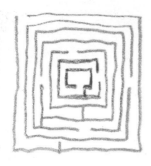

sion—all the varied dark and shadowy forces that whirl around like demons in the male psyche—these are things that we have tried to deny or ignore in order to be acceptable and admired.

But we have tried much too hard to be nice and we have essentially handed over the job of self-definition to others. This turns out to have been self-destructive. We emasculate and feminize ourselves to gain female approval—and then we hope against all available evidence that our powerful masculine energies will leave us alone. But is that likely?

Face it: For most men, the hope that our energy will fade away is vain. Witness the fact that our sexuality emerges at a very early age—usually much earlier than the emergence of female sexuality—and carries with it a beautiful immediacy, from spontaneous erections to wet dreams to vivid fantasies. This immediacy of male sexuality lasts well into our adulthood, even into old age for many men. Are we really going to be able to suppress all of that energy? And why *should* we repudiate such a unique and wonderful drive?

To use a Bly analogy, "The Widow Douglas wanted Huck Finn to be nice. And after he has floated down the river with a black man, Aunt Sally wants to adopt him and 'civilize' him. Huck says, 'I can't stand it. I been there before.' "

Sounds familiar, doesn't it?

The wildman lives in every man. He is beautiful and divine. He has enormous, fundamental energy and a great love for the world. He is just as much a nurturer and protector and creator as any female figure, but he will do that nurturing and protecting in his own masculine way. It is time for the wildman in us to be celebrated without shame. That celebration is part of what our revolution is about. It is our job as men to know ourselves better so that we can contribute more to this world and be more honest with ourselves. We have a right to our revolution, in other words. An absolute right.

Cut to a damp and cold weekend in November 1988 at a lodge somewhere in Wisconsin. I am attending The New Warrior Training Adventure, one of the only programs in the country that emphasize male initiation as a necessary rite of passage. It is late at night, I have been here for a day and a half already, and I am surrounded by a group of men who are asking me with focused energy to look deeply into my life. Who am I? What is my mission in life as a man? What is it that holds me back from completing my mission? What is my shadow, and how does it haunt me?

Understand that a number of things have occurred at this seminar before this moment, things that have pushed me and scared me and enlightened me and softened me up for the interrogation at hand. There have been some games, some questioning, there has been a rendition of

New Warrior Training Weekends are held frequently in various parts of the country. For a brochure and schedule, write or call:

Rich Tosi
New Warrior Network
4125 West Southland Dr.
Franklin, WI 53132
(414) 761-9810

"Iron John," a discussion of the shadow and what it means to men. I feel on the edge of a breakthrough. I am not sure that I like that feeling. I see myself as a man of containment and self-control, and yet here I am in emotional limbo. I feel like an astronaut on the moon.

I tell the men around me about what I perceive to be my shadow, my tendency toward aggression, my crazy childhood and difficult family life, how tough and defensive I became after early years of violence that seemed endemic in both my home and my neighborhood on Chicago's South Side, how combat-ready I always am, how I think that my turbulent mind-set interferes with my mission in life.

Rich Tosi, a former marine and one of the founders of the New Warrior Training Adventure program, challenges me on my description of my shadow as that of the ferocious man. "Bullshit, Baber," he says. "I'm not worried about you and your violence. You've explored that. That's not your shadow, because you've faced it. You know the kind of guy who scares me? The man who has never confronted his violence, the passive-aggressive bastard, who might freak out and lose control and get violent without any warning at all.

"Take a look. When are you going to admit to the grief you have for the men you've lost in your life? What about your father, for example, or your sons, when you lost custody of them, or the guys from your old neighborhood who never got out of there alive, or the marines you knew who were killed? You've lost a lot of men, haven't you, Lieutenant? Pick one of the dead ones, any one, and talk to him now. Go on, do it!"

I felt all my defenses crumble and I faced my grief openly for the first time. I mourned, I raged, I pounded the floor, I went down into the dark pond of my psyche and dredged up the forces I had been containing for too many years, I buckcted out my rage and my grief under the guidance of good men.

Tosi and Dr. Ron Hering, another founder of The New Warrior Training Adventure, lcd me down into the grave of the man I happened to grieve for most that evening, a marine named Mike with whom I served and who was killed in a chopper crash in Laos in the mid-sixties. Mike had been like a younger brother to me. His father had been like a father to me after my own father passed away in 1960. The secret war in Laos would kill Mike first, and Mike's death would kill his father a few years later. Losses? Mine were incalculable, and they had occurred in a very short time. Two fathers and many brothers dead in the space of a few years, and the additional specter of a full-scale war that had never been declared a war? I had not been able to handle the heartache of all that, so I had suppressed it, buried it. The heartache, you see, was my shadow.

Ron Hering and Rich Tosi and the other men working with me gave me room to grieve, let me explore my shadow, did not judge me or exploit me for my sadness, understood the losses that most men endure

The feminist critique of industrial society has put men on the defensive and masculinity itself on trial, as if there's something innately destructive in masculinity. The men's movement helps us reclaim and honor the beauty of healthy masculinity, which includes its generative, earthy and nurturing qualities.

—Shepherd Bliss

BABER

CALL

OF THE WILD

in self-imposed isolation, the denials we elaborately construct to hide from our grief.

Until then, I had always assumed that my physical survival was living proof of my cowardice and unmanliness. It was a certain kind of twisted male syllogism that is not uncommon: Men had died, I had not; therefore, I was undeserving of life; I should have died before them, possibly thereby saving them. That is a classic case of survivor's guilt, of course, and I had it full-blown.

Hering and Tosi and my peers helped me see that the men who had died wanted me to carry on the best traditions of manhood for them. They—all my fathers and brothers and sons from the beginning of time—were handing me the golden ball of masculinity with all its energy and beauty, and they were asking me to preserve it, protect it, and pass it on to the next generation of men. *That* was my mission in life.

With that realization, the shadow of guilt and grief that had dominated me faded in the light of my self-examination. I faced my shadow, battled it, tapped into my wildman energy and overcame it. Like Aeneas, I visited Hades and came away from the underworld with a little more wisdom.

In a very real sense, I was now an initiated male, a man ready to accept the joys and obligations of maturity.

"We are living at an important and fruitful moment now," Bly writes in his new book, *Iron John*, "for it is clear to men that the images of adult manhood given by the popular culture are worn out; a man can no longer depend on them . . . . [Men are] open to new visions of what a man is or could be."

New visions of masculinity: That is what our revolution is all about. Welcome aboard.

LONGING FOR THE GREAT FATHER

BY GEORGE TAYLOR

The magnet that draws most men into men's gatherings is the sense that here at last is a place where it is safe to explore and exorcise the long-repressed grief and anger over incomplete or unsatisfactory relationships with their fathers. Emphasis on this topic largely explains the extraordinary impact of the Robert Bly-Bill Moyers PBS interview, "A Gathering of Men," which brought the public an awareness that there even was such a thing as a men's movement. But as George Taylor's reflections suggest, men long not only for their personal genetic father, but for the Great Father, a transpersonal symbol of the majesty of masculinity. This desire is present even in men who had healthy, loving relationships with their dads.

RECENTLY I attended a men's conference in the mountains above Malibu near Los Angeles. As the wind off the ocean whipped through our large tent, I heard men talking in sad tones about how they felt abandoned by their fathers. Many told stories about fathers who absented themselves either physically or emotionally from the home.

I have experienced similar feelings myself many times, but lately I have been asking myself how I can reconcile these emotions with the father who clearly loved me, fed me, and sheltered me. The question in general terms is, How can there be so much father abandonment given the fact that many of these men (certainly not all) did their level best to raise us?

Since asking myself this question, I have had to reexamine these abandonment feelings. When I first started going to men's retreats, I felt that my main goal was to heal my wounds with my father and connect with other men. As time (half a decade) has progressed, I have certainly deepened my feelings toward my father—I have encountered, within my body and memory, love, anger, and anguish. I have also met some wonderful men friends, men whom I have laughed with, played with, retreated with, and advanced with. I have also learned about the difference between the mythological father and the personal father. It is no great insight to suggest that we live in a culture which has turned its back on the mythological, the spiritual, the soulful. In a culture like this, it's no wonder that we feel a sense of grief, of abandonment. The ground men used to stand on together has moved, like an errant continent, toward the material world, and away from the mystical, the mysterious, and the transcendent.

Now, when we focus only on our feelings of "father abandonment," we deny the loss of the men's lodge and our rituals of connectedness; we deny our need for the Great Father, our ancestors, our mythological heritage, and our masculine community.

In the old tribes, the men's lodge took on the training of the young

13

boys. This noble chore was not left in the personal hands of the biological father. The whole men's community participated in the education of the young men as they learned their place in the tribe's world. We have lost such ceremonies of affiliation and purpose.

Much of our male grief comes from that big loss, but we don't even know how to identify it. We mourn for that part of ourselves that's lost in the forest of the fairy tales, not knowing where to turn or how to live. We long for a community of men to come with torches to lead us back to the village. I'm not trying to say that we don't feel a desire to have more contact with our fathers. Sure, we feel that.

But think about the cry, "I was abandoned by my father." I hear in it the sound of the wounded child. While we must honor and heal this part

FATHER SONGS

Songs by men about their fathers or about the experience of being fathers. Here are some of my favorites, a couple of what must be considered "classics," and some more obscure cuts, not in any significant order:

Title / Artists:

"Seven Little Indians" John Hiatt *A spookly little tune about a spooky little family, the Big Chief Dad doing firedances for the kids around the television in his mucklucks.*

"Leader of the Band" Dan Fogelberg *Living up to the standards set by our fathers can be difficult. This is a beautiful song. Dad must've been proud.*

"Beautiful Boy" John Lennon *A simple love song from father to son.*

"The Walk" Sawyer Brown *A newer country tune about a father's deep understanding of the forces and changes in his son's life. A true love song.*

"Cat's in the Cradle" Harry Chapin *This classic piece reveals how a dad's workaholism/selfishness kept him from having much of a relationship with his son, who eventually responded in kind.*

"Yakity Yak" The Coasters *Golden oldie in which father tells his son he's got no time for joyriding with a "hoodlum friend" while chores like taking out the trash still need to be done.*

"Father and Son" Cat Stevens *An intense and lovely duet—both parts sung by Stevens—in which the father, while understanding his son's sense of urgency, pleads with him to take it slow. The son doth not heed.*

"Georgia Rae" John Hiatt *A high-spirited rocker which details the process by which little G. R. came to be conceived. "Lucky for you, child, you look like your mama!" Hiatt sings to the little one.*

"Seeing My Father in Me" Paul Overstreet *Overstreet has become the king of "family schmaltz" in country music primarily because he's so good at it. His portrayals of healthy marital and father-son relationships are a nice switch from the old dysfunctional country cliches.*

"The Pickup Truck Song" Jerry Jeff Walker *Going to the county dump, making up songs, and getting lost on the way back home is a pretty perfect way to spend a day with your kids, especially in an old beater Chevy, according to Scamp Walker.*

—List compiled by Lea Jones

David with his father's death mask.

George Taylor (left) with co-facilitator Doug von Koss.

of ourselves, we must also hear from the adult man, who might say something like, "I am a member of a generation of men who were born with a deep father longing; I long to experience the great, ancient masculine forces in the universe." No generation of men has ever been born so separated from our masculine traditions of power, responsibility, and wisdom, so of course we long to connect with something bigger than ourselves and our personal histories: our male community, our ancestors, our stories.

We long to connect, and so we do what men have done for millennia. We get together for an evening or a weekend, and we dance together, tell poems and stories, gossip, make up rituals, wrestle. We seek the connection beyond words with the holy masculine, the ineffable, the unspeakable. It is through giving into that deep desire that we feel our grief, our joy, and our anger. The longing for connection can take us out of our personal dramas and into our deepest feelings. Then we feel alive and human, full of rich emotional experience.

It is this longing to connect that connects us with our fathers, our ancestors, and finally ourselves.

RAINBOWS

Wherever you go.
    However far away it is.
Take my love
    on your shoulders, riding
                                as I did
    down those steep trails to our fishing place.
    (The only times I remember embracing you
              as a child)
    Smelling the cigarette smoke, the sweat
           the canvas vest
                        like perfume,
        the smell of a father
                                to a son.

Whenever you go,
    cast away your silent desperation
    like a dry fly into the current.

I will probably walk those trails
                     when you
                        are gone . . .

    crying, remembering how you were
        during those magical times.
    I felt your body move as it carried me
                down to the river;
you in search of trout
    me, hoping the trail

A poet's business is not to save
the soul of a man, but to make it
worth saving.
               —James E. Fletcher

would never end.
You will die a stranger to me.
   Unable to attend to my desires

                                   as a son,

   I wished you could be as gentle with me
          as you were
   when tying a fisherman's knot to the hook.
Perhaps I don't go fishing now because I fear
   the intrusion of those trips we made or
   confusing fragmented memories of them . . .
Only the two of us
   down that steep rocky trail

                        into the gorge.

You fishing for trout,

                          me . . . for you.

   I hoped you would look my way
          and leave the rod,
        the line and little fly,
    and reel me in.
When you go even as a stranger
   I will always hold those few trips
    like rainbows, in my little creel;
  and I will remember you
   carrying me down that trail . . . .

—HANK BLACKWELL

First published in *Talking from the Heart: An Anthology of Men's Poetry*, edited by David Johnson and Charles E. Cockelreas. Men's Network Press, P.O. Box 40300, Albuquerque, NM 87196.

RAINBOWS

CHAIN SAWS TO TOENAIL CLIPPERS
LOGGER TURNS FATHER
BY MARK JUDELSON

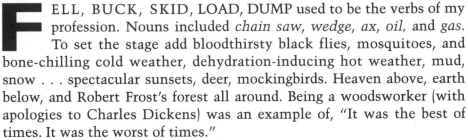

In contrast to all the grieving and regretting that surrounds much of midlife men's reflections on their relationships with their fathers is the joy and imagination that men are showing in their role as fathers. Society, which has made much of the achievements of women in the corporate world, has been much slower to acknowledge that most fathers are now present at their child's birth, that many dads carry kids in public as much as mom does, and that men's child-raising style may be more playful, but no worse than the more cautious and traditional style women have been taught. Besides capturing the whimsy and pride of fatherhood, Mark Judelson's essay neatly contrasts men's traditional role as worker outside the home with his even more important role as parent within the home. ✒

FELL, BUCK, SKID, LOAD, DUMP used to be the verbs of my profession. Nouns included *chain saw*, *wedge*, *ax*, *oil*, and *gas*. To set the stage add bloodthirsty black flies, mosquitoes, and bone-chilling cold weather, dehydration-inducing hot weather, mud, snow . . . spectacular sunsets, deer, mockingbirds. Heaven above, earth below, and Robert Frost's forest all around. Being a woodsworker (with apologies to Charles Dickens) was an example of, "It was the best of times. It was the worst of times."

The satisfaction of performing quality work in the woods was one of the highlights of my life. I took great pride in leaving behind aesthetically sculpted, eye-pleasing woodscapes . . . a community with species and age diversity whose individual members had space to grow. The stumps I left behind were no more than two inches high—this at great cost to sharp cutting chains. Branches were used down to ridiculously small diameter for kindling and what was left in the woods was cut so small that it all lay flat.

It was an honorable living and for most of the time that I did it, I loved it.

Then I began to notice that the older loggers were short and squat. I, on the other hand, am tall and athletically lean (never say "skinny"). I started asking the older guys, "Did you start out being tall and skinny and got short and squat because gravity just smooshed you down . . . or did you start out being short and squat?"

The older guys would smile their "now I can really zing this guy" smile and to a man they replied, "Kid, you finally got it. You tall, skinny guys don't last too long in the woods."

Although I've never seen exhaustive research on this critical topic, I think they're right . . . . So I went to graduate school.

But I still don my lunky steel-toed boots, odoriferous chaps, and *Star Wars* look-alike orange helmet with ear muffs and face mask and tread off into the woods for "recreational" cutting. After a couple hours, I gratefully limp back home, thankful that I don't have to do this for my living.

Meanwhile, my son Max emerged from the womb almost two years ago. Awesome mechanical challenges encountered in the woods are dwarfed by struggles to secure two safety pins to either side of his diapers while he squirms, thrashes, and kicks his way to freedom. To perform a quality job 1) the diapers must be snug and 2) both the diaper wearer and diaper installer not punctured by the so-called safety pins.

But the physical tasks are insignificant compared to the emotional tests. Creativity, patience, and energy are primary qualifications for the job. Being Max's father has been the most demanding and greatest joy-inducing experience of my life.

Let's get down to basics. What could be more basic than toenails? Some people are worried that if they're in a car wreck and an ambulance takes them to a hospital and in the emergency room a nurse is stripping their clothes off and the nurse discovers they're wearing dirty underwear ... I'm not sure what happens next, maybe nothing. All because they're wearing dirty underwear.

Soiled undergarments discovered in the emergency room is not my nightmare. Mine is unkempt toenails. I regularly trim my toenails as if a Marine Corps boot camp drill sergeant is about to inspect beneath my combat boots.

A slightly older Max returns the favor by shampooing his father

Max, however, wouldn't know boot camp from the Sears underwear department . . . . Well, maybe he would. The bottom line is he doesn't like having his toenails cut by someone else and he certainly wasn't about to do it himself.

Max's almost-every-night bedtime ritual since he came home from the hospital has been to share a shower or bath with me, be swathed in four diapers, dressed in pajamas, listen to stories, receive feet, hands, and head (in that order) massage . . . . All this while sucking for all he's worth on his juice bottle. When unsuccessful attempts had been made in the past to trim his toenails (finally, the toenails!), the little guy (again) had squirmed, thrashed, and kicked. It was like trying to drop a tree with a chain saw but the tree was madly hopping around trying to get out of the way.

Well, one night in the bath, he poked me with his foot and I recognized that the nails were just too long for safe cobathing. After he was settled into his crib, the story read, and he was awaiting his foot massage I said, "Max, I'd like to trim your toenails."

He quietly looked up at me, trust, sleep, and satisfaction in his eyes, gave me a nod of the head, and offered his foot.

JUDELSON
CHAIN SAWS TO
TOENAIL CLIPPERS

Never had I experienced the sense of satisfaction I felt as I trimmed away. No home run, no woodscape manicured, no story written ever came close. As I surveyed the completed task, each nail neatly, evenly, cleanly trimmed, I had not a worry in the world.

This was the right foot. I gently lowered this exquisite piece of art to the crib. "Max, I'd like to trim the nails on your left foot."

The same eyes looked toward me but no longer was the trust and satisfaction in evidence. Only impatience for his massage to begin.

"No!"

Nancy Reagan would be inspired by the determination and ease with which this person just said, "No!"

My choices were cajoling, begging, and/or ordering him to submit to the clippers. Cajoling failed. Ordering him to submit seemed excessive. Begging was beneath my dignity.

Okay, okay. Keep your toenails. I gave him the massage and kiss he deserved and he happily (albeit unbalancedly) drifted off to sleep.

I, on the other hand, was thoroughly dissatisfied. A job half-done is a job not done. For the ensuing 24 hours I was obsessed with images of Max's left foot. It clearly made no difference to Max that one foot's nails were perfectly trimmed and the other foot was the Mr. Hyde of Dr. Jekyll.

The next night, we shared our bath, got him ready for and placed in his crib . . . . The moment of truth.

I put on my most self-assured face (but feeling inside as unsure as my first lovemaking—well, almost as unsure) and said, "Max, I'd like to trim the toenails on your left foot."

FATHER-SON MOVIES

1. **All My Sons** (1948) *Sins of the father visited on his sons.*
2. **Careful, He Might Hear You** (1983) *An Australian film about a boy longing for his absent father.*
3. **Da** (1988) *An Irishman plagued by the ghost of his father.*
4. **Dad** (1989) *Three generations of American men in a contemporary tearjerker.*
5. **The Great Santini** (1979) *A sensitive boy brow-beaten by his military father.*
6. **I Never Sang for My Father** (1970) *A man cares for his ailing elderly father.*
7. **Kramer vs Kramer** (1979) *Father engages in a bitter custody battle for his young son.*
8. **Life With Father** (1947) *A nostalgic tribute to the head of a big family.*
9. **Nothing in Common** (1986) *Son spars with his cantankerous father.*
10. **The Three Godfathers** (1948) *Religious fable about three cowpokes and a baby.*

My precious bundle of love and emerging independence looked up at me with understanding (it was probably more pity) and nodded . . . ahhh . . .

That night, we both slept well.

BOOKS ON FATHER ISSUES

Phyllis Bronstein and Carolyn Pape Cowan, eds. *Fatherhood Today: Men's Changing Role in the Family*. New York: John Wiley & Sons, 1988. Collection of sociological essays (each with an extensive bibliography) on the many kinds of fathers in contemporary Western society—including black fathers, Chicano fathers, gay fathers, grandfathers, and stepfathers.

Arthur Colman and Libby Colman, *Earth Father/Sky Father: The Changing Concept of the Father*. Englewood Cliffs, NJ: Prentice-Hall, 1981. The Colmans relate five archetypes of the father (Father the Creator, Earth Father, Sky Father, Royal Father, Dyadic Father) to both married and single men's styles of fathering at various stages of fatherhood. Chiron paperback edition (1988) has a new preface and a new title, *The Father: Mythology and Changing Roles*.

Guy Corneau, *Absent Fathers, Lost Sons: The Search for Masculine Identity*. Boston: Shambhala, 1991. A Jungian analyst identifies ways that men can achieve the wholeness they were cheated of by growing up with distant, silent, or remote fathers.

John Lee, *At My Father's Wedding*. New York: Bantam, 1991. A collection of thoughts, feelings, and experiences with interwoven themes, relating the author's and other men's efforts to heal the father-wound, especially through men's work.

Samuel Osherson, *Finding Our Fathers: How a Man's Life Is Shaped by His Relationship with His Father*. New York: Fawcett Columbine, 1986. In addition to discussing the subject laid out in the subtitle, Osherson also examines the role of the mentor, a man's feelings when he becomes a father, and miscarriages.

Kyle D. Pruett, MD, *The Nurturing Father: Journey Toward the Complete Man*. New York: Warner, 1987. This supportive book by a prominent child psychiatrist shows males nurture just as well as females, only differently, and that caring for children brings out a man's full humanity.

Jason Shinder, ed. *Divided Light: Father and Son Poems*. Riverdale-on-Hudson, NY: Sheep Meadow Press. This moderately interesting collection of 20th-century poems, which is unfortunately hard to find, contains selections by Robert Bly, Gary Snyder, Etheridge Knight, David Ignatow, John Berryman, and Randall Jarrell as well as by less-known authors.

Gregory Max Vogt, *Return to Father: Archetypal Dimensions of the Patriarch*. Dallas, TX: Spring Publications, 1991. This gutsy, physical book demands respect for what is best in traditional masculinity. Invigorating sections on the Hunter's Body, the Body of the Builder, and the Philosopher's Body.

Gregory Max Vogt and Stephen T. Sirridge, *Like Son, Like Father: Healing the Father-Son Wound in Men's Lives*. New York: Plenum, 1991. Exercises, resources, and background to effect those difficult reconciliations between fathers and sons.

Lewis Yablonsky, *Fathers and Sons: The Most Challenging of All Family Relationships*. New York: Gardner Press, 1990. A sociology professor traces the stages in father-son interactions and suggests better ways of being a father.

MENTORING FOR MASCULINE LEADERSHIP

BY JOSEPH PALMOUR, Ph.D.
Archon Institute for Leadership Development

Mentoring is at the heart of the lifework of Joseph Palmour, Ph.D., the director of the Archon Institute for Leadership Development. The Archon Institute programs draw on classical Greek philosophy and mythology and modern psychoanalysis to awaken people's neglected aspirations to live noble lives. The institute's purpose: "Through mentoring and action projects, we clarify our goals, find our voices as speakers, writers and organizers, and advance our compassion, commitment and creativity."

The Archon Institute is located at:

3700 Massachusetts Avenue NW, Suite 121
Washington, D.C. 20016
(202-342-7710).

EVERYWHERE WE LOOK, we see the sad consequences of the absence of strong masculine energy and leadership in modern America. One of the reasons for this is that we've lost sight of what the ancients knew so well. It takes strength of character to be a strong man, and character has to be actively cultivated in people, not only in their youth but throughout their lives. The qualities of virtuous character were thought so important for manliness among the Romans that their word *virtus* (strength, virtue) was derived from their word *vir* (man). As late as the 19th century, mentoring for masculine leadership was always aimed at cultivating this kind of strength of character in gifted men. You'd search a long time today, though, before you found many teachers who recognized this instinctive connection between the development of moral power in a man's character and his being a virile person. Many of us are hungry to get back to this kind of mentoring, both for our own sakes and because we think the country needs the kind of strength of character we saw in a man like Martin Luther King, Jr., when we were young.

But like sex, marriage, and therapy, mentoring is the sort of thing that pretty much depends on who you do it with and what your goals are in working together. The mentoring I do with a small number of men and boys in Washington, D.C., is an effort to try to reestablish this practice of cultivating masculine leadership.

My work with both baby-boomers and the baby-boomers' sons has convinced me that the different generations need each other very badly and that the revival of a more ancient form of mentoring than we normally think of today can unlock the dammed-up energy inside of each. Boomers at midlife will stagnate if they don't learn to reach out to the young in friendship rather than feel contemptuously superior toward them. A more generative interest in young people can help men in their prime regain a sense of moral initiative in their lives and overcome a gnawing sense of guilt for having neglected their thoughtful idealism.

The admiration of younger men can inspire them to live up to the same values and standards they encourage in their protégés.

Younger men have become cynical and apathetic about their own identities, values, and goals because they don't connect with older men whom they respect and trust. A more intimate and encouraging relation with older men can help them develop a sense of what they really love and want to do with themselves. Such a tie to like-minded adults can foster more fulfilling friendships with peers for young people and make them less vulnerable to the pervasive cynicism and aimlessness in today's young subculture. Mentoring is thus a natural bridge between generations that can be greatly fulfilling to each.

THE EYES OF AN EAGLE

While there's much confusion about mentoring these days, most would agree there's a certain romance and even fear associated with having a powerful man hold you to high standards of mastery, whether it be in classical music, Zen and the art of archery, or brain surgery. There's also a more prosaic side of it.

Roman Eagle

Most often today in conventional society, having a mentor means having an older man in a profession or field you want to enter who agrees to show you the ropes. Such a mentor helps you find your way toward career advancement. He blesses your energy, believes in the promise of your unfolding gifts, alerts you to career prospects, and acts as both coach and cheerleader along a specific career path that he knows well. If you're good and he begins to identify with your success, he may even track your progress into the field with the passionate intensity of someone who wants you to do your work really well or to get the hell out of the way so someone with real competence can do it.

But at a deeper level, there's something menacing about submitting to a mentor's judgment of one's performance. It's not always pleasant having a master watch over you when he's a strong-willed man with a clear sense of what he expects. Seemingly with eagle eyes from the sky high above, he can fall on you from out of nowhere, ripping into you with powerful talons, and exposing little things that seem hardly worth noticing. But if you don't run away in prideful shame at being so sharply corrected, you soon realize that from his depth of experience, he is spotting carelessness and rookie arrogance that threaten your initiation into the inner circle of established professions in the field. At some deep level, he conveys a constant conviction of great value. You can accept the risk of paying your dues today in the hope that, sometime in the distant future, you will grow strong like an eagle yourself. Otherwse you must accept the certainty of continuing to live in the fear of being eaten alive like a rabbit in the field.

MENTORS AND FATHERS

Even with this inevitable tension over living up to standards, when mentor and student are worthy of each other, a special kind of father-son, master-apprentice feeling can develop that gives many of the same pleasures and heartaches of a biologically rather than socially based tie. A student's feeling for a beloved teacher no doubt comes to many people's mind at this point, so we need to be reminded that the traditional idea was that whoever truly labors for the development of another comes to love him in a very special way, rather like an artist loves his creation.

Parents and teachers were thought to love a child in their care far more than the young one loved them, precisely because they had labored for his development in this way. It's thus quite telling that as a society we don't seem to find it so natural anymore that teachers will come to love their students. But regardless of the nature of our teachers' labors these days, we need to see that there are important differences between a father's role and a mentor's.

As James Hillman has been saying at men's meetings across the country, it's only been in recent times that any society believed that the biological father was the natural person to conduct a boy's deeper initiation into the world of adult roles and responsibilities. (Most often in traditional cultures, the mother's brother would guide the boy into the process.) A father's gifts, calling, or education might make him totally unfit to initiate his own son into the discipline, the wisdom, and the personal relationships that would perfect a boy with radically different needs than his own. There is simply nothing to prevent a deeply intellectual father, for example, from having a highly athletic, noncontemplative son, and vice versa. An aggressive, bullish father can have a sensitive, artistic son.

Often a father merely senses the differences between himself and his son without being able to recognize very clearly what they are and how they contribute to his conflicts and disappointments with his son. He might give him a driving lesson or try to talk with him about schoolwork, literature, politics, or music, only to find his efforts ending once again in mutual frustration and recrimination. Whether spoken or not, each accuses the other of approaching things all wrong, of having a bad attitude or of just not understanding. What one of them loves and needs leaves the other cold, so over time they grow afraid to expose their most precious enthusiasms to each other. Talking becomes so painful they agree just to avoid each other. Rather than hope, they approach each other with fear, anger, and disappointment.

The fact that traditional societies seem to have grasped the practical importance of such a lack of fit between father and son makes it even more striking that we have not, especially given the fact that our division of labor is so much more specialized. A modern boy must master many more complexities than a tribal child before he can act with power and dignity in the adult world. A boy needs help to learn about his own gifts and identity, and help to learn how to identify someone who has mastered the skills that are the birthright of his own nature. With so many life options to choose from, our boys could actually use a mentor in the very process of finding a mentor.

Yet today, where youth should find guidance in knowing their own nature and in finding their rightful place in the division of labor in society, there is a gaping void. They have been left alone to fend for themselves. Their lives seldom expose them to mature men doing things of such quality as to inspire a boy's emulation and his willingness to discipline himself in anticipation of being ready for his own chance later in life. As a consequence, they suffer an absolutely natural confusion about where they fit in society and feel a desperate need to belong among their equally confused peers. In this light, we should not be surprised that our teenagers have grown apathetic about preparing for roles that are either invisible to them or that exercise no charm over their imaginations.

The problem deepens when we recognize that inside most grown men is an unmentored boy who hardly feels prepared to mentor anyone else. By focusing on their own neediness, many men ignore all that they do have inside themselves and turn their backs on all those who need their help. They simply miss the way in which a man's helping a boy can heal the hurt little boy inside of himself.

Many of us heard how the older men of traditional tribes would hold rites of passage to initiate fourteen-year-old boys into the world of men. They'd take them away from their mothers and away from a child's life in the world of women. (The mother of a fourteen-year-old recently told me now much easier it would be on her if we did this too and freed her from having to enforce and suffer through her son's testing himself as a young man.) Somehow it never quite made sense to me that the rite of passage into manhood would be done so young. A fourteen-year-old is hardly a man among us, and I doubt that he was in traditional society either. So what's going on?

One way or another, I've begun to hear my older students explaining this to me as we search for the roots of the attitudes holding them back from coming into their own power. My students have shown me that the years around fourteen are not so much the point at which a boy becomes a man as it is the period when he decides whether he *wants* to become a man. It is then that he must find the courage to test himself and pay his dues. A boy left without the help of men at this crucial stage tends to run away from life and remains inwardly a child while outwardly trying to fake his becoming a man. This is the period when so many of our best boys are being defeated, and it is thus the natural point when men these boys admire must help them. Many of my students had their spiritual backs broken in their early teens when they didn't get this help. Somewhere in the middle-school period, they lost their boyish enthusiasm and exuberance for life.

More specifically, they lost the confidence that they could live with real initiative without being embarrassed by their depth of feeling or by the aggressive passion with which they attacked any obstacle. They lost faith that adults would guide and encourage them to do the hard work that would earn them an honored place among their peers and in the larger society. They began facing life alone and demoralized, trusting no one, showing up unprepared and faking their way through every situation that would test what they're made of. Later in life, they're often ashamed, feeling they don't do their best to earn their pay.

As Americans, we all too readily assume that everybody is equal to everybody else, that there are no natural differences between people and that a person ought to be able to do anything that he really wants to do. But we ignore the fact that the same assumptions make it unbelievably hard for a father to admit when he is really a different kind of person from his son and is ill prepared to guide him in handling his radically different gifts and temptations. It is an uphill battle for us to establish how great such a father's responsibility is to find someone else to give his boy what he needs.

One current cultural assumption is that fathers have to feel profound guilt when they see they are not able personally to give their passionately gifted sons the direction and initiation they see their boys longing for. For many fathers, their sense of inadequacy is so great that they have to keep the feeling closeted away inside. Yet they must surely feel their boys' sullenness, distance, and disrespect as signals of their profound sense of betrayal and abandonment.

Younger men and boys, on their side, can just as readily believe that the only person who can initiate them into mature masculine roles is a father who is radically different from themselves. When this occurs, they languish in grief and anger for the lost father of their imagination. Not knowing about mentors and how to find one for themselves, they go despairingly through life never acquiring the discipline, purposefulness, and toughness of mind necessary to do anything really fine. Men like this grow reluctant to stake any claim to ground they want to make their own and defend. They refuse to put themselves to the test on any claims they do make and can't commit themselves to husband anyone. There should be little surprise, then, when their marriages fall apart and they can't stand up for quality in their work and justice in their communities.

Often the grown men who come to me for mentoring at first show

real passion only when blaming their fathers for not having made them into more of a man earlier in their lives. They trace their failings back to him rather than to themselves. When, by contrast, they describe wonderful opportunities they could act on in the present, they show no real enthusiasm or energy. At every point where their own plans for the future would require them to call on deep inner resources, they run away from their responsibilities—blaming their fathers, teachers, or other authorities.

We often have to spend months turning them around before they can face forward in their lives. How wonderful it is then for both of us when they begin genuinely to believe what men have always found. Profound hope and confidence come very naturally to gifted men when they submit to the training of a master at work they love. These are the fruits of beginning to monitor their accomplishments not against a childishly grandiose sense of what they ought to be able to do (if they really have the gifts they believe they have) but against their teacher's more realistic standards.

A mentor knows better than a student what a really gifted person from a given background ought to be able to do at a given stage of his development, and he knows how important it is to pace a student in order to bring him along properly. The greatest single threat to a student's progress toward mastery is his fearfully misjudging natural rookie mistakes to be a true reflection of the excellence he will be capable of when he has seasoned and steeled his skills. Thinking of himself as having the potential for greatness, he's easily shaken in this faith when he finds that great things do not come out of him without work. That's when a student learns whether he's got faith in his ability to work and when he realizes how much he needs a coach. A good mentor will show him that through pursuing an intelligent training program he can acquire that mastery for himself. He can reconnect to the trunk line of confidence and joy he so enjoyed in boyhood when he wasn't afraid to try and wouldn't quit until he got things done.

LIMITS TO THE FATHER'S ROLE

In both cases, for old and young alike, for father and for son, the reestablishment of a more classical understanding of the mentor's role can solve many problems. Creating the cultural awareness of the difference between the father function and the mentor function can in the first place free us from the illusion that our lives are poisoned for all time by having a father who could not mentor us. (This can be especially important in female-headed households.) When youth feel their whole lives will be lived under the shadow of what is in some respect the accident of the families they are born into, they enter life with a profound indiffer-

In Homer's *Odyssey*, Mentor (which means "advisor") was an Ithacan nobleman to whom Ulysses entrusted the management of his household while he was away fighting in the Trojan Wars. Mentor, or the virgin goddess Athena in his likeness, gave advice to Ulysses' son, Telemachus, and roused him to action. Later Mentor made peace between Ulysses and the people of Ithaca when he returned from battle.

ence to the greater possibilities for wholeness that lie around them. While it's true in one sense that we have to bloom where we're planted, there's another sense in which we're not plants at all. We can search for more sunlight and better soil to grow in.

We can strengthen fathers by relieving them of the illusion that they are the sole supplier of the developmental needs of their sons. When fathers feel they are responsible for something they can't handle, they are sorely tempted to deny that responsibility or leave it up to others, with no thought to their own role in the process.

Good fathering will always mean providing for one's family both the material and the moral security for their well-being and development. It will always mean a father's trying to give his children a mother who feels so loved, respected, and fulfilled in her own life that she's not tempted to keep her children from growing up in order to maintain a sense of meaning in her own life. To be a good father and husband requires a man to become secure and happy in his own power as well. That's why being a husband and father is such an important goal for men. For many of us, the desire to husband our wives and father our children has called us to come into a fullness of manhood we had never dreamed we were capable of. Loving our families then empowers us to fulfill more manly responsibilities toward the broader society beyond the limits of our families, whether it be at work, church, school, or other community groups. Through loving our families, we come to know what it means to husband people, and we love doing it.

But protecting and sponsoring our children does not necessarily mean a father must be able to satisfy their mentoring needs himself. As Hillman suggests, a father may much more naturally mentor another man's son than his own. Why should there be any stigma in a father's admitting when his son is a different kind of person and wants and needs to be a different kind of man than he is himself?

How wonderful it would be for everyone if we began to acknowledge the generosity of spirit involved in a father's actively encouraging his son to find his own identity. Fathers could be taught to participate more actively in helping their sons discover what moves and awakens them, and could be encouraged to rejoice in it even when it differs from their own interests and loves. With a humble and wondrous acceptance of our natural differences, a father could then proudly help his son find a man or men who will initiate him into a discipline and wisdom that might be different from that which the father has himself.

We must not kid ourselves into thinking this will be easy. Men are made so unhappy by their own working lives, and so seldom feel loved and encouraged to find and be themselves, that it will take exceptional men to give their sons so much better than they got themselves.

WHAT A MAN BECOMES

AN ESSAY ON THE BEST OF FRIENDS
BY EDGAR ALLEN BEEM

In classical times and throughout Western history up until the twentieth century, friendship between men was deemed a higher, purer kind of love than the one between a man and his wife. Enthusiasts inevitably quoted the passage from the Old Testament in which David laments the death of Jonathan, "Thy love for me was wonderful, surpassing the love of women." Since Freud, however, strong attachments between men have been made sexually suspect, and friendships between women and men valued more highly. Edgar Allen Beem uses chapters from his family history to illustrate contemporary views on male friendship. ✍

THE MALE-FEMALE relationship is a profoundly physical one—birth, nurture, intercourse, progeny. What a man needs most from a woman is physical companionship and comfort. The essence of a mother or a lover is her embrace. From another man what a man needs most is an example, someone to look up to, someone with whom he can identify. The essence of male friendship is the often unspoken reassurance that a man is not alone in his dreams and his fears. And after the divine spark has been imparted, who a man becomes depends a great deal on the other men in his life.

Edgar Allen Beem was a man's man. He loved baseball in the summer, deer hunting in the fall, golf on the weekend, an evening of poker, and a good stiff drink at the end of a day. He was a tall, handsome man who always drove Pontiacs and always wore his black hair parted in the middle and plastered down with Vitalis.

Born in Ohio in 1896, Ed Beem was descended from a long line of German-American farmers, but he was destined to spend most of his working life in the employ of the Metropolitan Life Insurance Company. He was 42 years old when Metropolitan transferred him from its New York headquarters to become the manager of its Portland, Maine, office. And that's why I live in Maine today.

My grandfather was a big man in a boy's world. His office was on the 10th floor of the tallest building in Portland, and everyone in that office called him "Mr. Beem." I just called him Bampi, and Bampi was the boss. What impressed me even more, however, was that Bampi was one of the founders of Little League baseball in Portland. Before I was old enough to play myself, Bampi slicked down my hair after supper and took me with him to the games. I was proud of the fact that everyone around the little ball field out behind Deering High School—including the players—knew who Mr. Beem was.

I am told now that my grandfather was warmer and more affectionate with his grandchildren than he was with his own children, but even before I knew that I learned from Bampi that a man could be distant and aloof in ways a woman was not. What I learned from my grandfather was that a man had a life of his own outside the family. A man had his work and his friends.

My grandfather was the product of hard times. His own father died when he was 14 and for the next seven years he was the head of his family. When, at age 21, he left home to serve in World War I, his grandfather gave him two pieces of advice—*A man's got to keep his self-respect* and *A man's got to keep his credit good*. These principles became the twin pillars of my grandfather's secular faith and he passed them on to his own two sons when they left home for war.

Edgar Allen Beem, Jr., my father, is a family man. He enjoys his children, his grandchildren, reading, naps, conversation, television, cleaning house, a glass of wine, staying home. A mild-mannered loner, he taught me by example about the sacrifices a man makes for his family.

Born in Ohio in 1924, my father was 12 years old when his family moved to Maine. After graduating from Deering High, he attended Maine Maritime Academy and then served in the merchant marine during World War II. During the Korean conflict he was in the navy, but most of the time I was growing up he, like his father, worked for Metropolitan. Then, when he was just about the age I am now, he made a dramatic midlife career switch and went back to sea, starting all over as an able-bodied seaman and working his way up to master mariner, certified to command any ship on any ocean.

Blessed with a gift of gab, a wealth of experience, and a great memory for names, my father knows hundreds of people but I think I was in junior high school when it first occurred to me that he didn't seem to have any friends of his own. All of his friends were my mother's friends, the couples they saw together socially. Noting my father's solitary nature at a time in my life when popularity was of paramount importance, I resolved not to let friendlessness become my own fate.

So I am the first son of a first son and I bear the first son's name. I am Edgar Allen Beem III, but I dropped the roman numeral as ostentatious baggage after my grandfather died in 1971. All through school, however, I was just Eddie Beem.

Eddie Beem was a bright, clean-cut, rather arrogant little kid just good enough at the things that counted to be included but never quite good enough to excel. And the things that counted in the Westbrook of my childhood were basketball and billiards.

The focus of all friendship was the school, of course, but the status of these friendships was regularly tested in the sweaty cage of the Cumberland Gym and the smoky cavern of Barrie's Billiards. Unable to make a bank shot or the basketball team, I went out for the track team and it was as a puny freshman hurdler that I first experienced the crude camaraderie of the locker room.

Throughout our trip we had caught people eying us oddly, no doubt certain that we were gay city slickers on a backroads sojourn. My one regret about the going public of male homosexuality is that it casts all men in pairs in a new and ambiguous light, before the world and before themselves. I don't mind being mistaken for gay, but I do mind the crowding out from the general consciousness of a kind of love between men that is neither romantic nor sexual, but is nonetheless terribly hard for most men to acknowledge to one another.
—Keith G. McWalter, "Hitting the Road"

Young men can be extremely carnal and dangerous beings, as I discovered one evening after track practice in 1963. I was all soaped up, skinny and naked, when I was joined in communal shower by Bob and Terry, two equally naked upperclassmen, who proceeded to grill me in the raw about my (nonexistent) sex life and just how far a guy could expect to get with Jane, my former junior high girlfriend. Mortified by their tactlessness but still wanting to be "one of the guys," I then made the mistake of accepting a ride home. As I sat between them on the front seat with a smile of brave fright plastered on my face my new friends proceeded to demonstrate that a Rambler sedan was capable of hitting speeds in excess of 100 mph on the crowded and slippery surface of New Gorham Road. I think it was then that I decided to become a poet.

What I learned from Bob and Terry is that you can show your vulnerabilities only to your *real* friends. My *real* friends in high school were Chris (now a legislative aide in Michigan), Earl (now a teacher in Westbrook), Roland (now a salesman in Portland), and Steve (now a gardener and caretaker on Islesboro). Ours was a fraternity based on attitude, and its rituals consisted largely of manning the corner booth at Deering Ice Cream and endlessly driving around town (or "bombing around" as it was familiarly known) in the days when there was still an inexhaustible supply of cheap gas.

The attitude we shared was one of irreverence, wit, and sense of the absurd and something like benign indifference. At one point we even discussed forming the Not Care Club ("If you'd care to join, you can't"), but no one seemed to care for the idea. Our heroes were anxious funnymen such as Woody Allen, Richard Farina's fictional antihero Gnossos Pappadopolis, Robert Benchley, Groucho Marx, and Oscar Levant (*Memoirs of an Amnesiac*).

Today, 25 years later and counting, if I want a good laugh (and months go by without one) I can call Earl and give him a little of the old attitude—"Hi, Earl, just called to see if you'd had your heart attack yet" —and we'll both be cracking up in no time, guaranteed. In all of our lives there is a depth of humor that can only be shared by people with whom we have a history.

And when I called Earl just now to ask him who wrote *Memoirs of an Amnesiac* he assured me I was still on his list of best friends even though we only see each other about once a year these days.

"When you're best friends," Earl said, "you can have a two-year hiatus and nothing really changes. There's an emotional bond there that can never be broken."

Chris, Earl, Roland, Steve—our lives spin in and out of each other's orbits with decreasing frequency, yet picking up the old thread is easy when we meet. And in the case of Earl and me, we have even carried out friendship through first marriages and into second.

Sad to say, but divorce seems to be the rule rather than the exception in this millennial endgame of ours. In fact, the circle of couples with whom we were closer than friendly in the 1970s has long since broken and dispersed. This epidemic of divorce, however, was the crucible for another fast friendship.

Don and I met when we were both free-lancing for the same alternative newspaper. Initially, our common interests were writing and baseball, and, pursuing a friendship based on both, we spent some truly productive summer months wasting our remaining youth on games of seaside whiffle ball. Then, as our marriages floundered and failed, we baby-sat each other through divorce and on into love again.

The complexion of a friendship depends a great deal on the soil in which it is planted, so Don and I don't laugh together the way high school buddies do. For that he has old friends from Bangor and I have mine from Westbrook. Instead when we get together we commiserate,

BUDDY MOVIES

1. **Brian's Song** (1970) *Above-average fact-based TV movie about cancer ending a friendship between two Chicago Bears.*
2. **Butch Cassidy and the Sundance Kid** (1969) *Comedy-drama about two famous outlaws.*
3. **The Chosen** (1981) *Friendship between an assimilated Jewish teen and a strict Hasidic one.*
4. **Dead End** (1937) *The film that introduced the Bowery Boys gang.*
5. **Dumbo** (1941) *Disney animated charmer in which Timothy the Mouse teaches Dumbo the Elephant to be confident.*
6. **Midnight Cowboy** (1969) *Naive male hustler and decrepit Ratso Rizzo fight to escape life in sordid New York.*
7. **My Own Private Idaho** (1991) *Partially inspired by Shakespeare's Henry IV plays, this poignant art film shows the relationship between a narcoleptic street kid and the mayor's wayward son.*
8. **Road to Bali** (1952) *The only color film in the "Road to . . ." series, starring Bob Hope and Bing Crosby.*
9. **Stand By Me** (1986) *Horror short story becomes the basis of a heartwarming tribute to boyhood friendships in the 1950s.*
10. **Three Musketeers** (1974) *All for one and one for all! Tongue-in-cheek version of Dumas' swashbuckler.*

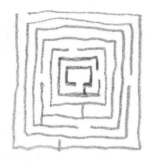

philosophize, and appreciate the tragic dimensions of life. Misery loves company, and ours is a relationship based on determining whose doubts and anxieties are more profound at any given moment.

Don now teaches writing at a college in upstate New York, and when I paid him a visit on Thanksgiving, we sat in his living room and watched helplessly and lovingly as our children—five in all, three his, two mine, one each on the way—filled the house with noise and life.

"Your children grow up and leave you," Don observed, "but your friends grow old with you."

Actually, at this stage in my life, I see more of new friends than I do of old, the society of my everyday world being determined primarily by work and family. If I'm not interviewing someone or related to them, I just don't have time for them.

In selfish moments I sometimes wish I were an old-fashioned man capable of finding masculine escape in fraternal organizations, veterans groups, or sporting clubs, but, damn it, I'm not.

"Oh, you're a modern man, aren't you?" a beautiful young woman said to me this summer. And with that she proceeded to bare her beautiful breasts and to nurse her newborn as we talked.

"Yes, I suppose I am a modern man," I wanted to say, "but that doesn't keep me from wanting to screw every attractive woman I meet."

The male-female relationship is powerfully physical. Other men understand this natural truth. Women seem to find it somehow reprehensible. I'm sure I will pay for admitting it here.

And perhaps because there are some primal truths that must not be uttered except in extreme confidence, a man needs at least one friend who is past the point of politeness. In my case, that friend was Mr. Rossolowsky.

Sergei Rossolowsky was a Russian artist born in St. Petersburg in 1895, one year before my grandfather was born in Ohio. By the time I met him 80 years later he had been pretty badly beaten up by history. His parents had been killed in the Bolshevik Revolution. His wife and daughter had been sent off to a Stalinist concentration camp and were never seen again. And he himself had survived imprisonment in Moscow during the revolution, forced labor on the Belmomor-Baltic White Sea Canal Project under Stalin, capture by the Nazis and forced labor in Poland during World War II, and the Dresden firebombing.

Old, sick, poor, and alone, Mr. Rossolowsky was a familiar figure on the streets of provincial Portland in the 1960s and 1970s. He was the little fellow in the greatcoat and beret pulling his portfolio and groceries behind him on a handcart. And the first thing I learned from Mr. Rossolowsky was how fierce a man must be in defense of his dignity.

I got to know Mr. Rossolowsky through the Portland Public Library, where I worked and he frequently appeared. A ferocious, unreasonable old tyrant, Mr. Rossolowsky won my heart immediately. During the last year of his life, 1975–76, I spent a good deal of time visiting him in his hot, fetid rooms on Cumberland Avenue listening both to his incredible stories of the modern age (novel-to-come) and his unending litany of low-income woes: inadequate medical attention, impenetrable bureaucracies, insensitive landlords, etc.

As it happened, I was with him in Bath (where he had gone because he insisted the doctors at Maine Medical Center were incompetent) the day he was told that a tumor in his stomach was finally going to do what Lenin, Stalin, Hitler, and U.S. bombers hadn't been able to do.

"Sic transit gloria mundi," said Mr. Rossolowsky philosophically. But he did not go without a fight.

So I sat by his bedside and I watched him die. At the very end his ancient, historical life was concentrated in his eyes, eyes which stared widely and intensely at the ceiling as his mouth gaped for breath. I kept talking until I was sure he couldn't hear me, until I was sure he was seeing wonders I will only see in my own time of dying.

I buried Mr. Rossolowsky on a cold, clear fall day in 1976. A frozen October moon rose in the midday sky and there were snowflakes like angels in the air.

What I learned from Mr. Rossolowsky is that a man never gets so old he cannot imagine living just one more year. What I learned from Mr. Rossolowsky is that no matter how routine your life seems at the moment, the forces underlying that normalcy are mysterious and unpredictable in the extreme. What I learned from my friend Mr. Rossolowsky is that it is entirely possible that my best friend has not even been born yet.

BOOKS ABOUT FRIENDSHIPS	**Brian Patrick McGuire, *Friendship and Community: The Monastic Experience 350-1250*.** Kalamazoo, MI: Cistercian Publications, 1985. Fascinating scholarly study of classic and early Christian attitudes toward and practices of friendship.

Brian Patrick McGuire, *Friendship and Community: The Monastic Experience 350-1250*. Kalamazoo, MI: Cistercian Publications, 1985. Fascinating scholarly study of classic and early Christian attitudes toward and practices of friendship.

David Michaelis, *The Best of Friends: Profiles of Men and Friendship*. New York: Quill (William Morrow), 1983. The most memorable of the seven accounts of contemporary pairs of best buddies is the one about "*Saturday Night Live*" stars Dan Aykroyd and John Belushi. Otherwise, the book has somewhat of a prep school, Ivy League orientation with portraits of pairs like John F. Kennedy and K. Lemoyne Billings as well as Buckminster Fuller and Isamu Noguchi.

Stuart Miller, *Men and Friendship*. Boston: Houghton Mifflin, 1983. Chronicling his attempts at midlife to make some male friends, the author found that most men's fear of homosexuality kept them from placing much of a priority on male friendships. Ironically, Miller discovered that the closest friendships were between gay males who were not lovers.

David W. Smith, *Men Without Friends: A Guide to Developing Lasting and Meaningful Friendships*. Nashville: Thomas Nelson, 1990. Conversational book written from a Christian perspective, full of discussion questions and personal inventories. Useful for church groups starting men's groups.

TOUCHING THE MASCULINE SOUL

BY BARRY COONEY, Ph.D.

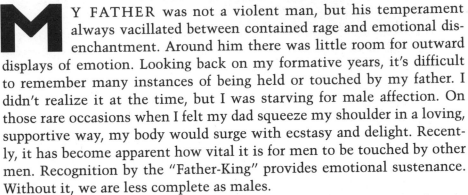

Next to drumming, rampant hugging is perceived as one of the hallmarks of the men's movement—and an easy target for ridicule. It's true that in some men's circles hugging has been cheapened into perfunctory gestures. Yet, elsewhere the powerful clasping of two men continues to hold its intensity. Self-consciousness about hugging another man, except perhaps in a post-touchdown jubilation, is largely an American hang-up; it is not a fear that arises naturally from the male psyche. . . . as Barry Cooney reminds us. ✏

MY FATHER was not a violent man, but his temperament always vacillated between contained rage and emotional disenchantment. Around him there was little room for outward displays of emotion. Looking back on my formative years, it's difficult to remember many instances of being held or touched by my father. I didn't realize it at the time, but I was starving for male affection. On those rare occasions when I felt my dad squeeze my shoulder in a loving, supportive way, my body would surge with ecstasy and delight. Recently, it has become apparent how vital it is for men to be touched by other men. Recognition by the "Father-King" provides emotional sustenance. Without it, we are less complete as males.

Latin, Mediterranean, and eastern European cultures seem to have a deeper understanding of this need. Anyone who has visited South America has witnessed the *abrazo*, or hug, that takes place when two or more male friends meet. I recall with stunning vividness my first weeks in Budapest as a graduate research assistant. There in the University Square, men of all ages walked arm in arm. At first, I was a little confused by their behavior. Gradually, I realized that this display of warmth and affection was not sexual, but arose from a deeper awareness of the need for males to bond with other males. Returning to the United States, I was shocked to see men recoiling from one another in crowded elevators or hands being quickly removed as soon as the shake exceeded its customary two-second limit.

Is it any wonder men in North America remain untrusting and self-centered, or why we bare our souls more openly to women than to our fellow brothers?

The taboos against males touching males in our society can be traced back to the thinking of our Puritan fathers. Their philosophy is one rooted in hard work, skepticism, and sin, with little time left over for anything else. According to their model, emotional expression is always suspect. (Life, it seems, was serious business.) The same is true in lovemaking, which was supposed to be carried out as a joyless procedure for procreating the species.

Prior to the men's movement of the last decade, signs of male affection were exhibited mostly by gay men. For those of us who took pride in being super studs, demonstrating physical affection to another male was definitely forbidden. However, in my case, the need to touch and be touched by a man was so strong that I knew I needed to search for someone who might be sympathetic to my plight.

I didn't have long to wait. The opportunity arose during my first job as a therapist in a large, East Coast teaching hospital. One of the chief psychiatrists (let's call him Bob) approached me after a staff meeting. Would I have dinner with him? "Sure, I'd be delighted," I remember saying. It was my suspicion that Bob was gay. However, the thought of Bob's homosexuality or of his invitation to dinner was in no way threatening to my sense of masculinity. To me, Bob was a sensitive, extremely bright, and highly cultured human being, a person whom I'd like to have as a friend.

We strolled along narrow cobblestone streets, talking about art and music. After a while, we stopped in front of an enormous, carved, mahogany door. Turning abruptly, Bob

struck the gold knocker, giving it two sharp taps. The door swung open and we were greeted by a tall, husky waiter with a huge handlebar moustache. Suddenly I found myself sitting in one of the city's most exclusive gay restaurants.

As we casually ate our superb meal, Bob talked freely about his homosexuality. He was the son of an alcoholic father who had abandoned both his mother and him when Bob was only nine years old. He developed a serious interest in men only a few years after that incident.

At one point during dinner, in the middle of a particularly painful part of his story, Bob spontaneously reached over and held my hand. It seemed an appropriate gesture, given the situation. I remember thinking how unusual it would have been for any of my friends or family members to extend themselves in such a manner. (The only exception to this

rule came at Irish funerals of distant relatives. Occasionally, amidst the arguing and crying, one could observe two or three men locked in a tearful, drunken embrace.)

As a result of our dinner meeting, Bob and I developed a close friendship. While he recognized that I was a "hard-core hetero," Bob was also aware of my own sensitivity. During the years we knew each other, I could always count on him for a warm hug at the end of a stressful day, or after my marriage ended, a needed shoulder to grasp when the pain became unbearable.

It's clear that my involvement with this gay psychiatrist was primarily therapeutic in nature. Being able to share the intimacy of touch, in many ways satisfied my tremendous emotional hunger for male affection. I felt stronger and more complete because of that friendship. Males who are denied appropriate physical affection with other males while growing up become people who never actually mature. In fact, many men who are so denied will strongly repress their need for manly affection. You can see these men in any football game or boxing match. They seem to thrive on the violent aspects of male contact, while distancing themselves from any form of intimacy.

At a recent workshop for men that I conducted in Toronto, I was working with a group of males whose ages ranged from 25 to 69 years. As is the case with most gatherings of this nature, there was a tremendous recounting of stories involving physically or emotionally absent fathers. As the workshop progressed and we moved through exercises that allowed us to express openly our emotions, it was clear that the supportive hugs and embraces being exchanged represented feelings that had been held in check for many years. For the men older than 50, listening to younger males speak of their need for the "fatherly embrace" seemed to break open their protective shells, allowing them to experience the deep healing that takes place when males begin to bond emotionally with other males.

One powerful aspect of the men's movement is its emphasis on this form of bonding. When men are allowed to freely experience the love and support of other men, they begin to question competition in our society. This questioning engenders a willingness to engage in more service-oriented projects and activities whose aim is to nurture and protect the planet.

Thus, the "feeling man" becomes fully initiated into manhood and carries out his role as a protector, healer, and teacher to other men. He enters, to paraphrase the late Joseph Campbell, a transpersonal state of consciousness in which service to his selfish ego is replaced by a desire to lend his energy and support to the greater good of humankind. Here lies the power of the New Masculine Soul. It all begins with an embrace.

MIRRORS ON THE WALL

BY JOHN GUARNASCHELLI, Ph.D.

John Guarnaschelli, Ph.D., lives with his wife and daughter in New York City. He is Associate Professor of History at Queensborough Community College, part of the City University. He is founder and present director of ON THE COMMON GROUND, a non-organizational Center for Men in NYC, which is located at:

250 West 57th St.
Suite 1527
New York, NY, 10107

PAYNE WHITNEY gymnasium with its towering gothic spires was a kind of cathedral of refuge during my years of graduate studies in history at Yale. Its apparently endless rooms and corridors housed every physical exercise from aerobics to weight lifting. And those halls provided welcome solace when the Hapsburg silver mines of the 16th century got to be just a bit too much.

Recently, I thought of the football team portraits that lined the corridors, in chronological order, from almost the first moment photography was popularly available to the present. I remember hurrying past them one day on my way to the pool and being struck by a really remarkable shift in the visual rhythm of those portraits.

The convention at Yale is that its football team should be portrayed casually draped over the Yale fence, which once marked its boundary with the town of New Haven. And with the teams from the 1880s, 1890s, and early 1900s, "draped" is certainly the word for it. The "Bubbas" and "Mooses" of that day seem to feel no inhibitions about sprawling all over each other. The men pose body to body, leaning against each other, sometimes with their arms over one another's shoulders. Their body language says, "We are the brothers of the football team, and we want the world to see that."

But suddenly, just about 1918 or 1919, everything changes. All of a sudden, the men in the portraits go bolt upright and stand very, very separate from one another. Bodily touching and arms over shoulders become things of the distant past. Now we stand staring at the camera with just the right space dividing us. And that's how the teams continue to pose right down to our own time.

The memory of those Yale photographs reminds me of the times the guys in my men's group and I have tried to approach the question of bodily contact. How skittish we become. How many jokes suddenly become necessary.

I remember a conversation on the subject one night with my good friend, Dennis. He points out that the only thing in the bar he isn't

allowed to touch is me. We're both careful to note how different we feel about the women standing around.

I remember how guilty and uncertain of myself I have felt when I discovered how good it might feel to touch or hold another man—or, God help me, be touched or held by him. What anger I've felt toward my father who never embraced me or really even touched me in a way that told me he had a body just like mine and that it was okay to have mine. Somehow these always seemed like very personal hurts—very tough to talk about. Somehow such feelings always skirt my dread of homosexuality. These are areas where it's just too tough to explore the answers my questions might offer me.

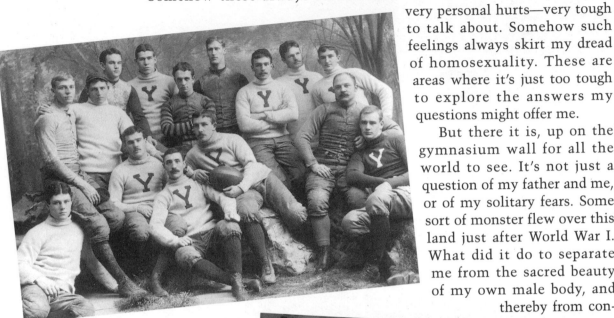

But there it is, up on the gymnasium wall for all the world to see. It's not just a question of my father and me, or of my solitary fears. Some sort of monster flew over this land just after World War I. What did it do to separate me from the sacred beauty of my own male body, and thereby from con- fidently knowing the sacredness and beauty of yours? How did we get so split from one anoth- er that we must over- come moun- tains of fear before we can hold one another

Team photos reflect the changes in the way Americans feel about physical contact off the playing field.

up? I'm sure I don't know the answer to that question. But whatever it is, I'm sure the foot- ball team led the way.

HUNG LIKE A HAMSTER
THE HEAVY WEIGHT OF A SMALL PENIS

BY GREG PERRY

I CAN'T REMEMBER how old I was when I realized that my penis was much smaller than the other boys'. But I can remember where I was when it hit me.

From an early age, I loved to swim, and was on several different swim teams. We'd already be in our suits when our mothers dropped us off at the city pool. We'd run through the locker room, splash across the foot bath and into the pool. One day, after swimming all afternoon, my neighbor's mother pulled up to get us. Instead of spreading towels across the seats to keep them dry, she handed us a sack with clean clothes. We were going straight to dinner from the pool and my mom had sent along some dry clothes.

I know I had considered my own penis by then—its purpose and the mysterious changes that happened sometimes—but until my friend let his trunks drop to the floor, I had never thought about its size. Which was, compared to my friend's, tiny.

Compared to my friends. Compared to my father. Compared to my younger brother. Compared to nearly every other man I've seen naked since then, my penis is smaller. And at once, I'm back in the city pool locker room, caught staring at my friend's dangling, slender penis.

During my orientation as a volunteer literacy tutor, we were told about some of the inventive ways nonreaders would mask their illiteracy. I could relate. My puberty, adolescence, and young adulthood were a study in ways to keep my underwear on. When our PE teacher would check to see if we had showered before going back to class, I'd wet my hair in the sink, and on one occasion with water from the toilet. In high school, when the swim team began to wear Speedo suits that hide nothing, I suddenly developed an interest in money, and quit the team to work. When I pledged a fraternity, it was because they had individual urinals and shower stalls which the dorm or other frat houses did not. I was constantly vigilant for situations that would expose me. I took showers late at night.

My lack of size below the belt was compensated for with obsessions of grand dimensions. At different times I've been addicted to good grades, good drugs, big money, and running. If I was accomplished in one small part of my life then no one could shame me about my other small part.

Which was true. No one ever did shame me. I was never taunted or snickered at. Lovers have dismissed my sheepish apologies after lovemaking. They were either pleased with how I compensated, or didn't notice a difference worth talking about. During a medical exam, my doctor noted to an attending medical student, an attractive woman, that "the phallus is normal." The doctor offered assurance, but words can't describe my embarrassment.

So the shame was self-created. I was the one who made comparisons with men in underwear ads, not them with me. Yet those ads do exist. And throughout the male culture, bigger is better and small is weak. I felt inadequate, impotent, and cheated. Not all the time, but often enough to keep me off-balance in my inner life, which was beginning to deepen as the men's movements matured. I could see no beauty in my own penis, which was the real shame.

What's the point of all this? I can't deliver an inspiring story of conquered humiliation, or witness for the magical transformative powers of the mythopoetic men's movement. Some days, the best I can do is feel sorry for myself. Some days I can write about it. When I'm feeling clear and whole, I can laugh about it. (After all, I titled this essay.) Certainly, my experiences with men's work have been rich and valuable; it's changed my life for the better and continues to feed me. Yet my shame, albeit somewhat diminished, persists. So I ask again, What's the point?

At one men's conference, I read this on the wall: By naming our wounds they will lose their power over us.

Consider it named.

Bly then takes the idea of wounds further. "Our wounds can eventually become our gifts." So, I offer this: my love and respect to all men who carry the pain of inadequacy—real or imagined. Believe me, I understand. I understand the fantasies. I understand the isolation. I understand the fear.

But let's forget it all for an afternoon, and go swimming. Naked.

42

Notes on Three Erections

BY MICHAEL VENTURA

Michael Ventura, columnist for *L.A. Weekly*, often turns out essays that exemplify the best in the tradition of that literary form. He brings together facts and insights from many different fields of learning and integrates them in original ways. Too much of a maverick to become an establishment figure in the men's movement, he recently collaborated with another iconoclast, James Hillman, on a conversation book *We've Had 100 Years of Psychotherapy and the World's Getting Worse*. The following much-admired piece appears in his collection, *Shadowdancing in the USA*. ✒

IF YOU'RE ever in Los Angeles, drive to the end of Wilshire and face the sea. Something stands in your way—something that purports to be a statue of Saint Monica herself. As to who Saint Monica was, the statue gives no clue; bullet-shaped, the stone stands without expression or gesture, giving nothing, asking nothing, and seeming to absorb any light or glance with no return reflection. The piece has an air of wanting to be ignored and it gets its wish. It is as though the sculptor had been frightened by his own idea. Plainly, whether he knew it or not, his idea had been to sculpt the image of a woman onto a phallus.

Walk around the statue. From behind, it is an erection plain and simple and only slightly abstract. From the front, a woman of minimal lines has taken her place within, or on the surface of, the penis. The conception is so phallic that once seen this way it is difficult to see it any other way, if indeed there was any other.

I think of lines from the poet John Yau:

> *Memory going one way*
> *the body another. Something wedged in*
> > *between.*

This minor sculptor was wedged in between, exercising his limited gifts while all but unbeknownst to him his psyche went back, far back, to the Neolithic era and beyond. In that day, it was not unusual to sculpt images of the Great Goddess onto carvings of the erect penis.

There were no gods then. Only goddesses. It would be thousands of years before the race would begin to sculpt male gods. Neolithic humans apparently felt little maleness in divinity. Or put it another way: Intense spirituality brought forth from them female images. Or another: for a long, long time in the youth of humankind, flashes of the spirit were felt primarily with the feminine aspects of both men and women.

We can only guess at what they meant by carving the Great Goddess

onto the cock. Was it the Goddess tattooing her claim onto the very maleness of men? Was it the man finding a passion in sexuality that couldn't be wholly satisfied by the physical, a yearning in him for something of the spirit to mix with his passion? Or was it the meeting not only of the divine and the physical, but of the masculine and the feminine *cohabiting the cock itself*? An idea to reckon with. If the cock is also feminine, then where does "feminism" hide and where does "macho" run?

We have made such easy distinctions in our society, and they suit so conveniently our prejudices of the moment. But simplicities like "feminine or masculine" and "straight or gay" are shallow beside these ancient stones. Robert Bly cites experiments in England that show that if a man suckles an infant regularly, after a few weeks his breasts will start to give milk. That secret was there all the while in those crude stone statues of goddesses on phalluses.

For us these can't be statues of precise meaning and shouldn't be. "Precision" in such things means to focus on one possibility while ignoring others. Rather, these are statues of the cock as a metamorphic possibility—a capacity to leap from meaning to meaning within the flesh itself. Very different from the singular thrust that "erection" means for us. Think of it rather as raw goddess-stuff and raw god-stuff that, like water from a fountain, hovers in a pillar at the height of its flight, keeping its huge erect form while engaged in continuous transformation.

But these are just words circling the image. Once the image gets into your consciousness it has its own life and doesn't need explanations so much as it needs to be savored, remembered. What is important in the image of the goddess etched onto the penis is that male and female energy meet in the cock without either one losing essence or form. And the first thing to "do" with such an image is to realize that we already embody it, no matter what we've forgotten and what we hide from ourselves. The erection, which the feminist and the macho alike have seen as such a one-note, one-purpose organ, is less a sword than a wand.

So, as an unknowing representative of ancient consciousness, that rather sad statue on Ocean and Wilshire transcends itself and becomes a piece of psychic archaeology. We have many a Neolithic stone in our heads. One of Freud's first and most important discoveries was that "in the subconscious there is no Time." Jung extrapolated from individuals to the entire race, using Freud's insight as a passageway down which he went to find the collective unconscious and his demonstration that ancient archetypes of thought live their own lives through and with us. Not that we are possessed, but that we are connected, and that the rhythms of our wills are often ancient dances.

Take that piece of stone, sandblast out "Santa Monica" and chisel in

*I am so **tired** of all this talk about "straight" and "gay." You cannot separate men into two camps, "straight" and "gay." That's just an effort to divide and weaken men. The truth is, there are two kinds of men: men who look good in a tank top and men who don't. And the ones who do are **insufferable**.*

—Roy Blount, Jr.

"Erect Male Member, Featuring Goddess" (marvelous word, *member*, a member of the group that is the person, a member both connected and somehow independent)—*then* people would stop and contemplate that statue. Or laugh at it—which would at least be a beginning, a step away from the monolithic notion of male sexuality in which we're all, men and women, equally trapped.

Put the Neolithic phallus beside another phallic image, this one some 17,000 years old: a painting in the innermost of the ancient caves at Lascaux, France. Deep in what is considered to be Lascaux's holiest vault, a wall painting depicts a bison hovering over a stick figure of a man with a birdlike head and an erection. This is thought (by such as Joseph Campbell and William Irwin Thompson) to be the earliest known depiction of a shaman. The birdlike head is thought to be his mask. His erection is taken as a sign that he is dreaming—for men very often get erections while dreaming. The shaman, who is reclining, is thought to be dreaming of the image of the bison that hovers over him.

Here again is an image to remind us of what the sexual deliberations of the last 20 years, mostly feminist and gay, have largely ignored: that an erect cock has more meanings than sex; that the act of ranging through realms of the psyche, which we call "dreaming," and which is how the psyche generates its images into composite sequences to give us signs, this act, too, causes erections. In fact, given the time we spend sleeping, it may not be too outrageous to say that dreaming causes most erections. Which is to say that there is something of the dream in every erection—the dream's complexity, its lineage, its imagery, and its metamorphic possibilities.

Go further and say: Every erection is, in effect, a dream. It rises from a dream, it is sustained by a dream, it seeks to penetrate a dream. Rilke wondered often in his poetry whether lovers ever truly touched. There are the man and the woman and all that each is and all that they want to be and all that they pretend to be and all that they think they are and all that they seek in each other, and all that is present in *every* coupling, making every coupling a veritable orgy! And the link through which all these aspects pass, the connector, is the erection. Again: the wand.

The shaman sleeping his vision in Lascaux, his vision seeming to hover above his hard-on, sleeps in us as well. We may have forgotten him, we may not like to think about him, but he dreams on, and his cock is also ours. What has happened to us, denying these subtleties of the cock? We've attributed all the mystery to the cunt, that's what. Projected it there, and then resented it there, because we had so little of our own. But the cunt has its own great claim on mystery, it doesn't need the inflation we men give it by denying what's inherently within us. It's a sorry way to be men, to live without our own physical mystery.

Who can say how much this denial's hurt us? And who can say how much it's wounded our world? Sexism is the need to suppress the women we secretly fear, and why do we fear them unless it is the suspicion that they contain mysteries, and therefore powers, that we can't equal? And while the mysteries aren't only sexual, the emblems of these mysteries certainly are. I am saying that men would have much less to fear of women if we were open to the equally sexual emblems of our equally mysterious natures.

In white men, this denial has been a cause of another horror: the racism that has plagued the world in the 500 years that European whites and their American descendants have sought to dominate it. We have looked upon black bodies, especially male black bodies, with utter horror for half a millennium, and why? Christianism has taught us that the body, per se, is wrong and that to deny the body is right. Christianism has saturated us with an iconography in which white is good, dark is not. It was a program for hate. When we came upon peoples who were not only dark but who moved with a suppleness that whites had denied in themselves—who were *in* their evil bodies without denial—then everything we've denied in ourselves came to face us. It was unbearable. For many, it still is. Rather than waken the sleeping shaman within our own cave, we ravaged a world.

We enslaved and hated and killed with the power of our own impacted mysteries. We were mad. A thousand years of denial had made Europeans restless enough to leave their homelands, and ruthless enough to seek mastery of everything. Peoples who hadn't denied as much, who were content with their homeland, and who wanted not mastery but the slow evolution of their traditions—these couldn't stand against the white jihad. We were like a horrible dream of the sleeping shaman within us.

He slept but was not dead. He has been stirring for a while now, half-awake, opening his eyes. In some men he speaks. In some he dances. He has enough mystery of his own, enough power, enough darkness in his light, not to fear or envy anybody else's. The ancients of Lascaux knew that you had to crawl down and down and down through the stone in yourself to find him, and this is something some of us are painfully learning to do. One thing that he will teach us is the ways of the wand.

To find the third erection, drive down the eastern coast of Mexico, where there are few Anglo tourists, and stop in one of the little towns about midway between Brownsville and Tampico. There are no flashy sights to see. These are simply working towns. Walk around in the early evening and go into one of the workingmen's bars (if you're a man—females aren't approved of here). There's usually a pool table, sometimes someone playing music, or a TV or radio. Mostly it's just a bar, no frills, just men drinking beer and talking. But on the walls you will often see two images. One is a rude wall-sized drawing of a *Playboy*-pinup-like woman (often not a Mexican woman) tied down, bloody with torture, being raped by some huge man, often an Aztec-like Indian. On the other wall, sometimes the opposite wall, there is likely to be a brightly colored drawing of a flying cock—often a winged and phoenix-like phallus rising out of the flames.

Those genial, grizzled, work-tired, and sweaty men drinking their *cerveza* are living between those two images. Most of us are. The incongruity between the men and the pictures would be almost comical if we didn't know that those pictures are painted on the inside of their skulls as well. On the one hand you admire how unself-conscious they are about it all—how readily accessible those images are in their lives. Most supposedly sophisticated peoples have to dig a lot harder to unearth the same materials. On the other hand, you have to feel for how without consciousness they are—bearing the weight of a culture that is somehow both tumultuous and changeless, exhausted by a struggle for survival that reduces them to a dependence on symbols that make it more difficult for them to survive. They drink their beer every night under the images that could help free them if they weren't too leaden with fatigue—in every sense, on every level—to think beyond what they've been given, to feel beyond what they know.

The winged cock: Is it a symbol of disembodied sexuality that will claim no responsibility and that wants no love, hence justifying and making possible the torture on the opposite wall? Or it is an unconscious counterpart to an equally unconscious image of torture, a vivid and poignant image of male sexuality trying to transcend the very walls on which the pictures are painted?

Both, I suspect. Here is the price of the macho code, yes, but that is too easy to say. What creates a macho code? Here is a household matriarchy governed economically by a societal patriarchy that emphasized being "a strong man" while denying men power over their lives or their work. Which means that there is no place for these men to be men. In work they are mules. And the home is the woman's domain. And so they are powerless except in their bars. And there they have no power but to play games, to talk, to pose, to get drunk, to fantasize. They don't paint pictures of their bosses and politicos being buggered because they would be arrested or shot, and most of them are too savvy to let themselves be so easily murdered. They can only burst their limits in that other place where they feel powerless, their homes. Their families. Their women. Their children. It is a miserable and vicious circle—no different from North American's ghetto bars and redneck bars. It is only that in Mexico it is more stark and less self-conscious, and both those qualities give us these wall paintings.

The rape is a fantasy of power over the women, the home, obviously; yet, on another level this usually Aztec rapist is torturing an almost-white Mexican woman, so this is also a fantas y of the ancient spirit of Mexico making Europe and the United States pay for their sins. It is no wonder that this is the only place where these men can relax; it is the only place where their rage is expressed honestly, however passive that honesty has to be.

And the winged cock flying from the flames—the one that I remember most vividly was so brightly colored, and its lines were so full of energy and movement, that you couldn't mistake its joy. Here was every metamorphic possibility set loose. Here was the rush of wings a man can sometimes feel in his pants. (Not to mention how a woman may want to feel it flying within her.) And here was the flaming psyche it rises from. Here was the want in its power. And, yes, that power must be grounded to be genuine, to be able to replenish itself. But we separate too easily the idea of being grounded and the "pure" idea, as the psychologists would call it, the idea of flying free. I think of how these concepts live together in a verse of Robert Bly's:

The Lingam–Brahmanic symbol of propagation.

> *A dream of moles with golden wings*
> *Is not so bad; it is like imagining*
> *Waterfalls of stone deep in mountains.*
> *Or a wing flying alone beneath the earth.*

A flight only occurs, after all, in relation to a ground—and what else is an erection but a rising, a flight, and then settling down to ground again? Bly's "wing flying alone beneath the earth" is such a resonant and satisfying image because within it the contradictions exist without needing to be put to rest by some compromise between them, some resolution. There are nights of lovemaking that are like flying beneath the earth.

The penis, which offers the same passage to piss and jism, to dead waste and creation itself, never resolves its contradictions. That's apparently not what it's here for. The want, far from being the monolith the West has made of it, has many lives that exist at once; its flesh is a medium of paradox, potent by virtue of the possibilities it calls forth.

There was much talk, in those eighties of ours, about masculinity and about the possibility of masculine movement through which men would begin describing themselves in a more full, more vital way than they yet have during the reign of Christianism. If this dialogue or movement is going to have some social force, it will have to have at its core a discussion of male sexuality, as feminism had at its core a discussion of female sexuality. I've offered these images of erections as a small part of a large beginning.

For certainly the weakest, silliest aspect of feminism—which for the most part has been an overwhelmingly beneficial movement—has been its description of male sexuality. It was a description that assumed a monolithic, monointentioned erection; it was a description that equated the ejaculation of sperm with coming. The three images here—and there obviously could have been many more—should be enough to suggest the many secret passageways within an erection. As far as the question of male "coming"—it is an immense and untried question. Ejaculation is a muscle spasm that many men often feel with virtually no sensation but the twitch of the spasm. To ejaculate is not necessarily to come. Coming involves a constellation of sensations, physical, psychic, emotional, of virtually infinite shadings. Coming may *sometimes* or *often* occur at the moment of ejaculation, when it occurs at all. *But many ejaculations for many men happen without any sensation of coming.*

Until a woman understands this she doesn't know the first thing about male sexuality.

Nor do many men. There is ample evidence in face after face that, as there are women who have never come, so there are men who have often ejaculated but never come. And they likely don't know it, as many women never knew it until a few began to be vocal about such things. These men live in a terrifying and baffling sexual numbness in which they try the right moves and say the right things but every climax is, literally, an anticlimax. It is no wonder that in time they have less and less connection with their own bodies, and are increasingly distant from the women they want to love.

Feminism has also gotten a lot of mileage out of the mistaken notion that men can't fake coming the way women can. Men can't fake the ejaculation of sperm, of course, but we can fake muscle spasms, hip jerks, and moans as well as any woman can. During an agonizing period of premature ejaculation, I ejaculated almost instantly upon entering but, remaining hard, I didn't let on but kept right on going through the motions, faking the muscle spasms and moans of orgasm when the women had (or faked) her own. Several male friends, when questioned, admitted having had similar experiences.

How are men and women to know of these things when they're never spoken of, and when even in literature you can search far and wide for a worthy, complex description of what it may be for a man to come. You don't find it, for instance, in Henry Miller. He describes brilliantly how it feels to be a cock inside a cunt, to truly enter and *be* there; and he describes his perceptions of women coming; and he is truly brilliant at writing of the shaman's dreaming erection—often he seems to write out of the center of those dreams themselves; but he never, in all my readings of him, gets inside his own coming. Nor does D. H. Lawrence, who is so fine at expressing the longing of the phoenixlike, winged erection.

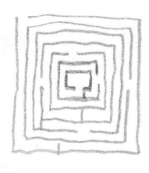

Their narratives stop before the ejaculation, pass over the experience of coming with some summary phrase and continue after it.

Norman Mailer gets close, once, but not in one of his novels—where, considering his aesthetics, his glossing over the issue is unconscionable. But he did it in an essay, a brief passage in his thought-sparking book *The Prisoner of Sex*. After chiding feminist writers (a brave move in 1971) for their "dull assumption that the sexual force of a man was the luck of his birth" he writes of ". . . orgasms stunted as lives, screwed as mean and fierce and squashed and cramped as the lives of men and women whose history was daily torture . . . comes as far away as the aria and the hunt and the devil's ice of a dive, orgasms like the collision of a truck, or coming as soft as snow, arriving with the riches of a king in costume, or slipping in the sneaky heat of a slide down slippery slopes . . . ."

A few sentences onward he gives one of the sentences of his life: "At orgasm," he says, "the eye of your life looked back at you then. Who would wish to stare into that eye if it was poorer than one's own?"

Who indeed. We are all paying the price of such moments. We pay for our own and for each other's. Men and women alike. Yet there are times when the eye of your orgasm, the eye staring back at you, matches your own; and times when it is richer than your own, leading you on to what you may yet be.

A single suggestive passage about male orgasm in years of sexually explicit literature is a poor showing. Doubtless there are more floating about, but not many, and they're hardly known and apparently unremembered.

We men, who have never spoken of such things, are squarely to blame for the consequences of our constipated silences. What more than spasms is to be expected of our entire culture of adult men who are frightened to wear colors during business hours? The neatly knotted tie is all that's left of our desert shawl and shaman robe. Most American and European businessmen, aped by businessmen all over the world now, still walk around in the black-and-white and brown-and-white color variations of celibate monks who spent a thousand years frightened of nothing so much as of all the imagery that might rise out of an erection.

One example of a reaction to the color fear are rock stars like Prince who, for all his childish and sexist lyrics, is on the cutting edge of these issues right now because he is bringing colors back to men. Or at any rate, back to boys who will one day be men. The hot-colored styles Prince inspires reflect the spectrum of the psyche much better than gray flannel.

There are many who would like the needed innovation and advances to occur on a more sophisticated and enlightened level than, say, Prince works on. But that is a luxury we can hardly afford. We are desperate people, and must take our signs as they come, whether from a rock star, or a sullen statue on Ocean and Wilshire, or a painting in a cramped cave, or a mural in a Mexican bar. They are the work of men, and so they are ours.

The body is such an immense place. We take so long to find our ways across it. And each of us has so many bodies. Sometimes they drag behind us, and we feel encumbered and earth-laden. Sometimes they race before us, making huge decisions in our name, while we scramble to catch up—and sometimes we call that "sex." And we know so little about these things. And one of the only ways we can test the little we know is to speak of it.

PHALLIC BOOKS

Eugene Monick, *Castration and Male Rage*. Toronto: Inner City Books, 1991. The author is an Episcopal priest and a Jungian analyst. This work begins by recapping many of the ideas in his earlier study, *Phallos*, and goes on to explore the ways that men feel psychically castrated by both women and other men. He then suggests some excellent remedies for this condition.

Eugene Monick, *Phallos: Sacred Image of the Masculine.* Toronto: Inner City Books, 1987. Though the book may be slow reading for those not familiar with Jungian terminology, it is one of the most appreciated works in the men's movement because it establishes the masculine principle as coequal with the feminine in the core of the psyche. Some men's groups make a project of discussing the book section by section.

Mark Strage, *The Durable Fig Leaf: A Historical, Cultural, Medical, Social, Literary, and Iconographic Account of Man's Relations with His Penis*. New York: William Morrow, 1980. This far-ranging consideration of men's fascination with their genitals shows that not much has changed since Adam.

Thorkil Vanggaard, *Phallos: A Symbol and Its History in the Male World*. New York: International Universities Press, 1974. An anthropological study exploring the significance of the penis as a symbol of homosexuality and of male aggression.

James Wyly, *The Phallic Quest: Priapus and Masculine Inflation*. Toronto: Inner City Books, 1989. Beginning with a survey of the fragmentary myths associated with the Greek god with the huge genitals, Jungian Wyly goes on to use literary sources and case histories to discuss masculine inflation and the need for deflation and compensatory balance by the feminine. ✐

VENTURA
NOTES ON
THREE ERECTIONS

MEN AND INTIMACY

BY DOUGLAS GILLETTE

Men have been branded with the stigma of being constitutionally incapable of forming (and staying in) close, committed relationships—or at the least of being naturally averse to such bonds. Because males' needs and ways of being intimate differ from females', men are found wanting when judged by women's standards. Douglas Gillette, coauthor of *King, Warrior, Magician, Lover: Rediscovering the Archetypes of the Mature Masculine* corrects some of the misconceptions. Though Gillette frames his discussion largely in terms of male-female relationships, much of what he says applies equally well to same-gender relationships. The artist-psychomythologist, Douglas Gillette, and the Jungian analyst, Robert Moore, have written a five-book series on masculine psychology which represents a breakthrough in our understanding of the structures and dynamics of the masculine Self. ✐

WINGSPAN
INSIDE THE MEN'S
MOVEMENT

MUCH HAS been written in the past 20 years or so about the reluctance of men, as a gender, to fully engage in "intimate" relationships with women. More responsible authors have shown that both sexes, for related but not identical reasons, often fear "intimacy." It seems more likely, however, that it is not "intimacy" itself that we fear. In fact, we *want* intimacy. Most of us are starving for it. The real problem is more focused. What we fear are specific behaviors directed against us by our partners in intimate relationship, behaviors which display an underlying hostility, but which we have been taught to associate with "intimate" relationship. We have been taught to make all kinds of excuses for these behaviors. We have been taught to whitewash them, to ignore them, or to accept them as the price we have to pay for being in an "intimate" relationship. Yet these destructive and abusive behaviors, perhaps not identified as such by either us or our partners, work like a corrosive to undermine the achievement of the deep and full sharing, the mutual respect and admiration, and the sexual joy which are the hallmarks of a truly intimate relationship between a man and a woman. What men fear—and rightly so—is humiliation, disempowerment, and annihilation at the hands of what they experience as the overwhelming feminine.

A man carries into his relationships with women a fear of disempowerment which arises not only from the painful memory of his Oedipal conflicts (and the *actual* disempowerment he may have experienced at that stage of his development), but also from his experience (also actual) of his gender-specific disempowerment in more general terms. This disempowerment and humiliation of his masculinity often came from his mother during his childhood and teenage years. There exists an inherent tendency for a boy to feel overwhelmed by his mother, and, thus, by the feminine. His mother was a seemingly all-powerful figure for him. She was the original and, even in modern times, the primary source of the earliest relationship dynamics of his life, dynamics which structured his perceptions ever-after of life in the world, which means life in relationship, both to self and others.

Leaving aside for the moment the vitally important dynamic of the "absent father," so much a feature of family life both in the recent past of our culture and in our present "latchkey" situation, it pays to face the fact that mothers often disempower their sons. The "absent father" compounds the problem. But the problem of masculine disempowerment, and the resulting fantasy of psychological, gender-specific annihilation, at the hands of the powerful feminine has its origins in the early mother-son relationship.

THE OVERWHELMING FEMININE

Even what the psychologist D. W. Winnicott calls "good enough" mothering tends to *feel* like disempowerment to boys. After all, the baby boy is, in reality, in a helpless position and in a relationship of utter and total dependence on the feminine. His mother may show him good-enough nurturing, or she may not. Even if she is nurturing, she may tend to stifle any moves toward gender-specific independence and autonomy on the part of her young son. To the extent that "good-enough" mothers are "smothering" they are disempowering of their sons.

The situation becomes much worse if the mother actually attacks or ignores her son. Her attacks may be verbal or physical, or both. If she ignores her son, she is, in reality, passive-aggressing him. Her passive-aggressive behavior and/or her emotional or even physical attacks upon him may come, in part, from her own anger, usually unconscious, against the masculine. Repeated incidents of the mother's disempowerment of her son often occur throughout the growing boy's and then the teenager's and the young man's life. These attacks take many forms, and may range from subtle attempts to undermine her son's masculine pride and exuberance to rageful displays of jealousy when he begins dating. She thus exhibits her own fears of mistreatment or abandonment by the masculine, and, even more primordially, by her own mother.

Fairy-tale witches often represent the "devouring" female.

In such a situation, the boy is left to fend for himself in a significantly, though usually unacknowledged, hostile feminine environment if the father is absent, either physically (because of his work or because he and his wife have separated or divorced) or emotionally. If the father is absent emotionally, he may, like the mother, either dishonestly (passive-aggression) or openly engage in verbal and physical assaults upon his son. Whatever the form, and whatever the underlying cause of the father's absence, the result is that the boy who receives such treatment is crippled in his developmental tasks.

GILLETTE
MEN AND
INTIMACY

53

One of the most important of these developmental tasks, which a boy must successfully accomplish in order to achieve satisfying intimate relationships with women later in life, is that of separating emotionally from the mother. The boy must come to experience himself as profoundly independent of his mother, of her emotional states, of her needs, and of her sexual identity. In order to achieve his own masculine identity, and security in that identity, a boy must first experience himself as radically differentiated from his mother, differentiated as a person and differentiated as a specifically *male* person. Then he needs to find a way to re-relate with his mother, and, through her, with the feminine—*as a man*. He can accomplish these difficult tasks, tasks which girls do not face in the same way because of their gender-identification with their mothers, most successfully when he has a strong, and present, father or other idealized male in his life. In the absence of such men, even good-enough mothers are frighteningly overwhelming to the fragile gender-specific emerging Self-structures of boys. But, as already noted, if the mother is less than good-enough, the threatening quality of the feminine in the early experience of boys is greatly amplified.

THE FORMS OF DISEMPOWERMENT

Disempowerment for boys takes two forms. The first is disempowerment and humiliation (with the attendant threat of annihilation or absorption into the "devouring mother") of the Self as Self. This Self, with a capital S, as the psychologist Carl Jung demonstrated, is bisexual. It is non-gender-specific in its essence. At this level of attack, the True Self (a closely related concept formulated by the psychologist D. W. Winnicott) of the boy—his original and appropriate grandiosity, his true feelings, his Self-expressiveness—is crippled. Since the Self on this level is both masculine and feminine, girls who do not have good-enough mothers (and/or fathers) may experience the same primordial wounding as boys. Here, the mother may be acting out her anger against her own humiliating and disempowering mother.

The second form of disempowerment and humiliation, in the case of boys, however, is aimed at the gender-specific Self, at the emerging *masculine* Self. The mother may launch "preemptive strikes" against the masculinity of her son even when he is still quite young. She may do this in order to a) revenge herself upon her husband, her father, and the masculine in general (which she has experienced, though usually unconsciously, as disempowering and humiliating of *her*) and b) to prevent her son from achieving what may seem to her to be the threatening status of the full-grown male.

THE VULNERABILITY OF MEN

Thus, many men—perhaps most men—to some degree or another bring with them into their would-be intimate relationships with women unresolved fear and anger about past feminine abuses of their masculinity. Many men are, consequently, extremely vulnerable to the shifting moods, to the criticism and anger, and to the sarcasm and ridicule of their women. They continue to try the various strategies they adopted as boys for coping with what feels to them like the invasive and overwhelmingly powerful feminine. These strategies, ultimately dysfunctional, were originally designed to preserve the boy's flagging sense of gender-specific Self-esteem. Men tend, to the extent that their early developmental tasks could not be adequately completed, to experience their partners in would-be intimate relationship as if they were their inordinately powerful mothers. The strategies which men often use to cope with their sense of "real and present danger" in their present intimate relationships include: a) macho bluff; b) studied or unconscious "insensitivity"; c) joviality; d) gentle, or not so gentle, ridicule of the woman or of the feminine in general; e) threat and emotional and/or physical violence; f) cajoling and whining; and g) "playing dead" ("Who me, I'm not a man! I'm no threat to you!").

In their present relationships, many men often find their inadequately drawn boundaries overrun by their women. Their boundaries *are* inadequately drawn because their mothers did, in fact, invade them and seek to merge with them and to submerge the boy's ego and Self, thus rendering the boy's task of constructing legitimate psychological boundaries extremely problematic. An additional factor in the generation of boundary issues is that their fathers were not present enough to show their sons how to consolidate their masculine identities or to empower them to exercise the *legitimate* masculine (and human) prerogatives of Self-affirmation and defense of psychological territory and integrity. These men, then, allow themselves to be overrun by the women they would like to be in intimate relationships with in exactly the same ways in which their mothers overran them, independent, macho, man-of-the-world exteriors notwithstanding. These men will often take an enormous amount of verbal and emotional abuse from women. They will, even though they may resist from time to time, allow their women to render them docile, compliant, and domesticated.

The more sensitive these men may be to women's reservations about masculine power (which sensitivity they learned in relationship with their mothers, reinforced, perhaps, by some feminist perspectives which they may have absorbed), the more they will cooperate in the systematic deprivation of their masculine joy and potency.

THE DISEMPOWERMENT OF MEN BY MEN

As already suggested, it is not only past humiliating and disempowering experiences with the *feminine* that cripple a man's capacity to achieve a truly intimate relationship with a woman. It is also past experiences of

In our civilization, men are afraid that they will not be men enough, and women are afraid they might be considered only women.

—Dr. Theodor Reik

humiliation and masculine disempowerment in the context of his relationships with other *men*. Attacks against the boy's masculine Self may have come from his father, his uncles, male cousins, male siblings, "friends" and enemies in school and in the neighborhood. Put-downs, subtle or blatant, as well as physical violence against him, are often a significant part of a boy's life. These attacks may vary. Vicious criticism may come from a father who feels threatened by his son's claim on the woman whose attention and affections they both share (his wife, the boy's mother), by his son's talents and abilities, by his son's sheer exuberance and aliveness, or by the boy's signs of weakness (reminders to the father of his own inner weaknesses). Psychological and physical attacks on the boy may also come on the school playground, or, in the teenage years, with an increased level of violence, on the streets of his own neighborhood. Actual life-threatening physical violence against teenage boys has become a regular feature of our inner cities.

Unfortunately, male attacks upon the boy's masculine Self tend to be repeated in his adulthood, where they are replicated in the hierarchically structured work world, and even in the world of academia. Women, in increasing numbers, have joined in the same practices as they have moved into greater positions of prominence in the work and academic worlds.

SEX LIFE

Over the course of time, such a disempowered man's sex life, at least his sex life with his mate, suffers. This is cause for alarm, even for panic, to men who fear intimacy. The disappearance of his sexual appetite, with, often, the consequent loss of firm erections, deepens this man's sense of humiliation, especially if his woman responds with anger, criticism, ridicule, petulance, or sarcasm, all strategies which she may employ to try to fend off her growing sense that she is no longer attractive or worthwhile. (She herself may feel humiliated and disempowered as a woman, playing out her own unconscious drama of rejection by the masculine, almost always precipitated originally by her actual rejection by her father.)

If the power struggle with his woman has not been satisfactorily enough resolved, and if he has not been able to formulate and to adequately defend his boundaries, the disempowered man's goodwill toward his mate may, at this point, completely evaporate. In a vain effort to feel his legitimate power, he may try to use the energy generated by his growing rage illegitimately through acts of verbal and/or physical abuse. Alternatively, he may play dead, withdrawing from the field of battle and exhibiting symptoms of major depression. Usually, his behavior will oscillate between these two extremes.

WINGSPAN
INSIDE THE MEN'S
MOVEMENT

56

EMPOWERMENT IS THE KEY
TO INTIMATE RELATIONSHIP

In order for a man to feel empowered, he needs, optimally, to have three factors come into play on his behalf. First and foremost, and fundamental to the recovery of his lost, or disowned, masculine power, he must develop appropriate contact with and reliance upon the archetypes of the mature masculine. Archetypes, as Jung defined them, are instinctual energy patterns built into the deep, or collective, human psyche; in this case, into the collective masculine psyche. Dr. Robert Moore and I have elaborated an archetypal theory which claims that there are four primary, or foundational, instinctual energies in the structure of the masculine Self. These four energies are the King, the Warrior, the Magician, and the Lover. These archetypal patternings of masculine thoughts and feelings, and of masculine behaviors (often resulting in societally defined roles and professions), interact in a complex and, ideally, complementary way with one another and with the accessing ego. In addition, a man needs to learn to know and to access appropriately his inner contrasexual other, what Jungians call the Anima.

Second, a man needs other men—especially older men—to bless him, to honor him, to encourage him, to point out his mistakes, and to raise

MEN CRYING SONGS

Songs that deal with men crying. Some of these tunes contain only fleeting references to tears or to the actual process of crying, while some hammer right down on it. Note that in most of these tunes, as with most pop music, *love* is the cause of all this pain. (Hmm....) Again, in no particular order:

Title / Artists:

"Tracks of My Tears" Smokey Robinson *She's gone and he's just pretending to be having a good time.*

"Little Bird" Jerry Jeff Walker *Thinking back on an old love. She's long gone, but it still hurts.*

"Crying" Hank Williams *She's gone and he's not happy about being nobody's sugardaddy now.*

"Hot Tub of Tears" Austin Lounge Lizards *Country music is an easy target for parody, but that doesn't mean we shouldn't do it. Fire away, Los Lizardos.*

"Til You Cry" Eddie Van Raven *No sooner do I make that crack about country music than I hear this tune on the local country station. It says that we can't get on with living and loving after a heartbreak until we cry.*

"Tears of Joy" Dennis Smith *A sweet song by this unsigned Oregon singer/songwriter—who happens to be a close friend of mine—which covers a range of sights and sounds in everyday life that tend occasionally to bring on the tears.*

"Gentle on My Mind" John Hartford *Another "tears of joy" kind of tune—this one a classic of friendship and tenderness..*

"Alone Again (Naturally)" Gilbert O'Sullivan *Sort of a whining tune, in that it seems that with an attitude like the one suggested in the title, this fellow is bound to be alone quite a bit. Nevertheless, his expression of grief at the loss of his parents is clearly genuine and very moving.*

"Crying in the Chapel" Artie Glenn *And now for something completely different . . . He's laid down his burden and found the Lord. A country-gospel classic.*

List compiled by Lea Jones

his status. The poet Robert Bly talks about this nurturing masculinity as the "male mother." We need not rely on feminine conceptualizations, however, unless they are Anima images, when we try to picture to ourselves what firm but generative older men might look like. We may have had at least *some* experience of such men in our own lives—a relative, a teacher, a coach. In addition, we may have encountered the nurturing masculine in our reading. We may have found supportive men in the arts, in the sciences, in history. But noncorporeal literary figures, while extremely valuable to the man struggling for a sense of legitimate masculine power and Self-affirmation (and struggling to get a vision of the mature masculine), cannot fully replace the *actual* experience of flesh-and-blood men "holding [him] in their hearts," as Bly says.

*A man accessing primarily the archetypes of the Warrior and/or the Magician will have a difficult time fully accepting the Lover in his life. The Lover is the most "vulnerable" archetype because of his inherent tendency to "merge" with others in general (including the world of nature), and his consequent lack of boundaries. This erotic energy draws all things together and all things "into" the psyche. This presents a problem for the man who has been unable to consolidate defensible boundaries. The mature Lover, however, draws upon the limit-setting and structure-building archetypes of the King, the Warrior, and the Magician. If a man is accessing this **complex** configuration in his deep psyche, he becomes a "tender Tarzan," a sensitive yet vital and "penetrating" lover.*

Third, a man's progress toward his legitimate empowerment is aided by a cooperative, admiring, and Self-affirming mate. A man needs to feel admired, appreciated, respected, honored, safe, and sexually responded to. He needs to feel loved. But love is not the most essential thing a man needs from his mate, unless love is *defined* by these other qualities. He certainly does not need the kind of love I have already mentioned, for that love came with the strings of humiliation, disempowerment, and the threat of annihilation attached, as we have seen. A woman can help empower her man to the extent that she herself has come to feel her own legitimate power, has resolved some of her own issues, and has come to terms with her femininity as well as with her contrasexual other, her Animus.

The man seeking legitimate empowerment, and his woman, must learn to cooperate with the instinctual man-woman, "Me Tarzan–You Jane" push from the primate past (a past which is always present in the deeper layers of the psyche). A willingness on the part of the man to participate in the animal spirit of the great male ape within, and a willingness on the part of the woman to participate in the provocatively yielding female ape within her psyche, along with a willingness on both of their parts to have their egos, temporarily at least, overpowered by instinct, will mutually empower *both* man and woman. This is nowhere more true than in their sex life together. They work together in a complex way to reinforce, affirm, and complement each other.

But the second and third factors frequently manifest only after the first—the accessing of one's own inner resources—has begun to take place. Once a man's psyche is moving in the direction of maturity, he will find nurturing men to bond with, and he will embrace, with wisely guarded enthusiasm, the chance for a truly intimate relationship with a woman.

BOOKS ON SEX ABUSE

It is only in the last few years that books geared specifically toward male victims of sexual abuse have been published—though, of course, the problem has been with society always. Incest and sexual abuse of boys by females has often been minimized or even regarded as lucky (early initiation into manhood by older woman), while similar acts with genders reversed have been branded statutory rape.

Mic Hunter, *Abused Boys: The Neglected Victims of Sexual Abuse.* Lexington, MA: Lexington Books, 1990. More clinical and thorough than other books listed here, it pulls no punches in describing the extent and horror of abuse of male children.

Mike Lew, *Victims No Longer: Men Recovering from Incest and Other Child Sexual Abuse*. New York: HarperCollins, 1990. The breakthrough book that drew attention to the fact that males deserve the same care and attention as female survivors. Addressed to "you," the survivor.

Thomas L. Sanders, *Male Survivors: 12-Step Recovery Program for Survivors of Childhood Sexual Abuse.* Freedom, CA: Crossing Press, 1991. Combines a workbook format with checklists and affirmations in the 12-step tradition with the author's personal account of his recovery. Christian in tone, but respectful of all spiritual traditions.

T. Thomas, *Men Surviving Incest: A Male Survivor Shares the Process of Recovery.* Walnut Creek, CA: Launch Press, 1989. Shortish book focusing on author's story.

BOOKS ON MALE-FEMALE RELATIONS

Barbara Ehrenreich, *The Hearts of Men: American Dreams and the Flight from Commitment.* Garden City, NY: Anchor/Doubleday, 1983. A history of the changing relationships between and the conception of the proper role of American men and women from the 1950s to the 1980s.

Warren Farrell, *Why Men Are The Way They Are: The Male-Female Dynamic.* New York. McGraw-Hill, 1986. Best-seller uses advertisements and cartoons to challenge assumptions about sexism, fantasies, and different kinds of power.

Herb Goldberg, *The New Male-Female Relationship.* New York: William Morrow, 1983. An examination of how both traditional gender roles and liberation philosophy fuel the battle of the sexes.

Gayle Kimball, *The 50-50 Marriage.* Boston: Beacon, 1983. Based on a survey of 150 couples who shared money-making, child-raising, and house-cleaning duties.

Rebecca Nahas and Myra Turley, *The New Couple: Women and Gay Men.* New York: Seaview Books, 1979. Examines both sexual and nonsexual relationships, including marriage between straight women and gay men.

Gerald Schoenewolf, *Sexual Animosity Between Men and Women*. Northvale, NJ: Jason Aronson, 1989. Taking a centrist position between feminism and masculism, the author sorts the causes for the escalating battle of the sexes, using literary sources, case histories, and religious texts.

Deborah Tannen, *You Just Don't Understand: Women and Men in Conversation.* New York: William Morrow, 1990. Anecdote-filled explanation of how men and women can benefit from understanding and at times adopting each other's conversational styles.

Women have often lamented that society judges them almost exclusively in terms of their bodies and looks, reducing them to "sex objects." Men are subject to even more impersonal standards; they tend to be judged by their career and salaries, standards which reduce them to "success objects." Many men have so much of their identity invested in their jobs that when they are forced to retire, they die because they see their life and value as inextricably entwined with what they do. How tragic then that so many men are trapped in stultifying jobs—not even when they are at work can they find fulfillment. In this excerpt from an interview, "I'll Answer It in Three Days," originally printed in *Inroads*, Michael Meade examines the relationship of work and gender. ✒

Work and Gender

MICHAEL MEADE

Interviewed by John Lang and Anthony Signorelli, editors of *Inroads*

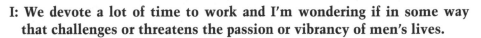

I: We devote a lot of time to work and I'm wondering if in some way that challenges or threatens the passion or vibrancy of men's lives.

MM: When we go to work nowadays, we feel a sense of loss, I think. What's lost is the meaning of work. And purpose—what's the purpose of work? Men and women need purpose and meaning in what they do for work.

Today, going to work means adding to the gross national product. It adds to what is gross and what is productive. And inside, we're smart enough to know that that's not the same as what we want. In tribal cultures, men and women both would spend two-thirds of their time doing ritual or working up to a ritual. Everybody would be involved in creating something for the ritual. Everybody would be involved in the art and beauty of the ritual work. The psyche remembers that and hungers for it. So the simple going to work causes us to feel a sense of loss of meaning and purpose. That is one reason, as fathers, we don't often take our children and say, "Come on. I want to show you what I do at work." The kid's going to ask, "Why? Why are you doing that?" "Well I'm doing that because I have to pay the mortgage." That's a good reason, but it makes us aware of the loss of meaning in work.

Another thing we feel in going to everyday work is the loss of rhythm. Everybody talks about the fast pace of life. Someone once said, "If you are going too fast you can't feel very well." You miss the sense of feeling, speed erodes feeling. So there is a way in which the pace and rhythm keeps us from feeling what it is we experience. When we get home after working, we feel a certain kind of isolated exhaustion. We don't have any depth of feeling or a story to tell, and often we don't have anyone to tell it to. If we are in a relationship, the other person has been doing the same thing. There is an exhausted alienation there, and there is not enough ground left to share on.

Because there is an assumption from the economic production

point of view that jobs are genderless—that anybody can do the job—there is no sense of care for who is in that job. The person working a job where there is no sense of care for them, knows it. He or she knows it on an inner level and feels it as a pain every day, as a suffering every day. Ivan Illich says in his book on gender that the modern industrial societies have removed the sense of a gendered caring for work. When that happens, we stop caring for ourselves. A certain amount of care has to come from the outside no matter who the person is. We need that sense of mutual care in the world.

When the care is gone, a job becomes something that anybody can do and jobs become scarce. Thus, men and women start to compete and envy for involvement in their jobs. The sense of dance is gone. The sense of mystery is gone. The soul feels that loss. According to Illich, that has not been the case in history before. Nowadays, we talk about life-styles as if all life-styles were for everybody. In the old way, gender alignments were guides on how to work, guides on how to care, guides to how to move, guides to how to live. There were styles of living but they had a gendered tone to them, a masculine tone or a feminine tone that was different in each place.

There are three conditions under which gender lines break down. First, all-out war. In war, everybody has to get down to basic protection; even though it is aggression, it's really about your protection. Second is plague or some kind of rampant illness. During the great plague the gender lines got demolished because they dropped to a much lower, more essential place of humanity or being. They had to forget gender. The third condition is in the breakdown of society. When a society's structures are deteriorating or breaking down, then the gender lines start to disappear. It's kind of a scary idea because we have been in this for a while. One of the reasons that everybody is in therapy, everybody is confused, everybody is suffering is that demarcation lines, the lines of the world, are shattering, and particularly the lines between men and women—they are broken and wrenched apart.

I: Job descriptions are being made to accommodate both.

MM: Yes. You read them and you can't even understand them. That is seen as progressive and positive but it is characteristic of a society coming apart, a society that is losing its sense of part. We are supposed to play a part, not do the whole thing. Since this has been going on for quite a while, it's as if we are going to work and going to love and going to family and going home under the conditions of all-out war or plague. We are all suffering the pressure that is felt in extreme crisis all the time. So by the time we finally get to an intimate situation, it's as if the love is going to be made in battle conditions. That's a tough way to live, and we all feel that. If we at least had a gender ground to stand

Some people have big ones; some people have little ones. Women have been shorted on them. Nobody really wants to know—but, on the other hand, everybody does want to know how his stacks up next to the other fellow's. It's not so much the size of them as what you do with them and what goes along with them. (Sure!) There is a taboo against revealing them. . . . Salaries.

—Roy Blount, Jr.

MEADE
WORK
AND GENDER

61

on, then we might feel more solid, and we might be able to handle more of our own emotion, our own imagination, our own spirit.

I: What do we do about the work part of it? We still have to make a living.

MM: What we have to do is bring as much as we can of our legitimate feelings and desires into work. And that's a hard thing to do. Work is supposed to provide the things that are needed for life. It's supposed to provide more than just the physical good, it's supposed to provide purpose and meaning, and interest, and discipline, and rhythm. And when work becomes a job, then it's good to start looking around for some other work. That's not an easy thing to do. I don't wish to say, in any way, not to participate in the culture, because that's all we have. But to be aware of the loss in going to work leads you to figuring out how to do something that is more meaningful. Without meaningful work, people die. Men don't have anything to fall back on in the sense of giving birth and that kind of thing. Women have that tremendous, mysterious ability to give birth to other beings. If we can keep an eye on the mystery of what we are doing when we are doing work, if we can see it as participation in something mythical, if we can find some mythos in that work it is a little less alienating. But that's hard work, too. It is another work in the work.

"MALE" IS NOT A FOUR-LETTER WORD

BY JACK KAMMER

Men's rights activists pull no punches in exposing what they see as society's misguided attempts to help women by shaming men. Men's righters are sometimes accused of "hating women," while they see themselves as refuting insidious lies spread by feminists (both male and female).

Though the mythopoetic men generally refrain from using language as hard-hitting as that in this piece, there is an increasing awareness among mythopoetic men that males have been getting a bum rap. And as Jack Kammer of the Baltimore Commission on Men demonstrates, even *Iron John* may be quoted to help sound the men's rights wake-up call. ✒

ITEM: FOR months after six men raped a woman in Big Dan's Tavern in New Bedford, Rhode Island, in 1983 the media reported that a barroom full of male patrons had cheered the crime. As University of Dayton English professor Eugene August observes, the news stories included "righteous denunciations of the average man as secret admirer and blood brother of the gang rapist." In a March 5, 1984, story on the rapists' trial, however, *Time* magazine quietly reported that "aside from the six defendants and the victim, only three people were in the bar, and that the bartender and a customer sought to call the police, but were prevented from doing so by one of the six." Professor August is left to wonder "why the media engaged in such an orgy of sexist caricaturing."

ITEM: Writing in a 1988 edition of *Spectator*, Fredric Hayward, director of Men's Rights, Inc., reports that in a sample of 1,000 advertisements, he found that men were 100 percent of:

- Jerks in male-female relationships
- Those who were ignorant
- Incompetents
- Those who smelled bad
- Those who were put down without retribution
- The objects of rejection
- The losers of competitions
- The targets of anger
- The victims of violence

ITEM: Warren Farrell devotes a chapter of his successful 1986 book *Why Men Are the Way They Are* to "The New Sexism." He analyzes dozens of anti-male cartoons, books, magazine articles, and advertisements, and, by reversing the gender assignments in his examples, helps readers see clearly the bigotry they embody. "In the past quarter century," Farrell writes, "we exposed biases against other races and called it racism, and we exposed biases against women and called it sexism. Biases against men we call humor."

ITEM: In 1991, before the National Coalition of Free Men succeeds in having Hallmark mend its ways, the greeting card company manufactures a product that shows on its cover a stylish young woman saying, "Men are scum." Since the card is from Hallmark, America's premier purveyor of sentiment and warmth, the incredulous shopper expects to open the card and read something like "S for sweet, C for cute, U for understanding, and M for magnificent." Instead the inside panel says, "Excuse me. For a second there, I was feeling generous." In announcing its decision to pull the card from distribution, Hallmark acknowledges that the product was one of its best-sellers.

This is male bashing—the mean-spirited mockery and categorical denunciation of American men. Sincere criticism it is not.

John Gordon, Ph.D., professor of English at Connecticut College and author of *The Myth of the Monstrous Male and Other Feminist Fables*, tells us that male bashing is hardly a new phenomenon. In Dr. Francis Baumli's anthology *Men Freeing Men*, Gordon asserts that "the ongoing flood of anti-male hate literature" is "a continuation of an old campaign. Men are the main targets these days because they always have been." He cites *The Feminization of American Culture* by Ann Douglas which "documents the history of two of the most popular and influential *genres* of the nineteenth and early twentieth centuries, the anti-male novel and the anti-male tract. These works—thousands of them—were part of a campaign," Gordon says, "to represent men as barbarians whose urges had to be leashed in by the forces of decency—meaning women—if civilization were to survive."

But clearly male bashing is more common and ferocious today than it was, say, 30 years ago. Why is it happening so prominently now? Obviously, feminism unleashed a torrent of simple, crude, unenlightened animosity toward men. Rather than suggesting an evenhanded redistribution of power between men and women, feminists chose instead to frame sexism unilaterally according to the by-now familiar victim-perpetrator model. Only men had power. Only men were using it selfishly. Only men required self-improvement. Only men were wrong.

Another interesting way to conceive of the current abuses of men is to accept the feminist allegation that men have treated women as children. Now that women are asserting their independence many of them are having what could be called a difficult adolescence, a still-immature stage which is often accompanied by a know-it-all attitude and haughty disrespect for former authority figures.

Farrell suggests that male bashing, the New Sexism, is at least in part some modern women's reaction to their failure to achieve their primary (and sexist) fantasy—being taken care of by a man who makes even more money than they. As women's earnings have increased recently,

Farrell points out, it is inevitable that fewer and fewer men will be able to fulfill that fantasy, and more and more women will feel angry, frustrated, and resentful toward men, whom they see now only in terms of their shortcomings. Furthermore, focusing on men's imperfections allows women to avoid the painful task of attending to their own.

This suggests yet another way to understand male bashing. Since male bashing is nothing if not offensive, and since, as the old adage goes, The best defense is a strong offense, we might ask, Are some women and their male protectors feeling a heightened need to defend something, trying to avoid an egalitarian sharing of some female domain or prerogative which men have begun to claim equally for themselves?

If in the early 1960s, when women were knocking on the door of corporate and academic America, seeking access to jobs, educations, and careers, men had mounted a scurrilous campaign about women's shortcomings, foibles, and imperfections, fair-minded people surely would have seen it for what it was. If, for example, a prominent male business executive had written, "The majority of women who compete with talented young men for careers and entrepreneurial opportunities are airheaded bimbos who have refused to study diligently, save their capital, work hard and devote themselves to the important and noble task of making money, who only want to file their nails, and who pose a serious threat to our hallowed American economy," no one could have failed to see that his real agenda was the exclusion of women from a male domain.

Perhaps, then, we can discern a clear payoff for women in male bashing, a classic example of which is found on the book jacket of Phyllis Chesler's *Mothers on Trial*: "Dr. Chesler shows that the majority of fathers who challenge nurturing mothers for custody are absent or psychologically damaging parents who have refused to pay child support and have kidnapped, brainwashed, economically intimidated and physically and sexually abused both their children and their wives." (For those readers who are unaware of her reputation we should mention that Dr. Chesler is considered a serious, sophisticated, and credible philosopher—not a ludicrous crackpot—of feminism.)

One of the most recurring and underlying themes of male bashing is indeed the unfitness of men to care for children. Certainly we cannot entrust our little babies to people who are sexually depraved, clumsy, selfish, hormonally inclined to violence, helpless, emotionally crippled, and generally morally inferior. We must leave that important work— "demeaned and devalued" as it may be—to women.

Since many men today are expressing an interest in being as involved with their children as women have been, it is understandable— as distinguished from acceptable—that some women will feel threatened. *The Motherhood Report*, published in 1987 by researchers Louis Genevie, Ph.D., and Eva Margolies, lends credence to this analysis.

Genevie and Margolies found that 1) only about one mother in four thought that fathers should play a fifty-fifty role in raising the children; 2) mothers want fathers to help more with the children, but not to overshadow their role as primary parent; 3) two out of three mothers seemed threatened by the idea of a father's equal participation in child rearing; and 4) mothers themselves may be subtly putting a damper on men's involvement with their children because they are so possessive of their role as primary nurturer. Male bashing in this light can be seen as a not-so-subtle damper on men's involvement with their children, especially when divorce, separation, or simple jealousy force the designation of one parent as primary and the other as second class.

Moreover, even the most amateur politician knows that the party who defines the terms of the discussion will win the debate. As long as feminists keep sexual politics focused on men's failings, they will enjoy total immunity from scrutiny or calls to make changes other than the ones they have found to be in their immediate self-interest.

Keeping attention focused on men's shortcomings requires that men's shortcomings be found—or fabricated—at every turn. Writing in the *Liberator*, Frank Zepezauer marvels at the resourcefulness and flexibility of the process. He describes how three sociologists working with three different types of raw material all delivered the same fuel for male bashing. The first commented on the fact that men still put in longer work weeks than women by saying that "men are trying even harder to maintain their superiority." The second sociologist saw a picture of Native American women grinding corn while the men stood watch. Her interpretation: "The men were as usual leaving all the work to the women." The third, after examining the many ways in which males, like the Indian men standing guard, took risks to protect women and children, concluded that this was another way that males maintained dominance, their own version of a "protection racket." As Zepezauer detected, the process is really quite simple. "Whatever a guy does, you find a sneaky, self-serving reason. He holds a door open for you? He's asserting dominance. He doesn't hold the door open. He's insulting your dignity."

Farrell has seen the same process in different terms. "*The Hite Report*," he writes, "found that *men* prefer intercourse more than women; the *American Couples* survey by Schwartz and Blumstein found that *women* prefer intercourse more than men. Hite interpreted her findings to mean that men preferred intercourse because intercourse is male-centered, focused on penis pleasure, an outgrowth of male dominance and ego gratification." But Schwartz and Blumstein, Farrell notes, interpreted their findings in the opposite way: "We think women prefer it because intercourse requires the *equal* participation of both partners more than any sexual act. Neither partner only 'gives' or only 'receives.' Hence, women feel a shared *intimacy* during intercourse . . . ." Farrell concludes that "the findings are diametrically opposed, yet both interpretations could only consider the possibility that women favor intimacy and equality, and men favor ego gratification and dominance. This is distortion to fit a preconceived image—or, when it is applied to men, the new sexism."

Speaking as he often does of men in terms of father figures, Robert Bly comments on the same problem. In *Iron John* he writes "that something in the culture wants us to be unfair to our father's masculine side, find self-serving reasons for his generous words, assume he is a monster, as some people say all men are."

Blaming men for each and every male-female problem, as John Gordon suggested earlier, is not new. Shakespeare confirmed it in *As You Like It*: "O, that woman that cannot make her fault her husband's occasion, let her never nurse her child herself, for she will breed it like a fool!"

Indeed, sometimes male bashing seems to be nothing more than some feminists' celebration of their ability to make men wrong, an out-of-control demonstration of their skill in framing issues just the way they wish, to make men and only men say, "Oh, yes, I'm so sorry. I can see now that I must confront and take responsibility for my attitudes and actions. Forgive me please and assuage my guilt!" Sometimes it seems male bashers must be laughing incredulously to themselves, shaking their heads and saying, "When are these chumps going to wake up?"

It almost goes without saying that along with its power to defend women from scrutiny and from encroachments on their domain, the

The wound that unifies all men is the wound of our disposability. The wound of believing that we were loveable if we sacrificed ourselves, if we died to help others. We are disposable as soldiers, as workers, as dads.
—Warren Farrell, 1991

strong offense constituted by male bashing can have aggressive applications as well. Male bashing can be like carpet bombing, softening up men's determination to defend themselves, destroying male morale, and inclining men to surrender at the first sign of hostilities, paving the way for dictators, tyrants, and aggressors of all sorts.

The offensive uses of male bashing can be broad indeed. The more widely one can assert the idea of male beastliness and comparative female virtuousness, the more one can justify whatever special treatment of women one seeks, the more likely one is to find ready acceptance of even the weakest accusations—whether they be of employment discrimination, parental unfitness, sexual harassment, rape, child sexual abuse, date rape, domestic violence, or simple social or marital impropriety, to name but a few possibilities. On the topic of domestic violence, for example, R. L. McNeely suggests in the November-December 1987 issue of *Social Work* that the popular and aggressively asserted misconception that only men commit spousal abuse may be contributing to "men's social and legal defenselessness."

Why do men not protest more vigorously against male bashing? The answer seems to be that we have been made to think we deserve it. We are, after all, male. We are, on the ladder of life, at least a rung or two below women, closer to the worms while women consort with the angels. It's not our *fault* really. It's just, you know, that nasty testosterone. We begin early on to learn what Dr. Roy Schenk has called the Shame of Maleness. We learned that we are not sugar, not spice, not anything nice. In the 1990s, little boys are learning only a slight variation on that theme: they are "rotten, made out of cotton"; girls, on the other hand, are "dandy, made out of candy." While young boys are learning to devalue themselves as males, the only defense with which our supposedly male-dominated culture equips them is a feeble response: "Oh, yeah? Well, you've got cooties!" It is easy to see the difference between boys' allegations of what the girls *have*, and the female allegations of what the boys *are*. Males—inherently—are inferior. We deserve what we get.

The idea that we deserve what females dish out carries through to adulthood. As Bly observes, "A contemporary man often assumes that a woman knows more about a relationship than he does, allows a woman's moods to run the house, assumes that when she attacks him, she is doing it 'for his own good.' "

Apparently we even think we deserve bashing in a physical sense. In his book *Wife Beating: The Silent Crisis*, Roger Langley includes a chapter on battered men. He says that "the response most often heard—from both men and women—to a story of a man beaten by his wife is: 'Good for her.' "

Is male bashing really all that harmful or are men's objections to it — as they have been characterized—simply "whining"? That's a fair ques-

tion to which there is a fair answer. Male bashing wounds men; it injures boys; it harms everyone who lives with or near them; it hurts everyone who seeks to have a relationship with them. In short, it is detrimental to everyone. It further rends our already tattered social fabric.

If we can agree that the American family is in serious decline, we might observe that the weakest element of the family is its male component. Male bashing only tramples fatherhood and husbandhood more thoroughly. In *Iron John*, Robert Bly, without referring specifically to male bashing, explains how it can damage marriages. "Conscious fighting," he wrote, "is a great help in relationships between men and women . . . . A good fight gets things clear, and I think women long to fight and be with men who know how to fight well." A man who has been bashed and browbeaten into guilt, shame, and submission, of course, knows not how to fight at all.

Male bashing also damages the young men families try to raise. In 1938, a social scientist named Tannenbaum articulated a theory of "labeling" that is still cited in the professional literature on juvenile delinquency:

> There is a gradual shift from the definition of the specific acts as evil to a definition of the individual as evil, and that all his acts come to be looked upon with suspicion . . . . From the individual's point of view there has taken place a similar change. He has gone slowly from a sense of grievance and injustice, of being unduly mistreated and punished, to a recognition that the definition of him as a human being is different from that of other boys in his neighborhood, his school, street, community. The young delinquent becomes bad because he is defined as bad.
>
> The process of making the criminal, therefore, is a process of tagging, defining, identifying, segregating, describing, emphasizing, making conscious and self-conscious. The person becomes the thing he is described as being.

Though Tannenbaum here refers to a boy being stigmatized in relation to other boys, we can perhaps see that male bashing stigmatizes all boys in relation to the rest of the human race. Researchers Myra and David Sadker found that "boys are more likely to be scolded and reprimanded in classrooms, even when the observed conduct and behavior of boys and girls does not differ." The effect of treating boys as if they are evil is to encourage and direct them toward evil.

Bly explains another deleterious effect of male bashing when he describes how undue harshness toward men saps our society of its vigor. "All the great cultures except ours preserve and have lived with images of . . . positive male energy . . . . Zeus energy has been steadily disintegrating decade after decade in the United States. Popular culture has been determined to destroy respect for it, beginning with the 'Maggie and Jiggs' and 'Blondie and Dagwood' comics of the 1920s and 1930s, in which the man is always weak and foolish."

Perhaps the most severe manifestation of male bashing may be found in the fact that for decades if not centuries the suicide rate for young men has exceeded the rate for young women, and that in recent years the gap has widened dramatically to a ratio of about four to one. In 1985, Edward S. Gold's doctoral dissertation at the Virginia Consortium of Professional Psychology investigated the "personal need systems" of a group of college students who had demonstrated suicidal or near-suicidal behavior. Among the males he found a common denominator: "lowered ego strength." "It is entirely possible," Dr. Gold said, "that the women's movement has had a lot to do with that. There has been a constant barrage of finger-pointing, a tremendous amount of criticism of men on nearly every front." Keep in mind that a whole spectrum of suffering exists between happiness and the extreme of suicide. Male bashing, simply put, can make men miserable.

But now let's turn to the optimistic part of this essay. What can we do about male bashing? A story from Bly in *Iron John* poses the question nicely:

> A friend told me [that] at about thirty-five, he began to wonder who his father really was. He hadn't seen his father in about ten years. He flew out to Seattle, where his father was living, knocked on the door, and when his father opened the door, said, "I want you to understand one thing. I don't accept my mother's view of you any longer."
> "What happened?" I asked.
> "My father broke into tears, and said, 'Now I can die.'"
> Fathers wait. What else can they do?

What we can do is stop waiting and get on our own offensive, an offensive in which the best masculine values constitute both the medium and the message. Calmly, patiently, fiercely, resolutely, lovingly, we can isolate, identify, and demand the cessation of that which damages us unfairly—especially the pervasive notion of the inferiority of masculinity—and replace it with a balanced analysis of the wounded relationship between woman and man, including a proper recognition of the strengths and weaknesses of both genders.

As a kid growing up I "knew" that male-female problems among my parents' friends were always the man's fault. Only the women would talk about them, and I therefore heard only the woman's side of the story. Nora Ephron candidly admitted that one of the reasons she wrote *Heartburn*, the story of her failed marriage to Watergate sleuth Carl Bernstein, was to control the version of the story that was told. Unlike my father and his male friends, and unlike the strong-but-silent Bernstein, we can begin to speak our truth, to confront the falsehoods and

Just as women started asking why the "glass ceiling" is all men, we must start asking why the "glass cellars" are all men.

Death Professions 94% of all people killed in the workplace are men.

Draft Draft registration is a male-only club. In the 20th century, over 99% of people killed in wars have been men. It is only men who enter the service who are required to serve in combat if needed. Why are women getting combat options but not sharing in combat obligations?

Suicide Why do men commit suicide 5 times more often than women?

Hostages Why does no one call it sexist when Saddam Hussein releases only women and children? Why does no one object to making hostages an all-male club?

Homeless The street homeless are approximately 90% men.

Assassinations Nearly 100% of political assassinations have been of men.

Prisoners Approximately 92% of all prisoners are men.

Executions Over 99% of the executed are men.

Early Deaths In 1920, men died only one year sooner than women; in the 1990s men died seven to eight years sooner. Why?

Disease Men die sooner than women from **all** of the ten most lethal diseases.

—Warren Farrell

half-truths about us and resolve never to let our sons say what Bly reports hundreds of men have said to him: "My father never stood up to my mother, and I'm still angry about that."

We should not only assert our truth to our female companions and partners, but also hold it out for our brothers to acknowledge, embrace, support, and share. All of us doing men's work know the power and the strength that arises from a man who says, "I'm glad you listened. I'm glad you understand. I thought I had a 'personal' problem. I thought I was the only one who felt this way."

Good, strong women will want to join our campaign once they see that good, strong men are at long last taking action. They should be invited and welcomed. In some circles, against some offenders, they can in fact lead our effort.

Finally, as we rise to our feet and signal "Enough!" we can take pride in knowing that it is precisely because we are good and always trying to be better that we have listened so long to the allegations that we are bad.

BOOKS ON MEN'S AWARENESS

Francis Baumli, ed., *Men Freeing Men: Exploding the Myth of the Traditional Male*. Jersey City, NJ: New Atlantis, 1985. Eye-opening anthology of men's rights issues covering everything from the men-only draft to battered and murdered husbands.

Richard F. Doyle, *The Rape of the Male*. St. Paul, MN: Poor Richard's Press, 1976. An angry book full of horror stories of men abused by women and the judicial system.

Warren Farrell, *The Disposable Sex: The Myth of Male Power.* New York: Simon & Schuster, forthcoming. The only man elected three times to the board of the National Organization of Women (NOW) of New York City issues his long-await-ed, heavily documented debunking of feminist claims that men hold most of the power in our society, concentrating on such topics as the draft, men as workers in 98 percent of hazardous jobs, perception that killing or beating up of men in movies is viewed as traditional entertainment, while even the slightest violence against women is viewed as intolerable, dangerous precedent-setting abuse. This book represents the first half of what Farrell originally intended as one volume called "The Ten Greatest Myths About Men." The rest of his material will appear in a book tentatively entitled *The Female FOE (Fear of Equality)*.

Roy Schenk, *The Other Side of the Coin: Causes and Consequences of Men's Oppression.* Madison, WI: Bioenergetics Press, 1982. Schenk blames the general belief in female spiritual superiority for many of men's social problems, especially their feelings of guilt for wanting sex. A strident cry for recognition that males are worse off in U.S. society than females are.

Kenneth Wetcher, Art Barker, and F. Rex McCaughtry, *Save the Males: Why Men are Mistreated, Misdiagnosed and Misunderstood*. Washington, DC: PIA Press, 1991. This reader-friendly book explores such men's health topics as workaholism, post-traumatic stress syndrome, depression, and substance abuse. 🖋

Charles Varon is a writer
and comedian based in
San Francisco. He is the
automotive editor of the
Green Letter, and a former
member of the Atomic
Comics. The author is
grateful to Jim Rosenau
for his help on this
address. ✒

STATE OF THE GENDER

BY CHARLES VARON

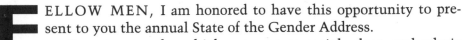

FELLOW MEN, I am honored to have this opportunity to present to you the annual State of the Gender Address.

Ours is a gender which cuts across racial, class, and ethnic lines as few others do. Men are currently represented in over 187 countries; we speak over 700 languages; and in total population we are second only to women. *(Applause.)*

This year, men continued to take leadership in science, business, politics, and communications. Feature articles on members of our gender were published in leading newspapers, and men appeared on the cover of *Time* and *Newsweek*. *(Applause.)*

It's estimated that in the past year, men fixed 400,000 small appliances and nearly 36 million automobiles. Men hit an all-time high of over 14,000 home runs this year *(applause)* though male pitching also gave up over 14,000 home runs.

On the down side of the ledger, hair loss continued unabated in our gender, with an average adult male losing 0.31 square inches of scalp to personal deforestation. Genderwide, gentlemen, this amounts to a total hair loss of some 27 acres. *(Groans.)* This was offset only partially by the 43 million boys who made the transition from fuzz to facial hair.

In all, 193 million male rites of passage were successfully completed this year *(applause)*, the most frequently performed being puberty, marriage, and driver education. We can rejoice that testicular cancer is now 90 percent curable, and we have reduced to near zero the deaths resulting from athlete's foot. *(Sustained applause.)*

In Geneva, our negotiators worked tirelessly, as is their habit. But they are proceeding with caution. Years of mistrust and misunderstanding cannot be erased hastily. Clearly, some provisions of the proposed treaty are in the interest of both sides, such as cultural exchanges between men and women. But let us be clear: We shall not submit to anti-male guilt tactics, nor shall we agree to give up even one more rib. *(Sustained applause.)* Our negotiators will not betray the vision and pride with which our male ancestors founded this gender over 2 million

WINGSPAN
INSIDE THE MEN'S
MOVEMENT

years ago. *(Sustained applause.)* We may forget birthdays, we may forget anniversaries, but we shall never forget our founding fathers, those men who hunted and fished, who pounded out stone tools, and who gallantly forged the foundation of the gender whose engine we have kept running smooth lo these many years. *(Wild applause and scattered chest pounding.)* I ask you: Would those ancestors have allowed on-site inspection of men's hunting lodges and treehouses by women without reciprocal access of men to women's bookstores and coffeehouses? *(Shouts of "No!")*

As we strive to find common ground with women, let us never forget that our two systems are fundamentally dissimilar. Their system is based on estrogen, ovaries, fallopian tubes. They give birth; we give advice.

VARON
THE STATE
OF THE GENDER

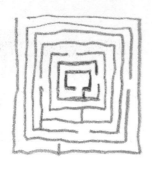

Clearly, gentlemen, security is our most important issue. We have lived too long with the fear of war and violence. If this means we must eventually give up war and violence, then so be it. We will bite that bullet when we come to it. In the meantime, we must seek tougher punishment for playground bullies, strict monitoring of fraternity hazing, and the formation of a blue-ribbon commission to decide once and for all whether it's nature or culture that makes us so bloodthirsty. *(Applause, with scattered shouts of "Culture!")*

So let us move forward together. The unbroken chain of masculinity, of which we males alive today are but one link, cries out for us to take action. Let us remember that our sons today will be the fathers of tomorrow and the grandfathers of the boys of the 22nd century. And if we wait for our sons to solve these problems, we will be up past midnight and then it will be another day. *(Sage nodding.)*

Internationally, from Lusaka to Budapest, from Beijing to Naples, from Key Biscayne to Kiev, men are still men. When heavy objects need to be moved, we are there. Who builds the dams, who clears the forests, who cleans out the sewers on rainy nights? *(Shouts of "We do!")* Who digs the graves? *("We do!")* I submit to you that it is we, the men. And wherever we are, whatever our garb—be it dhoti, kilt, pleated trouser, loincloth, or dashiki—we will continue to be men until the last drop of testosterone is gone! *(Wild applause and foot stomping; some dancing in the balcony.)*

Thank you very much, and good night.

II

IN SEARCH OF MALE COMMUNITY

SUPPORT GROUPS, COUNCILS, AND RETREATS

ISOLATION IS a demon that many men wrestle with. The average woman has been socialized to easily strike up a conversation with another woman and to compare very personal stories on a relatively short acquaintance. Men, on the other hand, have learned to preserve their dignity by either not talking to strangers or keeping interaction on an impersonal, joking level.

Despite their upbringing, men need outlets for their feelings and life stories every bit as much as women do. All too often, a man will confide deep feelings only to his wife or girlfriend. For many reasons, it's unwise to put all one's emotional eggs in a single basket. For one thing, these confidences can become very burdensome to the woman. When the relationship breaks up—and about half of them do—he is cast adrift. Separation from his wife usually means an ouster from a network of friends, who were really her friends. When the divorce is exacerbated by separation from a child, whom courts most often award to mother, the pain and loneliness may push the man hard enough to overcome his reluctance to confide in other men. But more often he is tragically kept prisoner by the lie that most males are stony creatures, contemptuous of another man's display of feeling.

What a blessed relief and revelation to discover that in the men's movement free expression is the norm instead of the exception! The man who has lost his moorings is consoled to find others who are in the same predicament or who, instead of looking down on him for voicing his grief or anger, applaud him for his courage in revealing himself. Better yet there are plenty of hearty, good-natured belly laughs to temper the sorrow and rage.

The men's movement offers a range of formats to suit the various needs of men. There are thousands of men's support groups that meet each week, hundreds of retreats during the course of the year, and scores of citywide council meetings convening each month. Some faithfully observe and elaborate on rituals, while others keep things informal and spontaneous. Some prize safety and respect for one another's feelings above all else; others make freedom to speak one's mind without fear of censorship the number one priority.

Some gatherings offer cozy cocoons; others are benign ordeals conducted by those who believe like Hamlet that they "must be cruel, only to be kind," confronting the participant with ugly truths he may have been running from all his life. There are even groups of male friends whose regular meetings over the years and supportive behavior qualify them as charter members of the men's movement, though they may never have heard the term.

The most important unit is the one we hear the least about—the small, weekly or biweekly *support groups*. Usually, these little bands of somewhere between 5 and 10 guys don't even have a name other than "my men's group." Members usually take turns meeting at one another's homes, although if they have tricky living situations, they may meet for dinner at a particular restaurant or congregate at some other neutral public spot.

Men's group members are different from friends. They gather, not simply to hang out, but to work on themselves in the presence of others committed to self-exploration. Men are there to practice being open, compassionate, and understanding of perspectives other than their own. There's no distraction of a ball game on the tube, cards on the table, or fish in the lake. Bonding certainly can take place wherever men spend time together, slowly letting one another seep in, silently sizing one another up, getting comfortable with one another. But the purpose of being part of a men's group is not to become buddies, even though friendships form as a natural conse-

quence. It's not unusual for one man not to like another man in his group, yet feel an affection for him born out of understanding.

Citywide monthly *council meetings*, which typically attract between 50 and 300 men, provide a less intimate, more ritually organized format. Most council meetings begin with drumming, whether it be free-form walloping of animal skins or lessons in polyrhythmic drumming by a drum master. Playing drums offers an excellent nonverbal but joyously noisy way for men to all settle into the same rhythm or wavelength.

After opening ceremonies and welcomes to newcomers, it's inevitable that some organizational business meeting must take place—even if it just means passing the hat to collect donations for room rent and plowing through announcements about subgroup meetings.

Some councils have a program presented by one of their number or by a special guest. Others use the talking stick format (see Joseph Jastrab's "Every Man's

Story, Every Man's Truth" in section V) to consider a question or take turns discussing a story.

Many councils set up literature tables with books and audiotapes for sale and with men's movement publications and fliers announcing upcoming workshops or special interest groups, organized around such topics as journal or poetry writing.

The drop-in, no-pressure, no-commitment quality of council meetings make them a likely first stop for men curious about the men's movement. Support groups can be intimidating because the small number of attendees sooner or later puts everyone in the hot seat, while at a council meeting with a hundred or more men, the shy or the tongue-tied can get by without saying a word.

Of course, the problem is that not every city has a men's council. Sometimes a lecture exclusively for men can serve many of the same functions as a council, such as spinning off support and discussion groups.

Inevitably council members become restless about their indoor meeting places, and the council finds itself organizing retreats—usually one in the fall and often another in the spring. Many groups schedule sweat lodge ceremonies on the solstices and equinoxes or at other regular intervals. October seems to be the favorite month for outdoor men's activity, but men's appetite for retreats has grown so voracious that retreats are now being scheduled year-round. In February men learn how to build igloos instead of the sweat lodges they might construct in less bitter weather.

Since the more luxurious retreat centers used by corporations are usually too pricey for groups that try to keep the cost of their events as low as possible, men's groups tend to rent summer camps, securing weekend dates just prior to the opening of a summer season or just after the close. Many directors of church-owned camps charge very modest rates because they want to encourage the exploration of male spirituality which is so much a part of many retreats.

The articles by Shepherd Bliss, Bill Finger, and Eric Pierson in this section describe three of the many kinds of retreats run each year. These special environments provide a respite from our oppressive routines and everyday identities, setting the scene for some rather astounding chance-taking and personal growth.

A man who normally wouldn't confide to the guy on the next barstool that he's afraid the boss is ready to ax him will stand up at a retreat and in front of 99 strangers give a straightforward account of the physical and sexual abuse he suffered as a child. What prompts a normally tight-lipped man to tell a platoon of other men things he never even told his wife?

One possible answer is that many men are more comfortable addressing a crowd than they are in moony, one-on-one situations. Many men are admittedly reluctant to imitate women's conversational patterns. Women's communication style is intimate and face to face, with a lot of give and take in the conversation; men prefer to be side by side, doing things together, either in silence or with superficial talk. At work they become accustomed to making speeches and conveying information to groups of people. Men's gatherings afford those who feel the need the opportunity to stand up and "give a report on" feelings that may have been festering for a long time.

Sometimes such gatherings resemble old-fashioned revival meetings. Certain men are able to muster the courage to speak only when they hear other men sharing feelings that one is not accustomed to hearing men express. For other men, one-upmanship dies hard: "I can top your horror story with an even more horrible one." Being brutally honest about oneself and one's failings can be a way of proving one's manliness—like holding one's hand over a flame without wincing. But if that dynamic of competition is what it takes to bring up the poison from a man's craw, at least the poison's out.

Many of the articles in this section come from small men's newsletters. They vividly convey the misgivings and suspicions that the authors had when they first ventured to a men's event. Very often first-timers torment themselves with one of the two following scenarios. A heterosexual man wonders if he will be the only straight guy there, if the etiquette of the gathering will force him to pay lip service to a notion that he may not really believe in—for example, that a male lover is just as acceptable as a female one. He dreads the prospect of being expected to participate in some sort of wild gay orgy.

A homosexual man, on the other hand, may worry that he will turn out to be the only gay man at the event. He fears that when the straight bullies discover this "faggot" in their midst they will vent their homophobic fury on him. Given the fact that the event is deep in the woods, miles from nowhere, the most he can hope for is a quick death. Neither of these scenarios ever materializes, but the fears are real.

Time and time again, first-time participants confess at the opening of a retreat that they are apprehensive and suspicious. At the end of the weekend, these same men report that time has flown by too quickly and that their fears and suspicions were unfounded. But these are discoveries each man must make for himself.

Note: Some of us have a tendency to dismiss descriptions of retreats and workshops too quickly as stale news or totally inconsequential history, like the old minutes of some now-defunct little club. These personal accounts have been selected because they vividly capture the essence of so many similar events, not because the particular gathering was especially momentous. They say as much about the present and the future as they do about a given moment in the past. 🖋

SUPPORT
GROUPS,
COUNCILS,
AND
RETREATS

DANCING IN THE CRACKS BETWEEN WORLDS

BY TOM DALY, Ph.D.

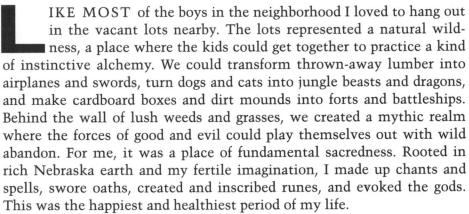

Beginning with a vivid evocation of the magic of boyhood, Tom Daly, director of the Men's Council Project, traces the gradual loss of gusto and meaning that he and many other men experience as they grow older and confront the hollow roles life seems to have assigned them. Those readers who can identify with Daly in his disappointment and dissatisfaction may also be inspired to follow him a few steps further as he rediscovers the sheer joy of brotherhood in the fellowship of like-minded men. ✐

L IKE MOST of the boys in the neighborhood I loved to hang out in the vacant lots nearby. The lots represented a natural wildness, a place where the kids could get together to practice a kind of instinctive alchemy. We could transform thrown-away lumber into airplanes and swords, turn dogs and cats into jungle beasts and dragons, and make cardboard boxes and dirt mounds into forts and battleships. Behind the wall of lush weeds and grasses, we created a mythic realm where the forces of good and evil could play themselves out with wild abandon. For me, it was a place of fundamental sacredness. Rooted in rich Nebraska earth and my fertile imagination, I made up chants and spells, swore oaths, created and inscribed runes, and evoked the gods. This was the happiest and healthiest period of my life.

About the time I left the primary grades, things began to change. I learned that the sacred belonged in church, that stories of mythic heroes and fabulous quests weren't for real, and that magic and witchcraft were bad. I learned that being dirty and sweaty and loud and passionate weren't okay. And all this at a time when my hormones were really beginning to kick in. I began a period of profound confusion and self-consciousness that lasted well into manhood.

Somehow I made it through the usual rites of passage into manhood. I came to live in a man's body and have a man's name. I got good at sports and drank beer with the guys. I did the mandatory flirting with death by climbing mountains in Colorado and driving like a madman. I learned to hide my feelings and act as though I knew what I was doing at all times, especially around women. I fathered two children, paid taxes, voted, and had a decent job. I was miserable.

Something was missing, and I had no idea what it was. I felt a deep longing, but I was so busy making a living and being a nice guy that I couldn't really touch some essential part of myself. In fact, I had been trained not to. The world was pulling too hard on the outside for me to notice the inside. I had to find out from others what I really wanted. My family and friends, the advertisers and authorities were more than happy to tell me. I needed "stuff," endless stuff, that I had to work my ass off to get, to keep, and to maintain. I needed to follow a lot of written and often unwritten rules if I wanted to be really successful. And it was totally my fault if I didn't make it.

I was convinced that there weren't any other guys like me out there. I never heard other guys expressing personal doubts about themselves, only complaining about their wives or girlfriends, talking sports, or expressing frustration about their jobs. I couldn't trust men; they were the competition. I found, however, that I could confide in certain women; they could understand my feelings. They could cry or express uncertainties. A deep part of me wanted that. I had been bonded to my mom; she had been my source of nourishment both physically and emotionally. I couldn't go to Dad for that stuff. If he and I talked at all, it was about how I was doing in school or at work and arguing about politics. So I found myself dependent on women for emotional needs, not really as adults, more as substitute mothers. I came to judge my manhood by comparison. All the cues about manhood were outside me, separate from my deeper self. With both men and women there was a constant need to keep checking. I felt manly if I could compete successfully with men and if I was very different from women.

I knew things weren't working, yet I kept trying to do more, and bigger, and better. Nothing seemed to be enough. After a divorce and a series of dead-end relationships with women, in desperation I reached out to a couple of men I knew at work. Slowly, but surely, I started to get the feeling that maybe there were other men like me and that I could talk to them about how I really felt. I began to trust those men more deeply and in the process started to trust myself more. I dropped some of my walls and the struggle to measure myself against others.

I read the works of Carlos Castaneda and Joseph Campbell and an interview with Robert Bly titled "What Do Men Really Want?" Something began to come alive in me: A more primitive, younger, and wilder side that had been suppressed for so long was awakening. I started to feel better about sweat and emotions and the passions of my youth. Suddenly, storytelling was okay again, warriorship was redefined and applauded, quests were real, and mystery and magic were natural. I found myself alone in the mountains on solo backpacking trips; I was rediscovering my roots in the earth and my roots in the mythic dimension. I began to see this as a quest for my true self.

Reading and being alone weren't enough; in fact, they just added to my frustration, my incompleteness. Here were mentors who spoke to a fundamental part of me, and yet I had no place to explore that, no place to live it. I began to see more gaps within myself and what those spaces might mean. I could feel the wounds of repression and disconnection from the child, the wild one, and the magician in me. I studied about

rites of passage and initiations of men from all over the world. I read
about Kalahari bushmen, Australian aborigines, Plains Indians, and
Siberian shamans. In the process I was reclaiming and honoring a lost
part of my childhood and recovering my soul.

Inevitably, I was drawn to workshops and retreats
that felt as though they

*The Root Kiva in
Council*

might be enactments of the prac-
tices that I was reading about. At one such event I met some men
of like spirit. We began to meet regularly and to explore these notions in
a very concrete and experiential way. We met every two weeks and took
weekend retreats together. We drummed, we danced, we did ceremony.
We talked about our worst fears, deepest wounds, our greatest joys and
our abiding passions. I came to know myself in ways I hadn't dreamed
of. The six brothers that I met then were the first brothers of the Boulder
Men's Council. Since that time, five years ago, the Men's Council has
grown to include many like-spirited brothers.

The Men's Council is to me a place like the vacant lots of my childhood. And, like them, it is not vacant, but simply wild and uncivilized.
It holds something that grows naturally out of the earth. The great mysteries are still alive there. This natural wilderness is the very soul of my
being, my source. And as wonderful as that is, I'm not contemplating
living there all the time, any more than I would try to live aboriginal

dreamtime, Plains Indian spirituality, or Siberian shamanism. Yet, all these traditions have value for me and have something in common: a connection to the sacred that is earth-centered, that is lived out in real community, and that honors the mythic realms of reality.

The Men's Council encourages this dialogue between the wilderness and civilization, a dialogue that is certainly heating up. Wilderness was the first parent, and all cultures are its children. The children have now grown, but many of us lack respect for the elder and this threatens us all. I feel this struggle within myself. I am not a primitive man and yet I am also not a civilized man. And I find that I am not alone. Most of my Council brothers are also questers and wild men and warriors and pilgrims, spiraling in and out of a great labyrinth. We are meeting and exploring ways to connect with our deepest selves and the earth, to bring that into our communities and to create a sustainable culture.

As we men gather to live out the truths of ourselves, we discover the value of our secular rites of passage and we cocreate new sacred ones that honor our manhood. Only when we have accepted ourselves and our brothers as men can we become fully humanized adults. This is not a one-time process. Nor can it be in this age. We are not conforming to a set of traditional beliefs or established doctrines. We are living in the mystery of what we will become. To do this, we need all our brothers. We must use the grief, the anger, the fear, and the wildness to take us down into our souls.

One of the beauties for me in this self-reclamation project is that I am now defining myself more from an internal place and can meet both men and women out of shared interest and not so much out of competition and dependency. Everything I do, be it writing for this book, changing my godson's diapers, or putting a supportive arm around a brother, is manly and comes more from myself. I can see the world with more clarity now, and paradoxically that makes the world far more mysterious. This awareness has a price. I feel the pain in others and in the earth. My choices seem infinitely more complex and difficult. Being adult and male is a huge responsibility. Fortunately, I now understand that this is not to be done alone. I have Council brothers and many sisters who enjoy this serious and blissful business of dancing in the cracks between worlds.

Tom Daly, Ph.D., is the director of the Men's Council Project, a co-founder of the [Boulder] Men's Council and the Men's Council Journal and leads men's workshops nationwide. Please feel free to call or write with your suggestions, comments, or ideas:

Tom Daly
PO Box 17341
Boulder, CO 80301
(303) 444-7797.

DALY
DANCING
IN THE CRACKS
BETWEEN WORLDS

83

BOX H

BY DOUG HUFNAGEL

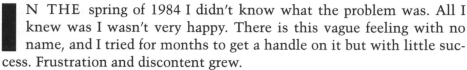

It's one thing to read about "wild man gatherings" and see rather startling pictures in magazines. But how do you bring all that faraway, slightly weird-looking activity into your own backyard? What does a man do when nobody in his neighborhood has even heard of the men's movement? Like so many fellows these days, Doug Hufnagel of Belfast, Maine, decided he would have to build his own men's group, his own men's community . . . and the fact that he had no idea of what a men's group was supposed to be didn't faze him. ✒

IN THE spring of 1984 I didn't know what the problem was. All I knew was I wasn't very happy. There is this vague feeling with no name, and I tried for months to get a handle on it but with little success. Frustration and discontent grew.

One evening Big Jake called from Florida. He had moved from town about a year before but would still visit Maine each summer with his boys. We talked for about an hour and in the course of our conversation "my vague feeling" became crystallized and found a name. The problem wasn't solved, but at least now I knew what it was. I felt better.

I had known Big Jake since the late sixties and after our talk I realized our conversations often had a cathartic effect. It also dawned on me that since he left town, I had no male friends with whom I could reach this same level of openness and honesty. There were women to talk with, but my sense was it wasn't the same.

A couple of years before I had read an interview with the poet Robert Bly in which he spoke about men and their struggles. He suggested that something was missing in men's lives and getting together to talk was helpful.

I thought long and hard about the problem and after about a month's hesitation, I put an ad in the classified section of the *Camden Herald*. It was July 1984, and the ad read:

> Changing with the times? The New Man, relationships, children, Vietnam, the '60s, sex, power, work, divorce, anger, sports. If you are interested in forming an ongoing men's group to discuss, study and explore these or any of our issues in 1984, please respond to Box H, c/o the *Camden Herald . . .*

At the time I didn't have the slightest idea of what a men's group was or even if anyone might be interested in such a thing. I was pretty nervous about the ad and could only wait for the response. The first week I got no letters. How depressing, I thought; maybe this is just too strange for men. The second week I got two letters, both nasty. As I recall now one went something like, "Are you crazy? I would never send my name into a Box H without knowing who was on the other end." It was a note full of fear. The second was a general gay-bashing diatribe chock full of words like "faggots" and "queers."

Very depressed, I thought about canceling the ad, but since I had run it for a month I decided to let it ride. Week three—a breakthrough. Two short notes, both cautious and hesitant. One had a number, the second only an address. I called one up and wrote the second. Both men were as excited and apprehensive as I was, but we agreed to meet. For the next six weeks we did nothing but put off "our first meeting." In the meantime, we managed to add two more men by means of conversations.

Finally, in October, after the summer had settled down, we held our first "men's group meeting" in a living room in Camden. We were six. After the first week we were five but all agreed to meet once a week for an hour and a half. During the first month we spent a lot of time on ground rules. Confidentiality and secrecy were two very important topics. We needed to make sure we could create a safe space within which we could all function. We also agreed not to reveal to anyone who the other members of the group were. We could talk about what we did in the group to our wives, girlfriends, or significant others, but not what anyone else had said. It was like belonging to a secret society.

For the first few months we spent our weekly time doing what came to be called "checking in." Each man would have his 10 or 15 minutes to talk about whatever he wanted. In this way we got to know each other's "story," so to speak. Histories were revealed, secrets slowly exposed, and each week our stories came alive as events unfolded. A decision was made to get a divorce. A man struggled with being gay in macho Maine. We watched helplessly as one of our members slowly went blind until he had to leave the state to return to his parents' home. A man lost his job and another his girlfriend. These were exciting and scary times.

As the months passed we fought to keep the group together. We changed meeting times to accommodate shifting schedules and even met at 6:30 A.M. for a few months. When checking in slowed down, we

HUFNAGEL
BOX H

85

picked a topic like our fathers to discuss for the week. Once in a while we'd go out to dinner and socialize or have a sweat lodge on a Sunday. We did anything to keep the group together.

Our group was leaderless. Occasionally someone would try to take charge, but he'd quickly be cut down to size. Our group was supportive in trying to help a brother through a rough spot and yet could also be confrontational if we saw one another slipping backward or repeating old patterns, which we knew quite well by now. Despite our differences and differences of opinion on many subjects, we hung together. I can still remember our breakfast meetings. Each week someone would be responsible for providing the food for the group. We ate some odd meals those mornings as groggy men cooked and fed each other. And on top of it all, it was fun.

At about the one-year mark two members moved out of state and another decided to devote all his energies to AA. Suddenly we were two. A decision was made to call upon Box H once again. Resurrected and changed slightly, Box H was a hit the second time out. Five positive responses, and within a month we were eight and off on our second incarnation. New histories were told and after a couple of months we again reached the level of trust needed to make the group work.

Over the next two years our group (we never did have an official name) saw 17 different men come and go. Lives changed, divorces were finalized, marriages took place, children were born, relationships ended, relationships began, homes were bought, real friendships bloomed. We watched each other grow. We helped each other grow. We played, joked, and cried together. I solved "the problem."

After about three years, we realized how important the group had become for us and decided maybe it was time to share it with other men. After weeks of talk we decided to hold a men's potluck supper. Not only did we each try to recruit our friends; we decided to print a bunch of posters and put them up around town. This was a public version of Box H, a further step in exposing ourselves.

No one knew what to expect when that cold Friday evening in February rolled around. Would anyone show? We all got there early and waited. It was Box H angst revisited. Slowly men began to wander in, carrying their hot dishes under aluminum foil. Within an hour 35 men were sitting around eating and laughing. Across the table I caught the eye of the original member of the Box H group from four years before. He was shaking his head in disbelief at the responses.

That night three new men's groups were formed and Box H was officially retired forever.

My conversation with Ernie

BY GEORGE MATHEWS

Getting a men's community up and running is often no easy chore; it's no job for the fainthearted and easily daunted. Even the most innocent and heartfelt of invitations to participate can be met with suspicion and contempt. Recruiters find themselves flouting traditional male communication patterns and paying the price. In this seriocomic account, George Mathews recalls how he fared when he agreed to do some "cold calling" to rustle up some newcomers for a men's dance. ✑

SOON AFTER the distribution of the first newsletter of the Men's Council of Boulder, Colorado, some of us were asked to poll our readers. We wanted to know their responses to the newsletter and in turn inform them about future Men's Council events. Things went smoothly as I ventured into the unknown territory of strangers, until—

"Hello?"

"Hi, may I speak with Ernie? This is Michael with the *Men's Council Newsletter*." (Note: Names have been changed to protect the ignorant.)

"Yeah. This is Ernie."

"Hi, Ernie. I'm calling to find out your reaction to the first issue. Did you like it?"

"Yeah. It was great. I really like it. I like the thinking behind it, and I like where it's going."

"Well, I'm glad to hear that," I responded. "Was there any article you especially liked?"

Ernie thought. "Let's see. I liked the photographs. (*Pause.*) I can't remember anything else in particular."

"Ernie, if you enjoyed the newsletter, then you might be interested in some of the upcoming activities of the Men's Council. In two weeks there will be a men's dance." My first mistake.

"Wait a minute. A *men's* dance? What's a men's dance?"

Boy, I could smell the homophobia across the telephone wires, as though all the transformers between here and Denver were exploding.

"Uh, you know, men getting together and celebrating their masculinity by expressing themselves physically in a safe place."

That's not how I wanted to say it, but that's what came out. I continued: "You now, in a Native American sort of way. Those men celebrate life through dancing and singing. They dance their agonies and

heartbreaks and dreams and victories. There's good reason for a bunch of white guys to take a clue."

Long silence. "Is this some sort of gay thing?"

Now, I'm one gay man, along with one, maybe two, other gay men, among twenty-five-plus straight men in the council, which is the ratio one would expect in just about any group of men. But there I was, wincing to myself, "Ernie, I'm not the guy you should be asking." As chance (ha!) would have it, it was me he was putting it to. Aloud: "No, almost all of the men in the council are straight. They recognize that homosexuality is a men's issue and they respect gay men."

Silence from Ernie. So I filled the breech. "Well, let me tell you

about another event. At the new moon in May there will be a sweat lodge."

Ernie's voice rose in amazement: "What's that?"

How was I going to convince this man, who clearly suspected that he was being lured into some queer, debauched, New Age intrigue, that a troop of naked men squeezed into a little underground autoclave to earnestly pray their brains away and to purify their souls? That's what I briefly tried to do, but it simply didn't work.

Ernie terminated the conversation: "Thanks, but I don't think I'm interested." I felt like a rebuffed salesperson.

Over the intervening months my seven-minute talk with Ernie has flourished into cumulative hours of digressive mental excursions and many a belly chuckle about my conversational ineptitude. These explorations have been mostly interrogative. More seeds have been planted than harvests gathered. Some of the questions must be answered by me, some by the men's community as a whole.

What kept me from telling Ernie, whom I didn't know from Adam: "I'm gay, but just about all the other men involved in the council are straight. They respect me. I respect them. And together we seem to be getting a lot accomplished about men's issues in general"?

How, and why, have ordinary American men been controlled into believing that expressions of their emotions through dance or singing are off-limits? Sure, I know men aren't supposed to express their emotions. That is a worn story. But to be forbidden to use one's whole body, arms and hands, legs and feet, eyes, chin, stomach, back, tongue, larynx (*aaaaaaah-rrr-rha!*), expressively—it's sort of like somatic castration.

Many straight men are afraid of gay men; many gay men fear straight men. I'm not talking about gang rape, or gay bashing, but interactions way this side of violence. What are we afraid of? How can we break down these prejudices?

How can men learn that there are times, much more frequently than we have allowed, when men need to touch and hold other men to be made whole, to heal, to grow whole? How can men learn that touching and holding are not necessarily sexual expressions, are more than sexual expressions? And, even further, how can men learn that if sexual feelings between men do appear, those emotions are natural, respectful, honorable, and wonderful?

That last one's a tough one for most of you guys, I know. This homophobia, it's a funny thing. It keeps popping up in the most surprising places. Take me, for instance. Sometimes I refrain from giving you straight guys, or gay men for that matter, a good hug or a kiss to let you know I'm glad to see you or that I share your sorrow because you might think I'm coming on to you.

We've got a lot of work to do.

DANCE

BY PAUL REITMAN

In the preceding piece, the wary Ernie manfully resists when the author beckons him to come to a men's dance. In this companion essay, we see what happens to a man brave enough to venture to such an event. Will he have to learn to follow after all those years of trying to learn how to lead? Will half the crowd be dressed like Carmen Miranda, and the other like Beelzebub? Will he ever be able to face the wife and kids again? Read on.... 🖋

I AM still naive. Naive at 33. I was invited to the Men's Council dance by a "brother" and I immediately thought about the time I was invited to a gay men's ball on Denver's Capital Hill. I decided to drop the kids off at the movies and go to the dance for some adult conversation, the kind of chitchat found at dances since we were all 14.

God, I remember those dances, rites of passage, dancing with (or for) newly turned women. We were such newly turned men. Invariably I went away from each dance ill. I did not want to dance; I had never learned how! I had never learned to do the social thing. Hell, I was usually too petrified to ask another petrified person like myself to dance the dance of puberty.

When I arrived at the Men's Council dance it was dark, and I was ushered into a candlelit hall. There was a circle of men ringing a bright candle on the floor, and inside the circle stood a man with a spear.

Oh, brother, I thought, what satanic mess I have gotten myself into this time?

My usher simply said, "Just follow along with what any of the other brothers do, if you like."

We held hands, connecting the circle. I had not held a man's hand since I was a child. One hand was warm, the other cold. I wondered what my hand felt like to the others—clammy?

The man in the middle, with the spear, began a poetic narration to the spirits (I think). He addressed the east, the west, the south, the north, the up above and the well down below. The words were uplifting, not satanic nor overly religious. And they seemed to come from the man, not from a book.

The circle broke and began spiraling in upon itself, becoming tighter and tighter. Weird. The circle got closer and closer and closer until we were all back on front and front on back. Strange, but in no way threatening. The compressed spiral of manhood began to groan, growl, reverberate. I felt it in my chest, too. I couldn't tell if the growling was coming from me or through me. It reached a peak and settled down reassuringly. The spiral began to sway for a few moments and then began to unwind.

Strange. Not knowing one name in this group, I now felt connected in a primeval sort of way. I felt as if I had growled a growl a million years old.

We began to move in a circle around the room. Dancing? The polka? A waltz? No. Not even punk slam dance. My only comparison would be to an American Indian dance. A dance of warriors. Peaceful warriors. Drummers took up the beat of big drums. The circle moved slowly at first, then faster, faster, until the circle broke into individual dancers doing their own dance. I did a dance, wobbly at first, never graceful, but full of energy. I also walked the room, looking at and touching the different items ringing the room.

Cloth, wood shafts with sharp metal tips, feathers, rattles, bags filled with smooth stone. Bells. I started ringing the bells. I played the conga; I never had before. I played the bongo. I played a tambourine and rang the bells again. It was wonderful. I ate apples. I watched a man, robed in a blanket, walk the room slowly. I rang the bells for him. I danced when I felt like it, but I mostly played the bells and watched. It all seemed right and good. Someone played the flute and someone else played a violin. All these men with raw talent, unpretentious, spontaneous. In the middle of the room two men began to wrestle as bear cubs might wrestle; not violently, but playfully. Some men danced with waving spears, not very carefully but never threatening.

I have never felt safe within a large group of men. Never during high school football. Not at all in the U. S. infantry. I had later avoided men for years. They were dangerous, I thought. I thought about my women friends' horrible tales of rape and violence. I have always feared men but I did not fear the group that danced in front of me.

I had to leave the dance early to go and get my children from the theater, so I don't really know how it ended. Was there a discussion or did everyone just silently go home? I don't think it mattered. I never spoke a word while I was there but so much was said to me nonverbally. So much was said in a physical, nonthreatening way. I left the dance with a new appreciation for the gender to which I belonged and which I did not highly regard. I left the dance feeling much better than when I arrived.

The dance was a celebration of men, and I felt a part of that celebration. It was not the social dance of my adolescence, but for me it was a rite of passage. For the first time in a long time, if ever, I was glad to be a man, and for the first time ever I had danced for no one but myself.

REITMAN
DANCE

91

THE FORCE OF UNSEEN HANDS

BY JOHN TAYLOR

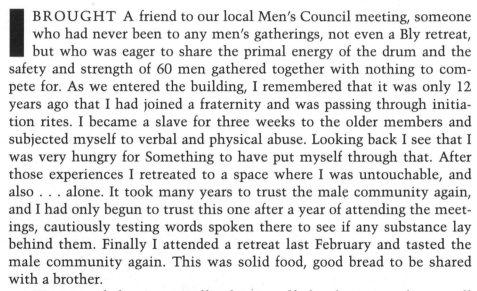

I BROUGHT A friend to our local Men's Council meeting, someone who had never been to any men's gatherings, not even a Bly retreat, but who was eager to share the primal energy of the drum and the safety and strength of 60 men gathered together with nothing to compete for. As we entered the building, I remembered that it was only 12 years ago that I had joined a fraternity and was passing through initiation rites. I became a slave for three weeks to the older members and subjected myself to verbal and physical abuse. Looking back I see that I was very hungry for Something to have put myself through that. After those experiences I retreated to a space where I was untouchable, and also . . . alone. It took many years to trust the male community again, and I had only begun to trust this one after a year of attending the meetings, cautiously testing words spoken there to see if any substance lay behind them. Finally I attended a retreat last February and tasted the male community again. This was solid food, good bread to be shared with a brother.

We entered the Great Hall. The Grandfather beat was alive in all drums and we joined in. My armor from the week began to slide from my body as I relaxed in the familiarity of the beat and faces scattered around the room. Fire shadows danced between us, creating heat and energy. Other beats joined Grandfather on the drum, chanting and dancing ensued, bringing us together in that spirit . . . I'll spare you any more words, you just had to be there.

The drumming ceased. Odor of sweat was in the air. We assembled in a large circle, where each was recognized by all. I find that powerful. Leaders for the evening stood and spoke of the journey we would be taking. All of us were instructed to leave and gather outside in the adjoining room and wait. Jere Truer told incredible stories about box elder bugs as we drank cider and munched chips and waited. One by one each man was blindfolded and bound and silently taken from the room. I was one of the last to go, and enjoyed many box elder bug tales and ate and drank most of the food. Finally, me. Hands bound and blindfolded, I was led through the doorway and in that moment slipped back again in time to 12 years ago, on the last day of my fraternal initiation. That day was spent on a farm, where we did every imaginable thing, acting out roles of slave and master. The initiation was consummated in a final act that seems unreal now. Alone, each of us stood blindfolded and bound on the end of a plank hanging over a large pit that all of us slaves had dug that day and filled with water, hay, and shit. In the final moment I bent over and took a final swat on the ass which launched me headfirst into the pit of sludge and . . .

Back in the Great Hall I was lifted by a force of unseen hands high into the air and carried about until I did not know where I might be. I was placed on hands and knees and unbound; my blindfold was removed; a voice spoke: "Go, The light is gold." A long tunnel lay before me with a light at the end. I crawled and nearing its end heard chanting and music. Emerging, I found myself with others who had taken the same journey. We chanted until the last of us was through and we were all together in the Great Hall warmed by fire shadows. Wounds of 12 years had been healed.

TAYLOR
THE FORCE OF
UNSEEN HANDS

MEN'S GROUP

You guys.
Mirrors of hairline, waistline, punchline.
We know how to eat.
We know how to feed our brains,
but not yet the alchemy to make a meal of our pain.

Our gathering of men.
Is it fun? Politically correct?
An adaptation to an increasingly alienating world?
How often do we sit with our backs to the source
at the center of our circle?
Who can name the fears that all our forms of pride
disguise? What is present in our silence?

You guys.
Magnetism. Polarity. The like forces repel if pressed
too close.
Effective builders large-scale and with raised little fingers.
Where can we find the wisdom to make a cradle small enough
to catch our tears? To sing until the lullaby is found?

Our gathering of men outscores church 96-24.
It isn't even close.
How often are we a small minyan of our unstated
congregation of yin-yang?
Where is our power?
Virtues abound. Humility. Generosity. Competence. Heart.
Do we cultivate self-control and toss passion with the other weeds?
Where is our wild man? Or do only our trusted women see
our wild man?

You guys.
We keep climbing.
We keep waking up.
We keep showing up.
To cast shadows on the living room cave walls,
to hug on the street, and be seekers without ceremony.
In our gathering of men.

—BY JAMES OSHINSKY

WINGSPAN
INSIDE THE MEN'S
MOVEMENT

WHAT HAPPENS AT A MYTHOPOETIC MEN'S WEEKEND?

BY SHEPHERD BLISS

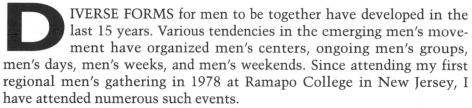

No synopsis, and no one perspective, can do justice to the profusion and variety of men's retreats. In attempting to gain some idea of the scope of men's work, it is important to consider the intentions of the leaders of these events as well as the reactions and perceptions of participants. This essay, addressed to the general public, sketches the theory and format of retreats led by Shepherd Bliss, a veteran of many phases of the men's movement. Shepherd calls himself a "group animator" and among other activities acts as the literary director of the Sons of Orpheus Men's Drumming Group described in Part V of this book. He can be reached at:

Kokopelli Traveling Lodge
P.O. Box 1133
Berkeley, CA 94701
(510) 549-1938

DIVERSE FORMS for men to be together have developed in the last 15 years. Various tendencies in the emerging men's movement have organized men's centers, ongoing men's groups, men's days, men's weeks, and men's weekends. Since attending my first regional men's gathering in 1978 at Ramapo College in New Jersey, I have attended numerous such events.

They range in size from the half dozen men who have met each week for over a year now at St. Johns Church in Oakland, California, to the thousand men who come to a men's day with Minnesota poet Robert Bly. They range in style from the political events of the feminist and men's rights gatherings to the culturally charged mythopoetic events. This article focuses on the weekend mythopoetic gatherings.

The dictionary defines mythopoeia as "the creating of myth" and myth as a "traditional story." I use mythopoeia to refer to that trend within the men's movement which is concerned with remythologizing and reimaging masculinity. The three main tools of the mythopoetic approach to men are storytelling, poetry, and drumming.

We use a variety of names to describe our weekends, selected carefully with those who are hosting us. "Journey into the Male Wilderness" has been a popular title. It implies a quest and movement—as well as something unknown and fresh. "Recovering the Deep Masculine" is another title we use. We describe our work as "recovery work, as well as discovery work, seeking to restore the male community." The deep masculine contrasts with the shallow, negative, or abusive masculinity, which we all know so well. The masculinity we affirm is vital, robust, zany, unpredictable, and spontaneous. It is bold and sensitive, vigorous and gentle.

In addition to the individual men who come to the weekend, there are two groups of men: the host community and the presenting staff. The men who have invited us to lead the weekend are important. Their role is to provide a helpful facility and keep things running smoothly, including providing nourishing food. They must insure a men-only space, even though women are often a part of those organizations who have invited

us. When the men arrive for the weekend it is important that they have contact only with men and begin to orient feelings and experiences exclusively toward men during these days. Host groups often have certain agendas, which we figure into the weekend. For example, they may want to emphasize the healing, spiritual, or artistic aspects of the weekend. Sometimes the inviters are members of a religious community or counselors.

I chose my staff quite carefully. In 1986 I began working with Bruce Silverman—a drummer, psychotherapist, and new father. We have entered into a partnership called The Male Lodge. When in the Midwest I sometimes work with John Lang, drum master of the Minnesota Men's Council and editor of *Manalive*. Other associates have included the visual artist, dancer, and poetry performer Doug von Koss; Movement for Men cofounders Alan Ptashek and Martin Keogh; and author Keith Thompson. Each man I've worked with has brought particular strengths to the weekend. In choosing whom to work with I am aware of several variables. I like an age range. I am 43 years old, a midlife man, so I prefer to have someone older than me and someone younger—an elder and a young adult. My strengths are designing the weekend and verbal presentations, so I am best complemented by men with movement, musical, and visual strengths. I always look for associates who care deeply for men and are able to work in an emotionally charged environment. I prefer them to be strong and flexible of body, mind, heart, and soul—and fun to be with.

All our mythopoetic gatherings occur in the countryside, at places like Neahtawanta Inn in Traverse City, Michigan. We want the men to leave the sounds and pressures of the city and come to a place with greater contact with birds, other animals, water, the earth, fire, and the rest of nature. The Neahtawanta, for example, offers us the Lake Michigan shore, a sauna, a fire pit, the lodge dog Ernie, and a single building which sleeps two dozen men.

The choice of a location, what we transform into our male lodge, is crucial. One of our favorite facilities is the Westerbeke Ranch in Sonoma County, California, wine country, where we meet in an old wine vat which has been converted into a conference space—quite dark, nice smell, Dionysus still resides there. The wood-burning stove helps, as does the sweat nearby. A sweat is a Native American custom of hot rocks under a container within which the men gather. The presence of a hot tub, sauna, or swimming pool can also be helpful.

Men arrive on a Friday afternoon in all kinds of conditions and in all kinds of vehicles: beat-up Datsuns and Toyotas, elegant Cadillacs and Mercedeses, sporty Porsches, and your basic Chevrolets and Fords. Sometimes a motorcycle comes. These vehicles are parked away from our gathering environment. Usually one man or more comes from far away, like Chris from Texas who saw us on national television and flew to Michigan.

The age range is teenage into the seventies, with the medium being around 40 years old, what the psychologist Carl Jung calls "the noon of life." Things begin to change around those midlife years. Carpenters, counselors, barbers, teachers, priests, corporate executives, and health professionals come. We've had policemen, firemen, stockbrokers, lawyers, and men from most occupations among the hundreds who have come to our weekends.

Men arrive with mixtures of feelings—including excitement, anxiety, and fear. They come from all kinds of situations at home and work. Some are well nourished and others are angry at bosses, coworkers, children, or lovers. We are always prepared for a range of feelings upon arrival, as well as during the weekend. We encourage the full expression of these feelings from the deepest grief to the highest ecstasy. We plunge into the vale of tears and rise to the heights of mountains.

Men have a lot of fear—of being with other men, of being hurt, of being rejected. So we seek to provide a safe—but not tame—environment. We stimulate the men and seek to move through feelings by heightening them rather than avoiding them. We rely on the release or discharge of feelings more than having insight into them, though understanding is important. We agree more with Aristotle that catharsis is a value than we do with Plato's warning that it is a threat.

We work more from the heart, body, and soul than from the head, though there is a clear theory behind what we are doing, why we are doing it, and when we do it. The cognitive component of our work is well developed. Timing is also important.

Our intention is clear: to form a weekend community of diverse individuals which can help restore the positive male community and facilitate the healing of each man and the context of humans, animals, and plants within which he dwells.

We seek to alter men's consciousness by means such as drumming and chanting, so we ask them to come without mind-altering drugs such as alcohol, cigarettes, and other substances which can be abused. However, we are not strict policemen; smoking does occur on porches and some drinking sometimes occurs. Whatever the mixture of fear, anxiety, and excitement a man has when he arrives, we welcome him. He is invited to join a small group of four to eight men with a facilitator—usually an animal group which he is drawn to or which recruits him. The small-group leaders meet the night before to get to know each other, receive a little training, and begin the creation of the weekend's community. They receive a detailed list of a dozen items which are their functions, which include the following: form your group; coordinate self-introductions; be available to your men; encourage feelings expression and release; listen, listen, listen; help connect the men and create a safe environment.

The opening circle Friday afternoon or evening usually involves a naming exercise, such as having the men each come to the center and say, "My name is _____." Then the entire group repeats his name three

BLISS
WHAT HAPPENS
AT A
MYTHOPOETIC
MEN'S WEEKEND?

times, "Your name is _____, _____, _____." A flood of energy moves toward the man. Depending on the group's size—they vary from a dozen to around 100—we have each man say one word about how he feels right now, either to the entire group or to the small group. The discipline of one word helps maintain an order which is essential throughout the weekend. Our groups are not leaderless. The leaders come well prepared to exercise power, take initiative, help ensure the safety of the weekend for all, and be flexible.

The first night includes the three main elements of the mythopoetic approach—the drum, storytelling, and poetry. The drum master teaches the men a simple rhythm, usually the samba, and they are off on it, usually quite quickly and joyously. The nonverbal, side-by-side intimacy of the men drumming together provides a valuable container.

We draw from the poetry of ancestors such as the Sufi Rumi, the Irish Yeats, the Spanish Lorca, and Rilke. Contemporary poets such as Robert Bly are also used.

"The Men of the Wound" is a story I often tell the first night. Or I might tell about the Greeks Philoctetes and Hephaestus. On that first evening we introduce some of our key concepts—the male lodge, soul making, and journeying. Sometimes we start the mask making. Our intention is to begin to take the men into the other world. Self-introductions by each man also begin on the first night, either in the small groups or the larger group, depending on size.

On Saturday morning we have the heaviest dose of cognitive material. I might talk about the mythopoetic approach, archetypal psychology as developed by James Hillman, catharsis, and storytelling. I work to evoke our ancestors, such as Francis of Assisi, Walt Whitman, and Henry David Thoreau. My partner Bruce Silverman sometimes appears mysteriously as Saint Francis—dressed appropriately and with a medieval Italian accent. We work on a certain theme, such as "The Father-Son Connection" or "Finding the Brother."

Later in the morning I may lead a guided meditation where the men relax, close their eyes, and develop a fantasy in response to a story I tell. Three guided imaginations we use are on the father, brothers, and animals. The father meditation tends to produce the greatest emotions—especially love and anger. Men often say things to their inner fathers which they have been longing to communicate to their biological fathers for years. Weeping is a common occurrence at our gatherings. It sometimes occurs the first night, or is initiated by the meditations.

In the afternoon we divide the men into smaller groups which go off with one of a number of teachers to work on drumming, mask making, and/or movement. Each group has also been instructed to put together a myth play or story to present to the gathering on Sunday afternoon, com-

Philoctetes was the most famous archer of the Trojan War, having inherited the bow and arrows of Hercules. However, Odysseus ordered that he be abandoned on the island of Lemnos because of the foulness of a wound Philoctetes received in his foot. Later an oracle ordered Odysseus to go back and rescue him, for only with Philoctetes' bow could the war be won. Also related to Lemnos and woundedness was the Greek god of fire, Hephaestus, known to the Romans as Vulcan. Hephaestus was hurled from heaven by Zeus for taking his mother Hera's part in a quarrel. He fell for nine days and his fall was cushioned by the people of Lemnos, but he broke one leg and was lamed forever, even though he was an immortal.

bining their personal stories, the mythological stories, music, movement, costume, masks, poetry, and whatever else. They are likely to rehearse in the afternoon.

In the early evening we have a community meeting at which men can talk openly about their experiences, complaining if they want to, asking for whatever changes they need. Then we go off to prepare for the weekend's celebration. Masks and costumes are donned and faces painted. A wild carnival ensues to samba music. The men dance, play games, beat drums, and tell stories. One man is clearly in charge—providing structure, safety, order, and a wildness. The carnival, Brazilian style, usually goes well past midnight and can go late into the night. We want the men to leave solar consciousness and give themselves to lunar awareness. Most men find themselves needing less sleep at our weekends than usual. The good food and the depth of contact provide substantial nourishment.

On Sunday morning we usually develop a new theme, such as "Man the Warrior," for which I use the award-winning film *Survival Run*. This film is about a vigorous, highly competitive run up Mt. Tamalpais, in which one of the runners is a blind man, assisted by a buddy. The film inevitably evokes strong feelings and the men talk about issues such as the side-by-side intimacy which it reveals, the trust, high level of communication, and the blind man's bravery.

On Sunday morning the men also do final preparations for their play-story-myth, which they present to the group as a gift. Whereas the Saturday night celebration has been one climax, these presentations are another climax. It helps complete a circle. Our closing ritual often involves a handshaking ceremony where each man gets to look each other man in the eyes. During the course of a weekend many extremes are touched—from sadness to ecstasy, remembering experiences from long ago—and ongoing friendships are often deepened or initiated. Though each man's experience is deeply unique, a community experience always occurs. Each weekend has a distinct flavor in my consciousness and is often symbolized by memories like the following:

- Ernie, the Neahtawanta Inn dog, coming from across the room to nuzzle me when the word "hound" comes into a poem.
- The tough Chicago policeman who arrived in full bellow on Friday and by Sunday was cradling the vulnerable young man from the South.
- The 41-year-old man who never knew his father, decided to find him, and reported three months later that he had found him.

The stories of men's lives which emerge on these weekends range from the sad to the joyous. The damage done to men in this society is much greater that I realized when I began this work. Given the chance to express themselves freely without judgment, men have much to express. Given an environment within which the deep masculine is valued, it can emerge.

FINDING THE DOOR INTO THE FOREST

["Finding the Door into the Forest" © 1992 William R. Finger]

BY WILLIAM R. FINGER

"When you're in trouble, remember the dances."
—MICHAEL MEADE

"THE FALCON erupts," Michael Meade is saying in his crisp, passionate way, hands resting on his drum. "When it erupts, it acts on impulse and does damage. It has a quality of wrecking things." Meade is sitting on a 15-foot log bench before a gathering of men, flanked by two of his coleaders. "The falcon has great style. But how does it carry its force without doing damage?"

The question darts about the dining hall serving now as a lodge, into the hearts and psyches and minds of 110 men. It's the second evening of a six-day conference. None of us can ignore this falcon, for it has already struck. Even the night sounds filtering across the lake from the mountainside seem muted. But it's not the image of the falcon that absorbs me as much as the theme Meade is discussing—initiation into a more powerful kind of manhood than I have ever known.

Friday night and Saturday morning, men arrived from Houston and New Orleans, Myrtle Beach and Massachusetts and Manitoba, Buffalo and Detroit, Sarasota and Saxapahaw. We came in car pools and airport shuttles, from 15 states and Canada, the majority from North Carolina and the D.C. area, to a secluded Blue Ridge Mountain church camp near Roanoke, Virginia. One black man (from the North) came to this first Southeastern Men's Conference; the rest of us were white. We ranged in age from 26 to 67—a dozen over 55, just three under 30.

Perhaps half of us (I learned as the week unfolded) had been to a workshop led by one of our leaders for that week last October: Meade, a drummer and teller of ancient stories; Robert Bly, the poet who has triggered what many refer to as the mythopoetic men's movement; James Hillman, the irreverent Jungian psychologist and internationally known author; and John Stokes, a tracker, whose grief sent him into the Australian bush for seven years where he became friends with the animals. Whether veterans of men's support groups or nervous initiates, we all were going deeper into our own forest of men's work.

WINGSPAN
INSIDE THE MEN'S
MOVEMENT

Before hauling sleeping bags to the cabins in the woods, all but the cooks and staff assistants passed through a registration ritual. Handwritten descriptions of three animals on a chalkboard beside the leaders' bunks posed a choice of clans. Many of the bulky and older guys gravitated to this phrase: "The black bear is father, mother, keeper of the forest. . . . As elders, they master and command respect. And hold the power to curse or bless."

The trout, in contrast, "dwell in pools of grief, reflect the upper world, seek wisdom in the water, elusively avoid capture. They regard fish and fishing as a holy thing, because one fishes for the wound and the wound that can be named can be healed." Some of the fieriest men became falcons, which "burn for what is difficult, beautiful and dangerous. They desire initiatory experience now."

The first night as dinner was ending, three falcons leapt from the edge of the dining hall, near the forty or so drums, into the front of the lodge, beside the log bench. With red cloth flying from their arms and legs (each clan had its color), they mocked at the trout, mocked a peace banner, and then as suddenly as they had struck, swooped back into the night. It happened so quickly that many of us hardly noticed the flurry. The conflict festered for a day before it came up at the Sunday afternoon general session.

Meade refereed the angry accusations, defenses, and explanations. As the volleys continued, Meade closed the topic, moving on in the week's program, called "Male Initiation and Isolation." That night, though, Meade returned to the issue, but on the mythological level, discussing images of "erupting" with an "impulse to do damage." From the falcons, who struck first with their small group skit, Meade swept to the full version of male initiation into the tribe.

"Initiation involves wounds," Meade says. "Initial statements are risky." It was the end of the evening, when men stand up and make brief statements to the group about who they are and why they are here. I was the second man to speak that night.

WHY I WAS THERE

I first heard of Robert Bly, the award-winning poet recently profiled by Bill Moyers on public television, in the spring of 1988, when the Men's Center of Raleigh, North Carolina, sponsored him in a workshop and poetry reading. I wasn't able to attend, but two of my friends did, both members of our seven-man support group, spawned a year earlier by the Men's Center. In February 1989, I did join 90 other men for a weekend with Michael Meade, where I learned to drum a bit and to talk and feel with other men a bit more. The most memorable part of the weekend came during a segment of the story Meade told over the two days. He asked us to identify with a detail in that part of the story and place ourselves in the room in sequence. Then Meade led us through that part

What I have discovered is that large retreats or weekend events with men can take a man farther than he can go in an individual therapy situation. There is an emotional experience at those events that is not only allowed but required. The Dionysian retreat world is the communal world, in contrast to the Apollonic lecture world, which is more reflective and conversational.

—James Hillman

FINGER
FINDING THE
DOOR
INTO THE FOREST

again, this time with each of us describing how our image related to our lives.

I was one of the three heads of the dragon the prince had to feed and pass over. We had been talking a lot about dragons and witches and fierceness and feminine energy that weekend. By identifying with the dragons' heads, I was confronting in mythological terms the powerful feminine energy in my life—my wife and two daughters. How could I find the strength to know how to be a man in my own home? It had been very hard.

Eight months later, on the first afternoon of the week-long conference, I sat in a circle with the kitchen staff, two professional cooks and seven of us assistants. I had written goals for myself before arriving, but they came from the head more than the heart. As I listened to each of the crew describe why he had come, I realized why I was there. Our task was to feed the bears, trout, and falcons. We had great powers to nurture—and great responsibilities. Our name for the week, with a color of royal blue, gave me the clue I needed to enter my forest. We were the Men Who Feed the Dragons.

Chinese dragon

After the first night's general session, including about a dozen personal statements, Meade led us through a ritual adapted from an African tribe. Several seasoned drummers beat the rhythms as we formed two long lines facing each other, 20 feet apart. Each line sang a section of the African chant, like warriors echoing a battle cry; at the same time the men would hop at the other line and gesture some type of insult. While one line chanted, hopped, and gestured, someone would race down the waiting group demonstrating the next insult to hurl back.

We got the hang of the odd-sounding chant and the accordion-like flow and moved into a feverish pace, impulses overriding reasoning. As others had done before me, I jumped out from my spot and raced down our line, holding a sneaker in the air and pinching my nose. It was a tame insult compared to many, but it burst from me with wildness and surety. As the opposite line retreated, their insult delivered, 50 of us moved forward, holding our shoes in the air, imparting our odors and grimaces and grunts and chants with the power of a pack of animal warriors. Back and forth we went until we could barely speak, hoarse and exhausted. When we ended, I was transported into the timelessness of the mountains and birds and trees and ancient men. We had begun, 110 men in our sounds and silences. And I was ready to speak.

On Sunday night, after Meade had transformed the falcon tension into issues of initiation, we moved to the personal statements. The first night, men had told moving stories mostly about their grandfathers, lineage, heritage. The second night, the statements took a more risky turn. A man who had earlier spent a week tracking with John Stokes spoke about his present life in a brave, passionate way. Then I rose, even though Michael had asked to hear from trout.

"I'm one of the Men Who Feed the Dragons, Michael," I said. "You really didn't say we could speak yet."

"Dragons can talk anytime," he responded quickly in a staccato way that I had remembered from the earlier workshop. Not until much later, until this writing in fact, did I realize how quickly the phrase "men who feed dragons" can be compressed into "dragons."

Permission granted, I spoke about my earlier weekend with Meade, about my place in the story as the head of a dragon. "This time, instead of having to be fed, I'm feeding the dragons. And that's what I've been doing at home more and more—nurturing my daughters and opening up to my wife, holding her and taking her tension into my body, instead of putting demands on her, demanding that she feed me. But this new nurturing role I'm playing still seems tenuous. I want it to be deeper, more solid for me. I want to know that it's permanent for me. And I need support for that."

I stopped, my words hanging in the lodge, bouncing among the men and back into my consciousness. I felt alive and alert, yet shaky that I had stated my purpose before so many, put myself on the line. Then I sat down. Meade nodded, gazing at me in a way that I felt he understood. But there was an unsettling challenge about his look as well. Again, only now do I understand what that expression foreshadowed. He had some instinct, even if operating in his unconscious deliberating as a leader, that I needed to find a new path: to a place where nurturing and being nurtured can merge together, where dragons and feeding the dragons can stand in tension but also as one.

After the night session ended, I went with Daniel, another cook, to make a mask. I had started the day at 5:30 in the morning, plugging in the camp's first pot of coffee. As I stuck with the kitchen duties, I was also stretching open the pores of my psyche—listening to poetry, participating in the body exercises, absorbing the short story Meade had told that day about a honey pot. I was mixing the responsible, provider side with sensual, passionate expressions, nurturing and being nurtured—which I find so hard to do at home.

At the den of masks (i.e., the camp craft shop), we lay on our backs with wet plaster of paris smothering our face, a small hole for breathing. I felt panicky at first and almost ripped the moist pieces from my eyes and mouth. One of the staff whom I hardly knew, Tom Daly, held my hand and reminded me to breathe. I felt better. He asked if I had ever had an operation. Suddenly, the feeling of suffocation I felt as a child came back, as the surgeon prepared to remove my appendix. And I talked of another operation as a man, when a urologist plunged his blade into my belly to cut a vein so that more sperm could grow inside me, and my wife and I could produce.

Finally, the mask dried enough to go onto a bench to harden. I sat beside my friend, revisited emotions as stark before me as the white mask, waiting for adornment. I didn't know what to create on this virgin plaster, so I looked around for ideas. One of the elders was gluing pine needles on his image. I decided to walk into the woods, now at 11:00 P.M., and found myself gathering berries and cones and twigs and mosses as if in a dream. That night and the next day, I added more of the forest, until there were great tears of grasses falling down one cheek, with shades of greens and browns covering my face, acorns and berries, red and blue, frozen in time on cheek and nose and jawbone.

ROBERT BLY ARRIVES

"Hillman seems like the mind, and Stokes is the body," one of the cooks observed after breakfast the second morning. "Bly, when he gets here, will be the spirit." He paused, looking for a neat completion to his pantheon. "And Meade is like the personality. It's like we have the full person with all four of them." And we did, but in unexpected ways.

A scheduling conflict delayed Bly's arrival at the conference. On Tuesday morning, after breakfast, we formed a snakelike corridor. This time, instead of charging and chanting at each other, we clapped a rhythmic welcome, as Bly walked through our canal which led to the log bench. We birthed Bly into the enclosure we had built over three hard days. In his trademark ascot and many-colored vest, Bly took his place beside Meade. Stokes and Hillman remained on the wings, body and mind anchoring spirit and personality.

Enclosure is a central concept for such a men's conference. A vessel must be formed where our psyches can roam safely with the spirits of ancestors and animals. Fears must be welcomed, demons must be recognized as part of us. First, we dealt with the fears among us, manifested in the unbridled falcon warriors. That fear was absorbed in the container, which made us stronger. We needed that unity to cope then with uneasy neighbors—the fear outside our vessel. The drumming had carried through the night air, into the valley over the hills, so a delegation of five ministers from our group negotiated with the church camp's administrator about our late night drumming. And on the second day, it was good. Finally, a much deeper and devastating fear struck, demanding many more such gatherings of human energy, and we coped as best we could with the news of the San Francisco earthquake.

Every morning after breakfast, the leaders sat on their log and read poems. Maybe D. H. Lawrence and William Blake started their day reading poetry aloud, but I had a hard time plugging my head into images so early in the day, whether in the main gathering or back in the kitchen, listening over the speaker our sound man had rigged for us. Bly recited his poems with the aura of an Indian holy man, waving his hands and chant-

ing in a high, almost nasal pitch. But instead of mantras, he spit out images with challenging and surprising juxtapositions.

On Monday morning, I was sitting out front when Hillman, the intellectual—not Bly, the poet—changed my view of poetry forever. Hillman started reading "The Race" by Sharon Olds, about a dash to catch a plane to see a dying father. Hillman choked with emotion by the fourth line, continuing though until the man was racing down the long corridor to the gate. Then Hillman stopped, sobbing. Michael reached his left hand across James's shoulder and held him. Then Hillman, who is in his sixties, resurfaced from his pool of grief and finished the poem. Tears were streaming down my face too, and I knew how it felt to have my heart opened at unexpected moments.

With those tears, I found another entrance to my forest. We Men Who Feed the Dragon didn't belong to any of the clans. During the first three afternoons, the three clans met with either Stokes for tracking, Meade for drumming, or in the mask-making den. When we had time off from the kitchen, we could join one of the clans. After Hillman's reading, I knew I would dance with the trout. Every man found his own paths into the forest during the week. The deeper I went into mine, the more discoveries lay ahead. But I would also confront more forks, more decisions, and need more courage.

The morning sessions usually focused on a theme. Bly talked a lot about shame and guided us through a one-on-one exercise which made shame more a feeling than a word. He spoke more than the others about concrete experiences, how we bring shame on our children and wives, then hate ourselves when we do.

He also spent a session on male archetypes, with brief but powerful ways of viewing the Warrior, the King, the Magician, the Lover, and the Trickster. "When you start thinking about the King," he said, "think about an apartment in ourselves for our fathers. It's a small room filled with demons. My job is to furnish that apartment for my father. Fix it up, see what's there. See if you can figure out ways he fathered me that I haven't thanked him for yet."

One afternoon late in the conference, I gathered with the trout in the leader's cabin. Men sat Indian-style on the floor and perched on bunks. Sitting on a blanket in front of a fire, Bly told a story, based on a myth but with a contemporary setting. In it, the man out of the army had to descend again and again to stir a pot, to earn money, which he brought back to the world. "The depth is the response to height," said Bly. "Failed ambition is what the plunge down is all about." Talking of ashes and grief, Bly suddenly reached back to the edge of the fire and brushed charcoal onto his forehead and cheeks. As we drifted back outside, the story over, many of us rubbed the ash across our faces too.

I sat against an oak then, the ash ritual over, listening first to the geese honk and frolic. Then a chorus of voices echoed across the lake,

Note: Robert Bly recounts and explains this tale "The Dark Man's Sooty Brother" in Part III of this book.

FINGER
FINDING THE
DOOR
INTO THE FOREST

where John Stokes was teaching the bears a Cherokee chant. The harmonies alternated to a soft verse which, in the magic of sound, whispered across the water in a way that penetrated my eardrums louder than the sounds of the birds. Like a Gregorian chant, it sent chills down deep, and I was filled with these voices of men.

Hillman spoke of many ideas during the week. "Our culture hasn't learned black," he said, discussing the darker side through a section on colors. He never addressed race and the South directly, though, nor did anyone ask about it. That week, we seemed to transcend our geographical location, even though more than half of us had southern accents. Hillman avoided Jungian jargon in his discussions, apparently sensitive to concerns of some conference veterans of too much talk of "anima" and "shadow."

Hillman also helped me think of fathers in an entirely new way. "As long as you complain about negative fathers," he said, "you remain a son. Use the negative in your psyche as an initiator. . . . Souls choose their parents. Mythologically, you choose your parents." The first step is to feel the misery, the wound, the victim, Hillman said. Blame your father. But then go to the second step, and use this scar tissue. "He should not have been any different."

During the morning discussion, Stokes would talk of his experiences with Native peoples primarily, often with sayings from his experiences tracking animals. "You can track anything," he said. "Including fathers." We took a break during the general sessions for Stokes to lead us in body movements. He seemed as much animal as man showing us how to be a deer, then a rabbit, then a tiger. From our spots in a large single circle, outside in clearings around the lake, we would move to the center, impersonating the animal. The tiger was the most fun—growling, opening our mouths wide, clawing at each other. I have had such fun with my kids but never with 100 men, snarling together, then returning to our places in the circle.

Meade talked some from his notebook during the general sessions, notably discussing the three levels of experience—concrete, psychological, and mythological—happening simultaneously, the vibrancy and the liabilities of each. But Meade leaves his mark in his drumming and storytelling, guiding men into their fears and vulnerabilities and wounds. What also sets him apart is the daring way he directs things. It was his personality that opened and closed the conference, that moved us as a group through the rough and joyous edges, even as it was Bly's spirit that undergirded the event.

Meade told a long story that spanned four days. He drums as he talks—a kind of chanting, really, his voice rising and falling in syncopation with the tall cylindrical vessel he holds between his legs, pulling the sound from it with different parts of his hand. The drum vibrations act as another voice adding unspoken details to the feelings pregnant in Meade's storytelling. "A story is like a forest," he explained before beginning the

long tale of a young man on an arduous journey. "You walk around it and find the right door, the right detail, and that detail is your door. . . . Look for a door you've not seen. Look for a facet of your psyche you haven't noticed for a long time."

Twice during the story, Meade stopped at a crucial point and asked us to go into the story ourselves. At the beginning of his journey, the young man was in a castle up in the sky; inside there was a door he was never to open. "But he could not resist and so he opened the door," Meade says, striking the drum very hard. A silence lands across the hall as he stills the vibrations. In his normal voice now, he asks, "What do you see in that room? Stay with the image that is filling your mind."

After five minutes of visualizing what we saw inside, Michael guided us into groups that had similar themes. Fear was the common element for about 15 of us who went outside on the bank by the lake. Behind my door was a high stack of books on the left, a men's chorus on the lower right side of the room, singing, encouraging me to cross the threshold. But behind the chorus lay a dark forest, spiraling away three-dimensionally like Alice in Wonderland. I was trying to move toward it but was, in my visualization, trembling at the edge of the room. In the small group, the fear became more approachable, these men becoming the chorus, there at that moment, helping me move forward.

THE POUNDING OF IMAGES

Meade and Bly advise against talking about the inner journey undertaken in the safety of such a conference. When we burst into deep sobs of grief, as men did throughout the week, men were there to hold us, to absorb the grief with us.

"Don't name it," says John Stokes. "If you ask someone the name of a tree and get a quick answer, you quit looking at that tree." I have done just that many times. "Instead of naming it," Stokes adds, "look deep into the colors of the bark, the textures of the wood, the curves of the leaves, the patterns of the veins."

But there is a time for naming, which Stokes and the others also discussed that week. "The wound that can be named can be healed," read the description of the trout. Such men's conferences as this one are designed not to keep women out but to open men's hearts. My spirit soared as I danced with the trout at our carnival, where we paraded by clan wearing our masks. The banquet had come earlier, where men gave toasts. I raised my glass to the founders of the Raleigh Men's Center, who were there to receive my blessing. "Thank you," I said, "for giving me the chance to open my heart."

This conference has helped to change my life. But it means nothing unless I continue the journey. I have a cache of memories from that week, some grasses and sticks in a rusty can found in the woods, part of the banquet decorations, together with waxed autumn leaves that came

in the flowers I bought for my wife before I left. In a mug decorated with unicorns, I've stuffed the blue sliver of cloth I tied around my body, two acorns gathered for my mask, the verse I was to memorize and recite, and one of my kid's whistles, which is like the one Michael used directing the drumming.

To return to my family and my life, I needed a reentry ritual. The Men's Center's monthly drumming session, scheduled just three days after my return, became that sacred gathering. Several of us cooks had brought fruit from our Virginia kitchen. At the drumming, eight of us who had been there stood in the center of the circle and offered the fruit to the others around us, to nourish other dragons.

As we chewed slices of grapefruits and oranges, we read poems and talked about our return. The men who had been in Raleigh talked of their lives as well. We were forming a new container of energy, a safe place to dance with the demons. I drummed that day and remembered Michael's advice, "When you're in trouble, remember the dances." And, that afternoon among these men, I read the poem I wrote upon returning:

HOMECOMING

A week with one hundred men . . .

The images pound against my sleep, push into my consciousness
Faces, colors, touching, dancing and hitting the drum
until I fall into the timeless wonders of rhythms,
my hands moving without instruction
The cacophony bursts as silently as the infinite sounds of the
forest,
waiting to be heard.

The memories flap with the swooping wingspan of the woodpecker
that soared away from the hardwood between the back of the
kitchen and the magical den of masks,
its red feathers bristling like the mane of a horse snorting
instructions to the herd.
With the birds, I fly deeper into the woods,
trusting my images but knowing they can vanish with the ashes—
Unless they are buried and tilled and sown, for the harvest
of the seasons is at hand!

Such a cutting is before me now, the last smell of mown grass for
the fall reminding me that I am home again.
My daughter snacks inside, happily alone.
My wife swims, bathing her bones—weary from nurturing
alone while I suspended myself in time.
And my elder daughter, at her friend's party, is enjoying a
magician.

I am home, with new spirits to guide me deep into the forest.

CREATING OUR OWN EVENT

BY ERIC PIERSON

On September 27–29, 1991, the Eau Claire–based Clearwater Men's Group in Wisconsin hosted a weekend retreat (or "advance") for men to explore their own masculinity. This lively account by one of the participants captures the perennial problem and only solution for men who want to conduct a retreat, but who don't have any specific models in mind. They relied on their own ingenuity and followed their noses! 🖋

WHEN WE decided to hold our Gathering, our group of men had been meeting each week for barely three months. We all had seen announcements for other men's retreats and workshops, and one of us had spent a week with Robert Bly and a hundred other men. We all wanted to experience something like these, but each event seemed too expensive, too distant, or too intellectual. So a handful of us took the plunge and agreed to create our own event, without a famous author or recognized expert on men's issues. We can be the best experts on our own lives. Democracy in action!

Setting a date was easy: Do it before it gets too cold. Finding a man to cater our meals turned out to be easy, too. Finding a location was harder: It had to be secluded but accessible, rustic but not too primitive, beautiful but affordable. Two possible locations had fallen through when Pat (a friend of a friend of our group) offered us the use of his homestead. As usual with things that drop unexpectedly into your hands, it was perfect.

We decided to limit attendance to 25, and we guessed that 8 or 9 of our own members would attend, so promotion was low-key. Writing a flier forced us to think clearly about the kind of gathering we wanted: We had to be specific enough to attract interested men, but vague enough to keep our options open. We tried to strike the right tone to attract the right men.

We sent out a few fliers and we got listed in some local newsletters. This minimal promotion was enough to get an encouraging response, and it got the attention of the local newspaper, which sent a (female!) reporter to interview a few of us. The resulting Sunday feature article attracted more men.

Sometime around then, it struck us: "This is really going to happen! What are we going to actually do?" If we had hired some more or less recognized author, professor, or human relations guru, we'd never have had to struggle with defining, describing, and doing the content of our

Gathering. But since we had decided to do it ourselves, we had to struggle. And this is what made the Gathering truly ours.

This is what we did at our Gathering of Men:

As men arrived, we each drew one of three kinds of stones from a bag. The stones signified the clans we would be in: warriors, magicians, or lovers. Each received a strip of cloth to wear about the head, neck, or arm during our time together: red for warriors, green for lovers, black for magicians. We met as clans several times, to explore these male archetypes and to plan our initiation of the other clans' members into our own clan.

We gathered in a circle at dusk for welcoming and logistical announcements. Each of us had a chance to introduce ourselves and say why we had come, using the "talking rock" to signify the gravity of our words, and to guard against interruption and less weighty talk.

In our circle of 21, we had men from 22 to 70 years of age. We had a garbage truck driver, a physician, a home builder, a counselor, a janitor, a homemaker, a computer programmer. We were students and workers; unemployed and retired; single, married, separated, divorced, and widowed; veterans and pacifists; religious and nonreligious; friends, acquaintances, and strangers; fathers, brothers, and all of us sons. As we spoke and listened, we quickly found that, despite our diversity, we had much in common. We wanted to be better at being men.

We broke from our circle to eat, talk informally, and examine our impressive battery of drums. Indoors, several musicians began to play. Their performance soon became a sing-along with extended free-form, high-energy drumming. It was loud, intense, and fun!

Some men lingered indoors, talking in twos and threes. Other wandered outside and gathered around a fire to talk and listen, share and support. Strong men took extraordinary risks in exposing their vulnerabilities, expressing feelings of fear and loss, hope and joy. Amid comforting hugs, there flowed tears of pain, grief, and recognition. We were getting real.

As the fire died down and the chill descended, we dispersed to our tents, not knowing what tomorrow would bring, but anticipating great and surprising things.

The night was cold and the ground was hard. We were awakened at dawn by the pungent squeal of bagpipes as a piper circled our encampment. Surprising things were happening already!

After breakfast we met in our clans. With such a diverse group, including men with no exposure to Jungian archetypes, it was unrealistic to expect that conversations would focus immediately on the attributes of the archetypes or how to get in touch with them. For example, two men in the magician clan resisted the idea that there were uniquely male personality structures. Our discussion shifted to a variation of the perennial question of what it means to be a man: Aren't we, men and women alike, all fundamentally human beings facing the same issues? Or are there gender differences that really matter? Are the apparent differences in personality and temperament "just cultural" or are they biologically innate? And what difference does the answer make?

These are provocative questions that go to the heart of the men's movement. Should there even be such a movement? As if by magic, we magicians were able to avoid debate and defensiveness. Our clan spent an enjoyable hour thinking about how we as men are different from all women, using some of Robert Bly's ideas about the male mode of feeling.

The clans then gathered into one circle for a "presentation," whatever that might be. No one knew what to expect—no one, that is, but me, and I had only a brief outline and a few quotations to read. How was I going to fill the time? Taking a cue from last night's expressions of vulnerability, pain, and woundedness, I led the discussion to different kinds of wounds and how we heal them; some wounds are experienced as badges of courage, others as badges of shame; some wounds are foreseeable and thus "only fair," others appear to be random and thus unfair; some wounds fester and remain sore, others get covered by tough but deadened emotional scar tissue.

Things got provocative when I focused on a wound we have all sustained: negative stereotyping of men, especially by feminists. Recalling Joe McCarthy's infamous challenge, I asked, "Are you now, or have you ever been, a feminist?" (I used to be one, but I've gotten over it.) When wounding is institutionalized by the dominant culture, it becomes oppression. Are we—white men who, we are told, rule the world and rule it badly—are we oppressed? It was a heretical idea, to judge from the uneasy expressions I saw around our circle. And as I began to challenge the feminist line, and how we have bought into our own demonization, I watched faces harden in resistance. Did they see me as a divorce-embittered woman-hater? A macho backlash nutcase? Maybe so. But not for long.

I quoted from Herb Goldberg, Robert Bly, Richard Haddad, and Robert Moore, building my case, owning my words, stating my points in the first person. I stopped often, calling out, "Are you with me so far?" And as I went on, the response from the circle grew from a tentative "Uh-huh" to shouts of affirmation. As it turns out, we are oppressed by the same kinds of social conditioning that feminists have rightly rejected for women. (Read the last page or so of *King, Warrior, Magician, Lover* and you'll see where I ended.)

As we all broke for lunch, I gratefully accepted thoughtful comments, thanks, and hugs. In my own polemical way, I had taken a risk by sharing, and I had found acceptance—following the initial resistance. I

felt pride in having honored our personal struggles by placing them into the historical context of the struggle of all men. I felt satisfaction in having done it in a provocative way, and in overcoming resistance to my truth. And I felt relief that my presentation was over. Now I could give even fuller attention to the Gathering.

Following informal conversation over lunch, we were treated to an exceptional display of courage. Some weeks back, in the heat of a high fever, Jim had received a vision. For his presentation, he decided to follow the example of Black Elk, acting out his vision for his tribe—with help from each of us, Jim assigned us our parts: One became a horse, another a deer, and six men standing in a line down a hill became a waterfall. The story was cryptic, and in another time and place we may have felt a bit silly acting our parts. But as Jim retold his vision and we moved in response I felt an unmistakable healing power in the vision, expressed in ritual and storytelling. No matter that I couldn't offer a rational interpretation; this vision made sense at some deeper level. And it took courage for Jim to trust that it would.

Inviting us further into the world of visions, symbols, and nature spirits, Jim brought out his staff: about five feet long, of rough wood, bearing bits of color and topped with a likeness of an eagle's head. He talked about how he found his staff and why he ornamented it as he did, then encouraged us all to go into the woods to find our own. We agreed to harm no living trees, and scattered into the woods.

Without knowing what I was looking for, but striving to put all images of staffs out of my mind, I strode into the trees farther than I thought anyone else would go. I looked neither to the right nor to the left, but straight ahead on the course I had set. I knew my staff the instant it appeared directly in front of my nose.

An hour later, we gathered to ornament our new staffs with paint, beads, fur, feathers, and other materials. Some tore strips from their clan insignias, exchanged them with others, and attached the strips to their staffs.

Then, without warning, the warriors burst into decisive action, moving magicians and lovers into pairs and blindfolding us tightly. Each warrior took two men by the elbows and led them off to the beat of a single drum, encouraging their sightless charges to walk by trust. We hesitated, staggered, then moved in growing confidence down a hill, across a space, over even and uneven ground, to where? When we eventually stopped, a voice told us to remove our blindfolds. We found ourselves beside a creek, standing shoulder to shoulder in an inward-facing circle, surrounded by grinning warriors. It felt good.

Late in the afternoon, we lit a fire to heat rocks for the sweat lodge. After supper and a welcome hour of free time, we gathered by the creek

Black Elk (1852-1950) was a famous medicine man, a Lakota of the Sioux people. As a child he witnessed the Battle of Little Big Horn and the Battle of Wounded Knee. At the age of nine he had a Great Vision of the future while in the Black Hills of South Dakota. His experiences were recorded in a book Black Elk Speaks (1932), which has become one of the most highly regarded works about Native American culture.

at the sweat lodge several of us had built a week before. It was the first sweat for most of us. In two shifts, we entered the hot darkness. Led by more experienced brothers, we crouched naked on the ground and voiced our prayers to the four directions. Not surprisingly, it was a powerful and moving experience, potent as any communion. We eventually emerged, steaming in the frosty night air, to plunge into the creek. Reverence quickly turned to exuberance as we splashed each other with cold water. We gathered our clothes and, to the beat of drums, headed up the trail to the house, feeling refreshed and restored.

Our drumming that night was different from our first night's. Maybe it was the afterglow of the sweat ceremony, or perhaps it was the brief instruction in drumming technique that transformed the first night's wild pounding into subdued, empathetic playing. At one point, at least a dozen drums pulsed quietly as one, never overpowering even the faintest whisper of a woodland flute. Gentleness in power!

After so much time together, having bared our bodies and souls to each other, our conversation around the fire ranged deep and wide. We shared proud moments and private fears, stories of our fathers and their sons, hopes for ourselves as fathers and for our sons. We told of leaving women and being left by women, and the struggles of relating to wives while wanting relationships with other women. As we spoke far into the

night, our respect, sympathy, and trust for each other deepened, enough that one man, for example, felt safe discussing his own impotence. But all was not heavy: Our serious conversation was lightened at unpredictable intervals by wisecracks, sexual (but not sexist) jokes, and a series of tales that all began, "The kinkiest sex I ever had was when . . ." I have no idea how late it was when I finally went to my tent.

Morning again. Bagpipes again! (The piper proudly showed me his instrument and let me try it out.) I washed my face in the icy creek, joined three men for a three-mile hike, and enjoyed a breakfast big enough for two. Thus fortified, I turned to the business at hand.

Following breakfast, the clan of lovers called us to stand in a circle and led us in singing "Amazing Grace." As we stood arms around shoulders, singing, humming, and looking each other full in the face, a warm, trusting peace came upon us. It was truly amazing!

We met as clans once more. The warriors retreated to their cabin fortress and the lovers stretched out on an open hillside. We magicians gathered at the fire pit, coaxed the ashes into reluctant flame, and sat in the swirling smoke to plan our ritual of initiation: As men began to gather for the closing, a magician approached and brought them, one by one, to our fire. As each man knelt, we marked his forehead with ashes and invoked a spirit of insight to master the inner technologies, while directing a stream of light energy into his crown. I do not know how it felt to receive this blessing but to conceive it and celebrate it felt like powerful magic.

You may have the impression that our entire time was spent in serious conversation, getting in touch with feelings, and generally being wise and spiritual dudes. But fortunately, and altogether naturally, we punctuated the heaviness with such traditional manly pursuits as king of the hill, Indian wrestling, and wood splitting, plus the ever-popular messing with the fire, making noise, and growing whiskers.

We gathered once again in a circle to conclude our time together. Once again we used the talking rock. Many men spoke movingly of what they had seen, learned, or felt in this brief weekend, and told of how grateful they were for the experience. One man confessed that he had never yet hugged his children, but vowed to start that very day. Another man knelt before an empty seat and poured out extravagant grief at the loss of countless brothers to war. Another man took the rock and leaped to his feet with a triumphant "Yee-HAH!" A father and his son embraced. And we all kept silence as an eagle circled overhead. I was flying, too.

Our experiences so far now led us to what they required to be complete: a celebration. We would celebrate a ritual of our own making, a ritual of striving, ascending, and joyous welcoming. We broke from the circle to plant our staffs in a double row, forming an aisle running fifty feet up a steep hillside. At the top of the hill we began to drum, building quickly to a throbbing boogie. Then one by one, beginning with the eldest, we descended to the bottom of the hill, entered the path between the staffs and walked, ran, or danced our way to the top to be hugged, held, and hoisted into the air by our new brothers' strong arms. As the youngest man reached the hilltop, the drums built to a new climax and we raised a triumphant chant: "WE ARE MEN!"

We are ordinary men in small-town Wisconsin, and we did it. We created our own event, and quite an event it turned out to be. As we broke camp that day, floating a few inches above the ground, not ten minutes passed before someone said, "We gotta do this again!" He was right.

MEN'S SECRET SOCIETIES
1890s to 1990s

BY CHRIS HARDING

Newspapers continue to run occasional stories about how yet another all-male bastion has fallen and women have successfully used legal and societal pressures to gain admission to a men's club or organization that formerly excluded females. Usually, the tone of these articles is "Good for her!" and "That'll teach those male chauvinist Cro-Magnons!" Such a simplistic feminocentric response ignores the consideration that there might have been something important and precious in the original conception of the group that made members feel it had to be exclusively male. While certain men's organizations have become calcified and need "liberating," not every men-only group is inherently evil, or supports the repression of women. As outdated men's groups disband or integrate female members, new groups arise to answer the need for all-male ritual space.

I N MANY ways the mythopoetic men's movement is just the latest manifestation of men's instinct to spend time in strictly male groups. It's hard for contemporary men to compare their private rituals and gatherings with the after-hours activities of men two or three generations ago because the details of men's everyday life have been left out of the history books almost as completely as the details of women's everyday life. Recent scholarly studies document the amazing extent to which in past decades American men were engrossed in secret society fever. Men left their homes several nights a week to participate in lengthy rituals and initiation ceremonies wearing masks, beating muffled drums, dressing in strange regalia. Like today's men who belong to the New Warrior Network or Justin Sterling's teams, they too left women at home wondering what could possibly be so interesting and why it all had to be kept such a deep, dark secret.

A brief look back over the last century of men's secret societies in America puts the current men's movement in a new perspective. It quickly becomes apparent that our great-grandfathers regularly held ceremonies that make our gatherings look tame, unimpressive, and unimaginative by comparison.

Though there are profound differences between men's groups of today and yesteryear, there are surprisingly many parallels. To name just four: exploration of ways to fulfill spiritual needs not adequately met by organized religion; abiding, unquenchable thirst for initiation; absent-father and role-model issues; and need for a safe space in which to shed everyday personas—where nobody clerks could be transformed into revered patriarchs, and responsible citizens could indulge in outrageous pranks that would be frowned on by women and "society."

Today many of us think of fraternal organizations like the Masons and the Elks as either antiquated relics or silly clubs like the Loyal Order of the Raccoon on "The Honeymooners." Many mistakenly believe that federal legislation has opened the doors of these once pow-

erful organizations to women as well as minorities. These impressions are largely incorrect.

While membership in fraternal organizations has declined greatly since the turn of the century, when one man in two belonged to at least one such group, several all-male organizations are still very much in business. Many of them prefer to be called "societies with secrets" rather than the more ominous "secret societies." In any case, most of their secret rituals are copyrighted and available to the public at the Library of Congress and other libraries.

The oldest, largest group and the model for virtually all others is Freemasonry, which counted 2,608,000 members in 1989—approximately twice as many as the Knights of Columbus mustered. (One British Masonic scholar sneered that the K of C was "a consolation prize for the good boys who might otherwise be tempted into Freemasonry," referring to the popes' long-standing ban on Catholics joining the basically Protestant Masons. In 1976 that ban was revoked, and Catholic men but not clergy were permitted to join.)

A candid picture of a Maine fraternity from the 40s

Though they keep a very low profile these days, men's secret societies are still considerable forces. At least 14 U.S. presidents have been Masons, starting with Washington and including both Roosevelts, Truman, and Ford. In 1978, a survey showed that 35 of the 100 U.S. senators were Masons in good standing.

As to the notion that proceedings at men's secret societies are a lot of ridiculous mumbo jumbo, it is important to distinguish between solemn rituals of the more serious orders and the burlesque ceremonies of "fun" orders. For example, while a serious order might dress an initiate in velvet robes, cover his head with a silk hood, and bind him with ornate chains, the affiliated burlesque group might strip him and subject him to hilarious but good-natured indignities before welcoming him as a full-fledged brother. The "fun" orders are not necessarily frivolous and self-indulgent. For instance, the Shriners, a suborder of or "playground for" Masons, is respected for its tireless work in raising funds to give crippled and burned children free hospital care.

Encyclopedias of fraternities like *Fraternal Organizations* (Greenwood Press) by Alvin Schmidt document the fact that many organizations have or had a very healthy and peculiarly male sense of humor about themselves. The Loyal Order of Bugs called its local chapters "bughouses" and their leader "the Supreme Exalted Bugaboo." And who would dare laugh at burly lumberjacks who boasted membership in the International Order of Hoo-Hoo? Many deriders of men's secret societies fail to perceive men's tendency to revel in pomp and ceremony and to undercut it and satirize it—often simultaneously.

One of the scholarly works that documents the former popularity of men's groups is Mark C. Carnes's *Secret Ritual and Manhood in Victorian America* (Yale University Press, 1989). It traces the evolution of loose bands of merrymakers into teetotaling secret societies whose members dressed up as Old Testament patriarchs, medieval knights, Roman senators, ancient Egyptians, or Indians.

"Many of the rituals written during the 1830s and 1840s made use of masks. Some were comical, some frightening; others simply obscured the face. . . . Within the lodge everyone acquired new and mysterious identities. The masks concealed one identity and conferred another."

The memberships' all-consuming popularity for initiation experiences forced lodge leaders to script more and more mysterious rites for advanced degrees. "In nearly every organization some leaders complained that the emphasis on ritual deflected money, time, and effort away from tangible political and economic objectives." But the fashion continued unabated until the 1929 stock market crash. Initiation fees at each level and costs of regalia required a serious financial commitment to the group. It was the depression and lack of money, not lack of interest, that cooled off the fever.

Though significant numbers of Protestant clergymen participated in these societies, these fraternal organizations propounded a philosophy that was at odds with the Christianity they preached on Sunday mornings. Countering the feminine notions of the goodness of God and faith in the perfectibility of man, Carnes goes on to note "the fraternal rituals taught that God was imposing and distant, that man was fundamentally flawed and that human understanding of religious and moral issues was imperfect."

Another work predicated on the belief that men are driven by an innate need to disassociate themselves from women is *Men in Groups* by Lionel Tiger—the book that coined or at least popularized the term "male bonding." Though readers must wade through lengthy documentation of various biological and anthropological theories, Tiger's thesis is plain enough. "Males bond in a variety of situations involving power, force, crucial or dangerous work and relations with their gods. They consciously and emotionally *exclude* females from these bonds."

Many of Tiger's claims will seem dated and sexist—the book was written in 1969—but he does have interesting observations on such phenomena as why some men don't mind barbecuing outdoors, but refuse to cook in a kitchen; why sports fans prefer individual female athletes like tennis players, skaters, or gymnasts, but like to root for men in teams; why Christ chose only males as his apostles. Tiger draws frequent parallels between behavior of modern man and his animal and primitive-society counterparts.

White American man's historical fascination with Native American ways has somehow been able to go hand in hand with his racism and exploitation of other peoples. One of the most popular secret societies was the Improved Order of Red Men, but until the mid-1970s only white males were allowed to join. Then at their 106th annual meeting in 1974, the group came to a turning point and invited Native Americans to join, sponsored adoptions of hundreds of Native orphans, and lobbied for Indian causes nationally.

Even today, however, despite claims about open-door policies, most secret societies remain basically white men's associations, and blacks have formed several groups that parallel the bigger organizations like the Masons and Elks. Prince Hall Masons say that initiation ceremonies at black lodges like theirs are considerably rougher than rites that white folks conduct.

Today, with all the hand-wringing done about lack of minority participation in the men's movement, the last thing men's group leaders may want to hear about is similarities between their organizations and men's secret societies with de facto segregation. Most of us have no problem with the notion of men's mysteries being separate from but equal to women's mysteries, but we do feel guilty about white men's organizations and black men's organizations. And even though the numbers of secret societies have dwindled, their surviving members far outnumber men currently attending mythopoetic retreats.

It is instructive to sympathetically explore why these men have felt the need to build barriers and why their groups have lasted so long. Perhaps then we can respond to those same fears and needs in ourselves, but find new solutions that don't exclude men of other cultures. And troubling as the thought may be, we need to consider that imposing a societal change because we believe it to be morally correct may exact a high price if it is unknowingly at odds with those half-understood clannish urges that warn us to cling only to our own kind.

III

LEARNING FROM MYTHOLOGY

WHAT OEDIPUS, NARCISSUS, AND SUPERMAN CAN TEACH US

Though today we think of religion, psychology, and literature as separate fields, in earlier times they were seen as inextricably interconnected. One's religion once included an explanation of why people thought and acted as they did; great literature and the visual arts had as their basic subject matter both the superhuman religion and the related human psychology. The later advent of scientific thinking largely devalued poetry and myth in people's belief systems.

Sometimes we mistakenly lapse into thinking that Sigmund Freud "invented" psychology. Freud synthesized and formulated new ways of talking and thinking about the dynamics of personality, particularly the way in which unconscious forces affect our conscious lives. But his new theories and vocabulary didn't much change the way people had been behaving and thinking. As Freud well knew, certain typical ways of thinking and relating had formed the basis of enduring stories in both folktales and high literature throughout recorded history as they doubtless did during the times before that when stories were transmitted orally.

Before he trained as a physician, Freud was an avid student of classic, English, and French literature. He particularly admired Shakespeare, Goethe, and Dostoevsky, whose works contain many brilliant psychological portraits. Freud cited the ancient Greek dramatist Sophocles rather than a particular case history when he named the Oedipus complex, perhaps the most famous and controversial stage in his schema of a male's psychological development. Freud also carefully analyzed Hamlet's relationship with his mother Gertrude in explaining this complex. Clearly he was acknowledging that two poet-playwrights had observed the same mother-son dynamic long before he did, but had chosen to express this pattern in a vivid narrative form rather than in a scientific treatise. They put their observations in a form best suited to the audiences of their time and, as it turns out, more attractive to audiences of successive generations (including our own) than the sometimes daunting prose of Freud.

The men's movement is rediscovering the interrelationships among psychology, spirituality, and literature and the notion that the heightened language of poetry and myth can impress truths more lastingly than a straightforward explication can. Like Mr. Keating, the inspirational English teacher in the movie *Dead Poets' Society*, movement leaders are proclaiming that it is not unmanly to be interested in poetry . . . quite the opposite: Verse writing is a time-honored male skill. Men are encouraging one another not only to read aloud or recite the works of others, but to write and share their own poetry and myths around council fires.

There is no simple or entirely satisfactory definition of "myth." Of course, we don't use "myth" here in the sense of a "popular misconception" such as in the statement, "It's a myth that men can't express their emotions very well." The term "mythology" can refer either to the study of myths or to the whole body of myths in a culture or religion. Myths or legends aim to explain the beginnings or meanings of things. In Western culture, tales of the Greek gods and mortals were more than entertaining adventures; they illustrated universal behavior patterns.

One simple example is the story of Narcissus, a strikingly handsome youth who fell in love with the young man he thought he glimpsed beneath the shimmering surface of a stream. Obsessed with trying to embrace what was actually his own reflection in water, he fell in and drowned, according to some sources, or pined away with unrequited love, according to others. This fate was meted out to him by the goddess of love, Aphrodite, because Narcissus had scorned the affections of the nymph Echo, who was so grief-stricken that she wasted away until nothing was left but her voice. While this sad story does not give a scientifically accurate explanation of how echoes work, it does provide a memorable metaphor for the dangers of egoism. Psychologists today use the term "narcissism" to refer to the condition in which a person is so absorbed with his or her own body or appearance that he or she cannot relate successfully to others.

The first important book in recent years to interpret a myth of masculine maturation and relate it in accessible language to the life of contemporary men was Robert Johnson's *He!: Understanding Male Psychology, Based on the Legend of Parsifal and His Search for the Grail, Using Jungian Psychological Concepts.* Johnson's short book showed how this Arthurian legend contains a detailed blueprint for the psychological and spiritual development of males. Since the work first appeared in 1974, it has been reprinted in revised editions many times. (Robert Cornett's "Still Questing for the Holy Grail" in this section outlines a multipart workshop based on the Parsifal story.)

The younger a person is, the less likely it is that his or her education will have included a solid grounding in classical mythology, much less a familiarity with the myths of non-Western cultures. Today it is in vogue to look down one's nose at Eurocentricism and the culture of DWMs (dead white males). Paradoxically, it is also fashionable to lament the lack of sustaining and undergirding myths in our impoverished culture. The reality is that we often don't recognize the prevailing popular myths of our own time because they seem so inconsequential.

For example, the modern myth of Superman is a central one for American males. How often have we consoled ourselves with the half-conscious thought that others who dismiss our unimpressive Clark Kent exteriors would be astounded to discover our true potentials and powers? How often have we feared that a woman like Lois Lane who got too close might expose our "secret identity"? The fact that countless comic book superheroes have similar dual personalities suggest how profoundly this Superman–Clark Kent myth speaks to and of our male experience.

In the section of the book you are about to read, movement leaders like Robert Bly and Michael Meade discuss the meanings of a variety of tales and share their techniques for making these stories come alive for audiences. They encourage men to strive to understand and embody culture-wide male myths. Various members of small men's groups have taken to boning up on different mythologies: One man may research Apache legends while another studies Celtic stories. These amateur experts then can help their group widen its perspective on how men of other cultures and eras have understood the kinds of problems men still face today. ✐

WHY USE MYTHS AND FAIRY TALES?

BY GEORGE TAYLOR

To many of us, fairy tales and folk stories can seem to be simple cautionary lessons, tailored to the limited minds of children. But libraries are crammed with studies offering conflicting explications of the moral, political, social, and psychological symbolism in these tales. Most of us haven't the time to weigh one interpretation against another, but we have become sensitized to the fact that when a detail of a story captures our imagination, it is offering a valuable clue to some aspect of our psyche that is crying for attention. 🖋

WE ARE currently attending men's retreats and groups because we find that the company, the truth, and the courage of other men supports our own quest for our deepest selves. At some of these meetings, leaders use myths and fairy tales, and encourage discussion of the themes and images of these stories. There are various reasons for this use of old tales:

1. Ancient stories of male gods and imaginary figures connect men to the lineage of the male community. Such stories help us to find images for the types of men we want to be. For instance, Odysseus expresses deep longing to return to his homeland, where he will find his wife, son, and father. Men can experience through his story permission to feel such deep feelings.

2. These stories and fairy tales are more anthropomorphic than familiar Christian myths. We see men and women in large families in which children, parents, lovers, and uncles are portrayed in relationship. The complexity of the father-son, father-mother, brother-brother interactions stimulates us. We are forced to ask ourselves, How would I act or feel? when Zeus mediates between the two brothers, the artistic Hermes and the rational Apollo, or when Hansel and Gretel are cast out into the forest by their parents.

3. These stories connect us with a part of our psyches which has been abandoned by our culture, a part of us which is nourished by the infinite, the divine, the Other. We feel connected to the Otherness of the world when we feel the majesty and the mystery contained within millenia-old stories. We ask ourselves, Why do these stories survive, and what do they have to teach us?

USE OF A HERMES MYTH IN A MEN'S GROUP

Introduction to Hermes

Jean Shinoda Bolen in her *Gods in Everyman* suggests that Hermes "personifies quickness of movement, agility of mind, and facileness of word; moving quickly, as a male image or as a metaphor, he crosses boundaries and shifts levels with ease." Hermes is the god of erupting energy, visitations, erections, and communication.

One of the most famous Hermes stories describes his first day of life; he creates musical instruments, steals the cattle of his brother Apollo, lies to him, goes before his father Zeus for trial, receives a pardon and approval from Zeus, and reconnects with his brother.

Method One: The Door into the Story

This method has been popularized by storytellers Gioia Timpanelli and Michael Meade. It is based on the idea that as a listener hears a story, certain images or details will stay with him or her. These details generally connect to some part of the listener's past and are called the "door into the story."

Hermes

I have used this particular method in groups and at retreats; rarely does a man have trouble associating some memory, episode, or feeling in his own life with "the door into the story," which in the magic imaginative world becomes an access point into the listener's own world.*

For example, in the Hermes story, Zeus and Apollo both notice Hermes's lying with reckless abandon and call him on it. Zeus says, "I want you to stop lying." Hermes replies, "I won't lie to you, but I won't necessarily tell you the whole truth." Not only does this line remind me of the hairsplitting I learned at my Jesuit high school, but there isn't a man in this country that doesn't tell half-truths to protect his self-image. That line was my "door into the story."

This storytelling method links men together through the common experiences and feelings; men who trust each other can go deeply into grief, rage, love, and other emotions as an evening continues. One problem with this method is that often it can stir up feelings without giving a way to work through them; good facilitation of this method requires training and experience in group process, I believe.

Method Two: Entertaining the Presence of the God Himself

Another method of working with the stories requires more attention and skill by the facilitator and probably works better in smaller groups. In

---

* Technical note: I usually play my drum while I tell the story, and then for a few minutes after it ends. Over the drumbeat, I ask the participants to find some part of the story that speaks to them; this usually takes three to five minutes.

this method, facilitator and participants notice behaviors and expressions of the god as they occur throughout the evening.

For example, a couple of years ago, on the night we told the Hermes story, a man, Thomas, spoke up as soon as I finished. He said, "I hate this topic. I feel frightened around Hermetic energy, like when people start moving in quick bursts of energy. I don't like phony backslapping. I'm especially afraid of those rounds of put-downs that men get into. I get so contracted, I can't talk. Then I heap shame on myself for not responding, so it gets doubly bad. . . . "

When I asked if other men experienced shaming behavior of this type, Vincent said, "Yeah, on my job site, I'm an electrician. I always want to get down and get connected to the other men. Well, it was happening at lunch the other day. We just broke through the usual conversational b.s. and were talking about real stuff, about AIDS, and our girlfriends sleeping around and all that, and it felt real con-

nected. Right when
lunch broke up I said, 'Yeah, I'm not stupid. My girl
and I are monogamous; we don't do that.' There was a laugh, but then I felt how I was cutting the other men down. Right when I was getting the kind of contact I always wanted from them. All that afternoon I felt sad."

"Hermes had leapt out of your mouth," I said.

Fred said something like, "We Scorpios tend to do that. . . . " The group laughed, although most of them didn't know what Scorpios do. And then Samuel said, "Yeah, and you deserve the trouble you get in."

An awkward pause fell on the room; Hermes had just entered. I said, "Does anyone want to respond to that?"

Vincent said, "What the hell do you mean? I didn't like the way you said that." Samuel thought it over. He said, "I don't know. It felt like one more comment to make in the same vein that Fred had opened up. . . . "

Thomas said, "Well, yours felt a little more angry or critical. . . . "

Samuel said, "I don't know. I don't know if I feel that way toward you two right now. . . . " Connection in the room was being reestablished as men went deeper with their own truth.

Then another man, Charles, said, "Hey, I know it's early, but I got to cut out. I'm going skiing this weekend." Hermes, guardian of boundaries and quick movements, walked out with him.

Final Thoughts

I see two main problems with using myths and fairy tales in the contexts which I have described. One is the tendency in men toward analysis, which is a constant challenge for facilitators of men's groups; we do not need more practice in staying in our heads. When men go mental, they are often isolated from their own experience and from the other men in the group.

Facilitators must pay attention to the isolation brought about by too much analyzing. Having the group talk directly about who feels connected to the speaker and who feels separate is a quick way to get men back into their feelings and to reestablish a group bond.

The second main danger of the story world is that most of the males we read about are operating in a patriarchal world, especially in myths. We have to realize that the models of domination of women are not ones we are supporting. These models (e.g. of Theseus kidnapping, then abandoning Ariadne) provide us with opportunities to "just say no."

Men have a lot of feeling about the lack of current models of equal, powerful relationship; truth telling on this topic provides an opportunity for men to heal and grow as they express the need for more models of loving behavior, especially between the sexes.

The gods often govern opposite-appearing forces. Hermes is the patron of all communication, including the truth, not just the negative, critical dominating we have seen in this essay. Invoking his presence must be done with consciousness, so that our language can create, rather than destroy, connection.

BASIC ASSUMPTIONS OF MYTHOLOGICAL MEN'S WORK

1. The primary purpose of men's work is to find ways to become more loving, wise, and powerful men.

2. The wounds that prevent us from feeling loving, wise, and powerful are stored in unconscious, numb parts of the body-mind.

3. Men (and women) can access these numb parts of the body-mind by using the imagination to connect consciousness with unconsciousness.

4. Storytelling, poetry, movement, music, and ritual are tools which allow the imagination to form this bridge.

5. Men can easily associate mythological stories and images with episodes in their own lives, and they can talk about these associations if they feel safe.

6. The sharing of these personal stories and associations in a group helps men to feel less isolated.

7. Talking about mythological imagery helps men to identify with the positive images of masculinity which are missing in our current culture.

8. On a personal level, talking about these stories and feeling them in the body helps men to release old wounds and bring new life into the heart and soul.

9. Once men have identified an emotional or historical memory with the events of the story, they can release it from their bodies through body work, breathing exercises, movement, or ritual.

10. Ritual helps to mend the male community and to connect men with the transpersonal and archetypal fathers. Rituals also can bond men in vigorous activity and creativity.

—GEORGE TAYLOR

THE DARK MAN'S SOOTY BROTHER
A GRIMM BROTHERS' STORY RETOLD

BY ROBERT BLY

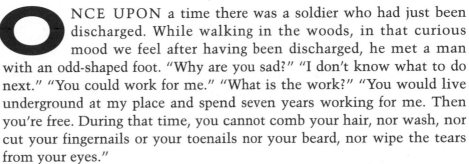

Soldiers appear frequently in middle tales and symbolize several tasks in middle years. . . . Consider first the life of ordinary soldiers. They slog through mud, polish shoes, and stand guard for hours on end. Like beasts of burden, soldiers are expected to work without complaint. They offer a poignant metaphor for the toil of middle years, applicable to men and women alike.

—Allen B. Chinen,
*Once Upon a Midlife:
Classic Stories and Mythic
Tales to Illuminate the
Middle Years*

ONCE UPON a time there was a soldier who had just been discharged. While walking in the woods, in that curious mood we feel after having been discharged, he met a man with an odd-shaped foot. "Why are you sad?" "I don't know what to do next." "You could work for me." "What is the work?" "You would live underground at my place and spend seven years working for me. Then you're free. During that time, you cannot comb your hair, nor wash, nor cut your fingernails or your toenails nor your beard, nor wipe the tears from your eyes."

So he went with a man who took him underground and showed him the three pots. "You'll be tending my three pots and keeping them boiling. You will not look into the pots. Is that clear? And the shavings you will sweep behind the door. Can you do it?"

"I can," he said.

He chopped wood, put the wood chunks under the huge, black covered pots, kept the fires going, and swept the shavings behind the door. After three or four months, he said to himself, "I think I"ll peek into the first pot." He did, and to his surprise he saw his sergeant sitting there. "Oh ho!" he said. "You had me in your power, but now I have you in my power." And he added more wood to that fire. He worked a few more months, and then felt the desire to peek into the second pot. He did and saw his lieutenant sitting there. "Ah ha!" he said. "You once had me in your power, but now I have you in my power." And he added a lot more wood to that fire. Six months or so later, he couldn't resist his longing to peek into the third pot. He lifted the cover and who did he see but his old general—General Westmoreland!—sitting in that pot. "Well, well!" he said. "Once you had me in your power, but now I have you in my power." He chopped extra wood and added good dry oak under that pot.

When the Dark Man returned to see how the work was going, he remarked, "By the way, you looked into the pots, and if you hadn't added more wood, I really would have punished you."

Time seemed to pass faster now, what with the extra chopping each day, and week by week the time went by, and the seven years were up.

The Dark Man returned and said, "You've done your work well." He swept up some of the shavings behind the door, put them in a gunnysack, gave the sack to the man, and said, "Here are your wages." The man was disappointed, but what can you do? Always remember to arrange your wages beforehand. The Dark One said: "When anyone asks you where you have come from, you say, 'From under the earth.' If they ask you who you are, you are to say, 'I am the Dark Man's Sooty Brother and my King as well.' " It didn't really make sense, but he memorized the sentence and prepared to go back to the world.

He left the workplace and the strangest thing was this: as he made his way up to our world, the shavings in his bag all turned to gold. That pleased him, of course. Eventually he came to an inn and asked for a room. "Where do you come from?" asked the innkeeper. "From under the earth." "Who are you?" "I am the Dark Man's Sooty Brother and my King as well." He hadn't shaved for seven years, or wiped the tears from

BROTHER MOVIES

1. **American Flyers** (1985) Two brothers—one seriously ill—force themselves through a grueling bike race.
2. **Beau Geste** (1939) Three brothers battle gallantly in the Foreign Legion.
3. **The Brothers Karamazov** (1958) Dostoevsky's tragic novel about four brothers, sensitively adapted to the screen.
4. **Dead Ringers** (1988) Jeremy Irons plays identical twin gynecologists in an unpleasant but based-on-fact story.
5. **Dominick and Eugene** (1988) Sentimental tale of young doctor sacrificing himself for retarded fraternal twin.
6. **East of Eden** (1955) James Dean's debut in this Cain and Abel story.
7. **The Fighting Sullivans** (1944) Sleeper hit of 1944 based on true story of five brothers enlisting and dying together on a battleship.
8. **Rain Man** (1988) Selfish Tom Cruise learns compassion and caring for his autistic brother Dustin Hoffman.
9. **Seven Brides for Seven Brothers** (1954) Rowdy redheaded brothers dance spectacularly in this musical.
10. **The Sons of Katie Elder** (1965) John Wayne, Dean Martin, Earl Holliman, and Michael Anderson, Jr., avenge wrongs committed against their dead parents in this Western.

his eyes—you remember that—so the innkeeper did not find him to be an appetizing guest, and said, "I'm sorry, but I have no rooms left for tonight." Then this worker made his first mistake—he opened the sack and showed the innkeeper his gold. The innkeeper now said, "Well, as I think of it, I remember that my brother, who has been in number 10, is going away this weekend, and you can have his room tonight." So it was. In the middle of the night the innkeeper crept into the room and stole the gold. Our friend felt bad about it, but he said to himself: "It was through no fault of mine," and decided to go back underground.

He found the Dark Man, told him what happened and what he wanted. The Dark Man said, "Sit down, I'll wash you now and comb your hair, and cut your nails and beard, and wipe your eyes." When that was done, the Dark Man gave him a second bag of shavings and said, "Tell the innkeeper you want your gold back. If he doesn't do it, he'll have to come here and take your place. I will come for him." So Hans told the innkeeper that and reminded him that if he went down, he would end up looking just like Hans did. That was enough; the innkeeper gave him the money back and more. So Hans was rich now.

He started off to see his father, brought a white coat of coarse cloth, and made a living traveling around the country and performing music on an instrument he had learned to play while underground. Eventually, the King of that country heard his music and offered Hans his oldest daughter. When she saw the quality of his coat, she said, "I'd prefer to jump in the river." So, he married the youngest daughter and got half the kingdom. When the King died, Hans inherited the entire kingdom. That was luck. As for storytellers, we still wander around with holes in our shoes.

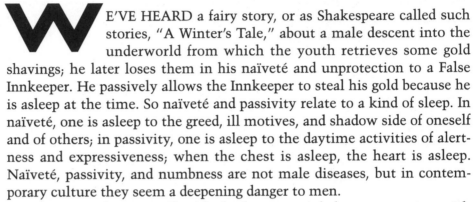

MALE NAÏVETÉ AND THE LOSS OF THE **K**INGDOM

BY ROBERT BLY

Robert Bly's commentary on the Grimm Brothers' story of "Iron John" or "Iron Hans" was no one-shot wonder. Those who have longed for "further adventures" and insights from the movement's foremost figure will appreciate this exploration of the 100th story in the Grimm collection. As Bly notes, this story is recorded as "The Devil's Sooty Brother," but in his retelling, Bly avoids Christian terms like "devil" and "hell." Comparing Bly's version with the Grimm original sheds light on the story and the mind-sets of the Grimm Brothers and of Bly himself. (This essay, which first appeared in *Inroads*, vol. 2, no. 1, is an adaptation of a talk prepared for the Friends' Conference on Religion and Psychology in Philadelphia in 1988.)

**WINGSPAN
INSIDE THE MEN'S
MOVEMENT**

WE'VE HEARD a fairy story, or as Shakespeare called such stories, "A Winter's Tale," about a male descent into the underworld from which the youth retrieves some gold shavings; he later loses them in his naïveté and unprotection to a False Innkeeper. He passively allows the Innkeeper to steal his gold because he is asleep at the time. So naïveté and passivity relate to a kind of sleep. In naïveté, one is asleep to the greed, ill motives, and shadow side of oneself and of others; in passivity, one is asleep to the daytime activities of alertness and expressiveness; when the chest is asleep, the heart is asleep. Naïveté, passivity, and numbness are not male diseases, but in contemporary culture they seem a deepening danger to men.

This story begins well with the lostness and the conversation with the strange-footed man. The job underground embodies the old mythological theme of the underworld, and suggests some form of initiation for young men, guided by an old earth type. In Grimm, the story is named "The Devil's Sooty Brother," but one needn't pay too much attention to the word "devil." I would guess it was added in Christian times to a tale already thousands of years old. The being is probably some old earth god of northern Europe—we remember Pan's goat feet. A sculpture of the wild man built into a Spanish cathedral of the Middle Ages shows him with one animal foot. So we could call this underworld being a "dark man," a relative of the Wild Man. It is interesting that the young man who descends with him is required to retain some characteristics of the Wild Man—long hair, uncut nails, and unconcealed grief. He agrees "not to wipe the tears from his eyes."

He agrees to go underground. That is the most important detail in the story. Sometimes a man will embark on "men's work" but refuse to go underground. Men of this sort become consumers of myths, connoisseurs of fairy tales, judges of the conference leaders, playboys of growth.

To go underground is to go into Hades. The dark men one meets there may not be, as James Hillman says in *The Dream and the Underworld*, symbols of virility but messengers of death.

Perhaps they are the horses of that heathen Attila or the black messengers sent to us by death.

—VALLEJO

To go into the underworld is to go into eclipse. A shadow moves across the moon woman, whose circle lights the waters, and the shadow thrown by the very earth we live on overwhelms the circle. The animals and birds normally making sound in moonlight fall silent. Baboons howl in nervousness. This underworld state can go on for years. This is a Winter's Tale.

The Descender's job is to keep three kettles boiling. For that he has to chop wood, but strangely, the shavings turn out to be important. The Dark Man's instructions are precise: Sweep the shavings behind the door. If we try that, we find that when we open the door to let our friends or enemies in, the shavings will not be visible, for the opened door will hide them; but when the visitors leave and we close the door once more, all these shavings will be visible to our own eyes once more. So the story recommends a beautiful little dance of hiding and revealing. The Iron John story urges the young man to hide his gold; here he is to hide the shavings as well.

What are these shavings? We know that certain insights come only when we are depressed. If we go down in order to bring up a poem, let's say, certain lines will get written and then thrown away, and therapy when done well produces many prethoughts and afterthoughts. Certain ideas about our life which we come upon, say in therapy, don't seem to amount to much at the time—but when we come back up into "our world" these insignificant ideas turn to gold. That's good to know.

And this chopping one does when "underground"—what's the point of it? To keep the pots boiling, our story says. The shavings are an extra gift. To his surprise, the fire tender finds people sitting in the pots! It turns out that our old sergeants, lieutenants, and generals have come to sit down in those pots. We should remind ourselves that there are no people in a fairy story, so no person is being boiled. These are nonmolecular creatures inside our soul. The first pot holds an image of the sergeant. We could say that it is an image of authority. Some of us might need to glimpse a high school principal there, or a harsh grandmother, or the critic who offered humiliation when we showed our first poems. Usually we sit hunched up beneath these critics, inert, resigned, stuck; so it is a great advance just to get them off our backs, into a pot, sitting in hot water.

Our story says that being passive toward these beings is not the thing—one has to be active toward them, boil them. That requires a "dark man," apparently, an underground place, some pots, chopping, heat, ashes, soot. We notice also that the completion of it requires active disobedience of the first orders the boss gave us.

Apparently images of the sergeant and other officers change when

A man who has not passed through the inferno of his passions has never overcome them.

—Carl Jung,
Memories, Dreams,
Reflections

BLY
MALE NAÏVETÉ
AND THE LOSS
OF THE KINGDOM

boiled, as milk changes to cheese. Some trancelike power that the authority figures had gets boiled away. "Once I was in your power; now you are in my power." What is that like in daily life? I would say to get a hold on the main lines of your father's life would be a boiling. To see which people shamed you in your childhood and how they did it, and who in this place continues to shame you would be a boiling. Power works on us namelessly when we are children, and as adults our job is to name it. That in itself helps get rid of naïveté, and encourages shrewdness to develop. When the young man looks in the pots and piles wood on the fire, he is doing well. When he is about to go back up, the old earth god warns him about the importance of language. When

Robert Bly in "A Gathering of Men" with Bill Moyers

someone asks who he is, he is to say: "I am the Dark Man's sooty brother and my King as well." He is not to say: "I have spent three years at the Jung Institute in Zurich under Marie-Louise von Franz and I am a licensed Jungian therapist," nor "I am a Quaker since birth and now an overseer in my Friends Meeting," nor "I am a young intuitive working on my individuation." Those would be naive answers that would call up inflation in the speaker and an urge to kill in the listeners. He is to say: "I am the Dark Man's sooty brother and my King as well." He isn't the Dark Man's shiny brother, but the Dark Man's sooty brother, and he is "my King as well." That phrase makes no more sense in German than in English, but it suggests that the process of boiling has freed him from some reliance on outer authority or outer kingship, so that he is to some extent his own King. That's very good.

But, alas, when the young man shows his bag of gold ingenuously to the Innkeeper, it's clear that he is still a fool, even after the seven years of boiling. This complicated experience hasn't cured his naïveté. The naive quality in young men hangs on. So I think we could profitably spend a little time talking about naiveté.

"Naïveté," according to the dictionary, is "natural simplicity or artlessness; ingenuousness." But looked at from behind it is a state of feeling which avoids the dark side of one's own motives or the motives of others. Naïveté discounts anger, fear, or greed, and assumes more goodness in the world than there is. The naive person often refuses confrontation or combat, and, if thrown into combat by circumstance, often fails to notice that he has in fact been defeated. Wearing a white suit he rides about the field where the defeat took place, waving to the onlookers as if he were the victor.

Naïveté seems to be characteristic of American men in the last 40 years; we could say that Hemingway represents a successful fight against

it—he tried to see defeat as defeat. But in Kerouac and the "sixties writers" in general the fight is lost. At all times in history, men moreover appear to be naive in relationship even when they are relatively shrewd in their worldly dealings.

We've mentioned that the naive man doesn't see his own defeat even when it takes place in front of thousands. He also doesn't notice when an invader crosses his border. He doesn't know "manners." When in earlier times in Japan a guest arrived at the door, the host must have said something like this: "For a humble and utterly worthless person such as myself it is an unspeakable honor for my family and all my ancestors to greet the celestial person that you are." He doesn't believe a word of it, but the sentence reminds the other soul and his own of boundaries around both parties. Such sentences prevent inappropriate mergings, and make invasion of the psyche less likely. Goethe said:

Tell a wise person or else keep silent,
because the mass man will mock it right away.

The naive person doesn't fear the mass man, and many idealize him. The naive man at a party will tell utter strangers his most intimate experiences. It was a mass man who invented the encounter group. "During this weekend," says the encounter leader, "I want you to get everything out. Don't hold back anything. We want to know how you feel about your mother."

The story says that when you are too naive in your offering, an Innkeeper, whom we'll call the False Innkeeper, called forth by the naïveté, steals your gold, and he has to. He has no choice. The naive man often puts much emphasis on "sincerity." He feels for example that if he tells a person sincerely what he has done, that person should forgive him right away. "It's true I betrayed her but I did tell her right away. I don't know why she is so angry. I was really frank with her." He thinks his sincerity should protect him from a long look at his shadow side. He enters a tunnel without noticing the tendency of a tunnel to become narrower and darker. "Let's hope for the best." The hopeful way the American politicians entered the tunnel called the Vietnam War was highly naive; and the Russians were equally naive in entering Afghanistan.

During the last few decades both men and women have begun to love the word "wholeness" even though none of us has ever met anyone who is whole. All this use of the word "wholeness," then, holistic worldviews, wholeness and healing, whole earth catalog, wholeness newsletter, encourages naïveté, and inflames the False Innkeeper to outrageous acts of theft. Naïveté, as our story says, works hand in hand with betrayal. The naive man trusts the charismatic leader such as Ronald Reagan, who immediately steals the gold. The naive man trusts his boss and the boss overworks him. His children turn him into a slave, his wife leads him by the nose and recognizes that all he can do is to forgive, and daydream about wholeness.

Once his gold has been stolen, the young man has lost the payment or reward for all his work. One could say that his therapy has failed; or one could say that he has slipped back into some childhood state of dependency and denial; or if he is an artist, one could say that he has settled, as kitsch artists do, for a comfortable work of art that ignores "the ugly facts." One could say that his initiation process has gone off track; or that his inward emotional body has not become activated.

We'll look at the latter possibility. I have heard person after person at men's conferences testify that they grew up without any model of what an activated masculine emotional body is. Some men describe scenes in childhood in which the mother flew into a rage, directed at the father or at men in general, and their father said nothing, sank into silence and guilt, or disappeared from the room, having defended neither himself nor the boy. Others have known only robotlike fathers, or victim fathers without a job, or playboy fathers without depth. The man without an activated emotional body may alternate between abusive behavior and impotent gentleness that isn't really gentle. Robert Moore remarked that two distinguishing marks of the uninitiated man are wife beating and the contrary softness.

Sometimes sons will try to activate their own emotional bodies through rock music or gang activity, but it does not succeed. A woman who notices that a man's emotional body is not activated will sometimes offer to activate it for him, by helping him to express his feelings, or teaching him to be more sensual. It may be that sex deepens the integration of physical and emotional body in a woman, but the same thing doesn't seem to work for a man. In general, I would say that the emotional body of a man cannot be activated by a woman. That's the job of old men, such as the man in our story. In some cultures the older men give years and years of their lives to just that.

The old men who still today initiate boys in Australian aborigine tribes in New Guinea and in African tribes take the boys away from the mothers between the ages of 8 and 12 and begin a complicated sequence of adventures, teachings, trials, and dances. The old men recite poems, act out myths, say outrageous things, and may themselves dance all night. The boys experience close up what the emotional body of a man is like when it is activated. The boys in some African tribes are taught to dance for 24 hours straight.

"The Dark Man's Sooty Brother" doesn't go into detail on how the emotional body, once the young man has come up, is activated, but it provides a brilliant image for the second part of the work: "I will go back down." So the young man has to go back "down" a second time. The False Innkeeper has stolen his "insights"; the old patterns have returned; all the work has apparently been for nothing. That state of diminishment we all know of. The response, the story says, is not resignation, beer drinking, season tickets to the Bears, more talks on male mythology, but rather: "I'll go back down."

All the details are fascinating in this part of the story. We know that the young man agreed not to cut his hair or his fingernails when he took the job, and he kept that promise; but when the seven years are up, the young man says nothing about any obligations the Dark Man has in that area. The Kettle Keeper goes back up with his hair still uncut, his fingernails long, etc. Inertness in the emotional body shows itself in failing to ask others for what we want and what we deserve. The young man is too agreeable, too helpful; one could say he keeps on giving to those parts of the psyche that are insatiable. A wife, a boss, a son, a daughter, a guru, can stand in for that clawed part of the soul that eats and is never satisfied.

But when the young man goes down the second time, he says to the Dark Man two things: "Give me some more wages" and "Cut my hair, trim my fingernails, wipe the tears from my eyes, cut my toenails." I love this part; it seems to me so brilliant. Jung remarked: "American marriages are the saddest in all the world, because the man does all his fighting at the office." How difficult it is to say to a wife, "Cut my hair." Instead men live through years of a relationship secretly resentful, dimly enraged, passively hostile. And we are not only talking of marriage here, or agreeabilities in the outer world. Doesn't the dark one inside deserve some orders? Or rather, suppose the Dark Man inside is waiting for an order? We know that the dark ones in the psyche do not act until asked to. Some readers will remember Kafka's story about the doorkeeper and the suppliant. The suppliant waits by the door for months, for years, waiting for the moment the door opens or when the doorkeeper falls asleep, or when he will be invited in. Years pass. Finally when old and dying he calls the doorkeeper over, and whispers to him about the injustice of it all. The doorkeeper says, "Oh this was *your* door; you could have gone through at any moment." And the suppliant dies.

Sociologists report that 48 percent of American men are now employed either by one of the top 10 giant corporations or by the United States government. We have to expect that the passivity Kafka talks of will deepen. Writers in eastern Europe, where a characteristic state bureaucracy has been in force for several generations, have described in Kafka-like terms the emotional stagnation, mingling resentment, malice, and shame, that results from bureaucratic control. "As Gregor Samsa awoke one morning from uneasy dreams, he found himself transformed in his bed into a gigantic insect." ("Metamorphosis" by Kafka.) Fundamentalist religions require a dependent mind. Ollie North's story makes clear that furious and independent activity in one area does not rule out a sheeplike and passive attitude toward higher authority in another.

Disciples in Oregon allow the guru to do all the Rolls-Royce owning; devoted traditionalists allow Jimmy Swaggart to have all the biblical interpretations; channelers allow the unearthly spirit invading them to state all his or her opinions without objection or discussion. "I don't have any responsibility; I don't even know what the spirit says, because I'm

not here during the channeling." The channeler's audience is equally passive, and hears outrageous assertions without asking for evidence. Americans during the last administration acted as if Reagan were a channeler; most citizens agreed with his optimistic opinions on the economy and the poor, even when they had to stumble over the homeless on the sidewalk to get home to watch TV.

We begin to understand now the meaning of the last phrase in the sentence: "I am the Dark Man's sooty brother, and my King as well." Evidence of kingship is the ability to say to the Dark Man in a convincing voice: "Cut my hair." The inner King is the one inside who can decide on one's course for the next six months, the next year, the next 20 years, without being overly contaminated by the ideas of other people on that subject. Our story says kingship also involves telling inner people—who are not Kings, Warriors, or Lovers—what you want.

What else can one say about this marvelous story? It turns out that while he was in the underworld, probably his long first period, he learned how to "play music." That is a cunning reference to the emotional body: We remember that Kabir mentioned several times that he often heard music coming from his own chest, even though "no fingers were touching those strings." When we learn how to play a "musical instrument," when the body itself makes music, then a woman hears it, or birds hear it, or other men hear it, or a "king's daughter" hears it. And then this underworld worker, the man earlier "discharged from the army," who later did not "wipe the tears from his eyes," gains "half the kingdom." We should be so lucky.

BOOKS ON UNDERSTANDING FAIRY TALES

Bruno Bettelheim, *The Uses of Enchantment: The Meaning and Importance of Fairy Tales*. New York: Vintage Press, 1976. In this study that won a National Book Award, a famous child psychologist uncovers the psychological meaning of "Jack and the Beanstalk," "Little Red Ridinghood," "Cinderella," the tales of the Arabian Nights and a host of other familiar and not-so-familiar stories. He also explains how the cathartic impact of these tales is heightened when these stories are told to children as opposed to merely read to them.

Marie-Louise von Franz, *The Feminine in Fairy Tales*. Zurich: Spring Publications, 1972. Von Franz's discussion of "The Handless Maiden" and other fairy tales illuminates the feminine principles in men as well as in women.

Marie-Louise von Franz, *Individuation in Fairy Tales*. Boston: Shambhala, 1977; Rev. 1990. Jung's collaborator focuses on the bird motif as a symbol of psychological and spiritual transformation in tales from Spain, Persia, Turkistan, Iran, the Balkans, and Austria. She also discusses how fairy tales can offer guidance in therapy.

Maria Tatar, *The Hard Facts of the Grimms' Fairy Tales*. Princeton, NJ: Princeton, 1987. In a lively style that belies her subject matter, Tatar investigates why so many fairy tales revolve around terrible things like murder, mutilation, incest, cannibalism, and infanticide.

STILL QUESTING FOR THE HOLY GRAIL

BY ROBERT CORNETT

Reading about the interpretations of myth or even hearing a lecture on the subject is still basically a passive activity that allows us to keep our distance, insulated from the powerful transformative spell of the story. To fully experience a myth and to become convinced that it can really impact our lives, we must get actively involved with it—by relating our personal histories and current behavior to various details of the myth. Here, Professor Robert Cornett, in an essay condensed from a two-part series in *Wingspan*, recounts the specific activities he and his workshop participants used to relive the adventures of the good knight Parsifal in his search for the Holy Grail.

   Robert Cornett is a human resource specialist, consultant, educator, actor, and counselor living in Cape Elizabeth, Maine. He holds a master's degree in counseling and the history of religion from Harvard and is the former director of the Interface Graduate Training Program in Holistic Education in Boston, Massachusetts. He has been leading men's groups and workshops since 1976. His current work explores the mythic and archetypal dimensions of male development through drama, art, ritual, and personal growth activities.

I WAS RECENTLY blessed to facilitate a series of weekend gatherings in New Hampshire on the theme of "The Journey Into Manhood." This was a call to interested men to come on a quest—a sacred journey—to the mythic roots of their male souls. Calling upon the legends, symbols, and images of the legendary quest for the Holy Grail, I sought a group of "noble Grail knights" who would be willing to create together a Round Table of shared experiences and to take risks together as we looked into the symbolic significance of this ancient myth and its relation to our lives.

   The medieval story of the quest for the Holy Grail and the related Arthurian tales embody many powerful symbols and archetypes of the human soul's quest for wholeness and integration. They can offer us awareness of the deeper patterns of experience that our souls long to know. Myth can take us to that interior altar—the sacred sanctuary of Psyche (soul)—where dwells the reservoir of love and spiritual power that sustains us on our journey. Indeed, if the sages are correct, that reservoir may be the primary aim and end of our journey on this earth.

   In designing a structure within which to invoke the images of the Grail Quest I came upon the format of a trilogy: a series of three weekend gatherings for men, spread out over a nine-month period. During the first gathering we sought to summon forth the Grail by initiating a quest to understand the inner woman and the related principle of love— what depth psychology calls the Eros principle. A key step for men in the process of recovering our souls is to enter into the dark, mysterious realm of feminine energy within us. This is the territory that Carl Jung called "the anima." The Grail Cup itself is a major symbol of the feminine aspect of soul. (Contrasted to it in Arthurian legend is the sword Excalibur, which can represent the masculine qualities of firmness, strength, and discrimination).

   Finding and contacting the inner woman can allow a man to touch and experience a deep capacity for love and for union with the divine. This area of the psyche contains a powerful creative force that poets and

artists describe as the muse. She has the capacity to inspire the greatest artistic work. The road to the anima, however, is fraught with difficulty and delusion. A man must learn to sort out his true inner woman from the projections of her he has of psychic necessity placed upon real-life women in his external world: his mother, his wife or lover, his daughter, and his sister in particular. Because the inner woman is so hidden, so deeply imbedded in his unconscious, a man can hardly know her except through the ways in which these women remind him of her or mirror her qualities. Often a man goes a lifetime without ever recovering or reclaiming these qualities as part of his own soul. Instead he allows the women in his life to do the feeling, the nurturing, the intuiting, the artistic expression that he so longs to do himself.

During this first weekend gathering we entered the realm of the anima by exploring four archetypes of the feminine found in the Grail story. These four figures were Parsifal's mother, the maid Guinnevere, Blanche Fleur, and the mysterious Lady of the Lake. These four represent four key aspects of the inner woman that men must come to terms with on the path of individuation and self-integration.

There were two other weekends dedicated to exploring our own maleness and the principle of masculine power through the Grail characters of Parsifal, King Arthur, Lancelot, and Mordred, Arthur's bastard son. For men to grow, they need to contact and access not only the anima or feminine aspects of soul, but also the masculine aspects of firmness, power, strength, and will.

The figure of Parsifal in the Grail story holds a powerful key to the unfolding of our male soul. Parsifal represents the fool and the inner child. In Jungian terms he is *puer aeternus*, "the eternal youth." Parsifal's innocence, his lack of pretense, his curiosity and vulnerability gain him entry to the Round Table of Grail knights and ultimately help him of all the knights to find the Holy Grail. Parsifal, too, is associated with the fool of the Tarot deck: the young lad with head in the clouds standing on the edge of a precipice without a care in the world. He is also the clown, the joyful trickster and risk taker; the one who takes on both the happy face and the sad face and so shows us the vulnerability of being a man. The clown face, found in so many cultures of the world, is the true soul face of the man, showing us both the profound joy and the deep sorrow of being human.

Parsifal, the fool, the clown, is a powerful symbol of vulnerability. The word "vulnerability" comes from the Latin *vulnus* or wound, and it means our ability to be wounded. This willingness to acknowledge and to express our pain and suffering is key to accessing our power as men and is why Parsifal, the fool, is the central hero of the Grail quest.

To uncover the Parsifal energy in our own lives we went back to a time in early youth or adolescence when we felt like a fool, a moment or event that was painfully embarrassing to us. We sat in small circles and told these stories and talked about our learnings from these events. How did these events change our lives? How did they release the fool in us or force him underground and keep him hidden? We talked about that embarrassing first sexual encounter, the time we were beaten up by the school bully, or the time our father made us look foolish on the baseball field with some critical or sarcastic remark.

We also painted on clown faces and ritually acted out these scenes in short skits. In so doing, we gave both name and face to our inner fool, to the Parsifal energy within us. We celebrated together our power to be wounded and hurt and to learn and grow from those wounds. We discovered that our brothers can be compassionate witnesses to our wounds and supportive and loving guides to the growth and healing that comes from recognizing and acknowledging our pain.

Another important aspect of male power is found in the figure of Lancelot, the noble warrior and Grail knight of the Round Table. As Parsifal grows in manhood, he must take on many battles and learn from the heroic and courageous knights of the Round Table. On the inner level of soul making, Lancelot, the grail knight, is symbolic of the spiritual warrior: the man who takes on the obstacles and antagonistic forces to his growth, who battles with inner dragons of doubt, fear, and loneliness, who fights for his right to be a whole, creative, and loving being on this difficult earth.

In the Grail workshop we served as warrior guides to one another as we talked about the internal struggles and dragons that are holding back our growth as men. As a way to celebrate and acknowledge the power that is within us to overcome these obstacles to growth we created short power statements which represented the battle cry of our souls' inner intention to break through the obstacle or constraint.

Seated in a circle as knights around the Round Table we each stepped to the center, taking hold of a sword—the magic sword Excalibur. We raised the sword in the air and shouted out our battle cries to acknowledge our intention and our power to overcome the forces within us that keep us from growing and living to our full potential.

The third aspect of masculine power that we explored is found in the image of King Arthur, the legendary king of the Round Table. Arthur represents many things in the Grail story, one of which is the power of creative authorship and of fathering. As the spiritual father and leader of the knights of the Round Table, Arthur represents the ability to come into one's full authority and power as a man and to be the author and creator of one's own fate and destiny.

We accessed Arthur in the workshop by sharing photographs of our fathers and telling our fathers' story. We tried to discover and to name

CORNETT
STILL QUESTING
FOR
THE HOLY GRAIL

the central wound in our fathers' lives and to see how in our lives we may be attempting to claim our power by addressing and healing our fathers' wounds. Robert Bly alludes to this phenomenon in his poem "My Father's Wedding":

Then what? If a man, cautious, hides his limp, somebody has to limp it. Things do it; the surroundings limp. House walls get scars, the car breaks down; matter, in drudgery, takes it up.

We also spent time looking at those qualities both positive and negative that we are carrying forward from our fathers. How are these qualities helping us to grow and assume our creative power in the world and

Grail Quest workshop participants literally making fools of themselves

how are they hindering that growth? By understanding and knowing who our fathers are and the wounds they carry, we can begin to free ourselves from blindly "limping" that pain for them. We also begin to free ourselves from resenting our fathers for what they could not give us as men by knowing and accepting them for who they are as human beings. In so doing we call upon our capacity to nurture and to father our own inner child and at the same time to symbolically "father" those creative acts and deeds that our souls are capable of.

We ritually honored this Father energy by visualizing our fathers standing behind us and our grandfather and great-grandfather behind him all the way back to the Great Father Creator and at the same time imagined in front of us our sons and grandsons and great-grandsons carrying forth the quest for male wholeness and integration on into the future.

Finally we came to the character of Mordred, who was Arthur's bastard son in the legend. Arthur's denial of Mordred and refusal to acknowledge him ultimately leads to the downfall of Camelot and the fatal battle in which Arthur and Mordred fight to the death. Mordred may be considered as a representation of the male shadow—the dark, unconscious, repressed aspect of the self that holds all that is undesirable within a man. The shadow represents all that is violent, ugly, primitive, and destructive in the male soul. And like Arthur, a man who refuses to acknowledge this dark part of himself may end up having the shadow erupt from the unconscious and wreak havoc in his life and relationships. Like the Greek god Hades, the shadow is the one who visits us from beneath the earth. By recognizing and understanding the dark part of our nature we can begin to reclaim this part of ourselves and so reduce the possibility for harming ourselves and others through dark thoughts, words, and deeds.

One way that we worked with the shadow was by thinking of men we really dislike and despise and listing their qualities, such as "arrogant," "competitive," domineering," "cold and unemotional." Then we ask ourselves how those dark qualities are reflected in ourselves. Because the power of projection is so strong in the human psyche, it is often easier to access and see our own shadow side by describing what we see in others. This awareness alone is enough to make a man stop and examine how he is living his life and how his darkness may be unconsciously hurting and affecting others.

Another powerful way to work with the male shadow is to ritually acknowledge and confess its presence and power. We did this by reflecting on a time in our past when we did a dark or evil act or contemplated such a deed. Then each man writes down on a piece of paper what the deed or thought was and puts the paper into a clay pot. After mixing up the slips of paper to retain anonymity each man pulls out one of the slips of paper and then in seriousness and respect reads out loud one of the slips of paper. After hearing 15 statements the effect on the group was powerful and devastating. Here was the range of male shadow and its capacity to wound and injure! The tears flowed from many men. Many felt relieved to release these dark parts of themselves and to realize other men too had darkness and guilt that they were carrying inside. Afterward we ritually burned the slips of paper in the clay pot to ask forgiveness and to purify our lives through a symbol of the flames of that inner hell that we all hold inside.

In the final weekend of the trilogy we explored the integration of the love and power principles and the male and female energies within us. We reviewed all of the learnings from the work on the inner woman and the inner man and created an altar with images of the eight archetypal characters that were worked with. On one side of the altar were the feminine images of Parsifal's mother, Guinnevere, Blanche Fleur, and the Lady of the Lake. On the opposite side were the masculine images of Parsifal, Lancelot, Arthur, and Mordred. We meditated and talked about

the role of love and power in our lives and thought about ways to balance and integrate them in ourselves. As Carl Jung said, "Love without Power has no effect; Power without Love is blind ambition." In the middle of the altar were the Grail Cup and the Sword Excalibur, indicating the marriage of male and female, the conjunction of opposites or the *hieros gamos* (sacred marriage).

During this workshop there was one more character from the grail legend that we needed to meet and that was the magician Merlin. Merlin represents the power of the magician to synthesize the opposites, to bring about the internal alchemy that produces true wisdom in our lives. Also as an archetype of the wise old man, Merlin represents that profoundly creative aspect of the male soul that can both touch the sacred mysteries of the earth and fly like a hawk to the heavens and so integrate spirit and matter, body and soul, heaven and earth.

After visualizations and dialogues with the inner wise old man and magician, a ritual celebration and invocation of the spirit of Merlin was performed. Each of the men created a short dance that expressed the integration of the male and female energy within him. A joyous celebration of drumming, music, and dancing around the Grail Cup and the Sword and amid the symbols of the Grail quest followed. In that magical moment truly the spirit of Merlin had joined us in the room.

BOOKS ON THE GRAIL QUEST

Ashe, Geoffrey. *Camelot and the Vision of Albion.* Canada: Granada Publishing, 1971. (Historical, archaeological, legendary overview of Camelot.)

Cooke, Grace, and Ivan Cooke. *The Light in Britain.* England: White Eagle Publishing Trust, 1971. (Esoteric role of Britain.)

Johnson, Robert. *He: Understanding Masculine Psychology.* New York: Harper and Row, 1974. (Psychological explication of the Grail story.)

Jung, Emma, and Marie-Louise von Franz. *The Grail Legend.* London: Hodder and Stoughton, 1960. (The classical Jungian work.)

Matthews, John. *The Grail Quest for the Eternal.* New York: Crossroad Publishing Co., 1981. (Excellent and easy-to-read overview.)

Stewart, Mary. A series of four books on the Arthurian legend, including:
The Crystal Cave. New York: Fawcett Crest, 1970.
The Hollow Hills. New York: Fawcett Crest, 1973.
The Last Enchantment. New York: William Morrow and Co., Inc., 1979.
The Wicked Day. New York: William Morrow and Co., Inc., 1983.

Stewart, R. J. *The Prophetic Vision of Merlin.* London: Routledge and Kegan Paul, 1986.

White, T.H. *The Sword in the Stone.* New York: Dell Publishing Co., 1939. (Arthurian Legend.)

Wyatt, Isabel. *From Round Table to Grail Castle.* Sussex, England: Lanthorn Press, 1979.

RENEWING OF THE FLESH
MICHAEL MEADE ON STORYTELLING

BY JOHN LANG AND ANTHONY SIGNORELLI

Editors of *Inroads*

One element that gives structure to any conference co-led by mythologist-storyteller Michael Meade is the multipart, cliffhanger way he retells old stories accompanying himself on his conga. Presenting a single story in segments, pausing at turning points to consider dilemmas with the hero, savoring the tale as it unfolds, Meade has won himself many admirers and imitators. Here is an excerpt from a longer interview called "I'll Answer It in Three Days," published in *Inroads*.

I: How long have you been telling stories?

MM: About 10 or 11 years.

I: You always memorize them when you tell them, right?

MM: Not actually. What I call it is memorizing-forgetting. The first step is to memorize it. The second step is to forget it. I don't want to tell a story from memory. When I'm telling a story there are two things I want to have happen. First, I want to get the bones of the story right. I want to get the structure, the skeleton of the story, right. That's my responsibility to the story. But then there is also the business of what is going on right then. The immediacy of the situation, and what is going on in me, in the room, and in the people listening. To tell a story by rote can miss that. Some words are key for me in the story, then the rest of them are the words that happen to be there when my mouth is open. And that puts the element of risk in it, too. And that wakes up the psyche—at least my psyche. It gets the psyche very intrigued because there is an opening. Anything could come out. All of a sudden, there is that tension that comes when you have a situation with danger in it. There is often a surprise for me, too, so that means I'm paying more attention. I always hope to learn something from the telling of the story.

I: From the telling of it?

MM: Yeah. Because there are always two things. There is the thing that strikes me in the story that I hadn't thought of before, and then the thing that I forgot. I usually forget something and I then try afterwards to remember what I forgot. And that tells me something that I am not paying attention to. And then whatever comes out that was surprising to me tells me something else. One reason I like old stories is because there must be something strong there for a story to survive. A story that survives for a couple of thousand years has some good bones in it.

But then for a story to continue, the story has to have a renewing of the flesh. There has to be fresh blood, so to speak. The skeletal structure has to be kept accurate but the flesh can be changed. Part of my job is to bring some blood into it. To change the flesh. That's what keeps the story going.

I: In the story, "The Two Fathers," where the father strikes the son with an ax, everyone feels it in a different part of his body—that's that flesh.

MM: Exactly, and everybody listening to a story is putting his own flesh on it. If you overtell the story then you ruin the imagination of the people listening. People don't like it.

I: Right, it's like watching TV.

MM: Yes, and it is another reason why I don't like to work strictly from memory. Because not all the words will be alive the next time the story is being told. The story is deadened. The American Indians considered stories to be animals. Like an animal, it needs to be fed. They are only partly tame, only partly domesticated. So you have to be careful what you feed them. I mean, stories have teeth.

I: How does the drum work with doing the story?

MM: I don't know. When I started telling the stories I was having a hard time just telling the story. I would walk around and gesture a lot. One time I was trying to figure out a phrasing for a part of a story, working on the sentences of a scene, and my drum happened to be there. I just decided I would drum while I thought about it and the images just started to come out.

I: What is going on in the psyche with the drums?

MM: I'm not sure. I don't know anything about the drum once I start. I was telling a story recently and someone said, "You are drumming too fast." I had already started the story and I said, "You know, you're right. And I wish there was something I could do about it." My hands were going. Once it starts, I'm not paying attention to it. What I sometimes say at the beginning of the story is that we are going to get on the drum, as if the ground has changed from the seats we are sitting on to the rhythm of the drum. The idea of stories is that they are intended to unify, to bring us into the same imaginal space for the purpose of working, in the positive sense of work. Exploring, hunting, all that stuff that happens in the story. Story is like a terrain, so the drum, by putting a rhythm in there, puts everybody in the same rhythm.

I: I was thinking how the beat seems to mesmerize. Not quite a charm but . . .

MM: The way I imagine it is that there is a certain amount of anxiety and nervousness always present whenever a bunch of people get together because everybody's psyche realizes that there is a lot of power in the room. You get whatever number of people together and they come together to hear about stories and myths and psychology, and you know these are serious people here. So if that is the case the psyche goes, "Wow. We've got a lot of power in the room." So the drum captures that anxiety and gives you the rhythm. Then the people start to settle in. Drums were often used in war, to prepare for war, and so it is as if the drum sets up a little protection. But mostly I see it as a unifying thing.

I: When you do go through the process of memorizing a story, what's going on? What awakens?

MM: My sense is that you can't go through the story, whether you are telling it or listening, without imagining most of the details. When you stop imagining, when the images stop coming, you won't hear the rest of the story. You won't hear the part where there aren't any images. Or if a startling image occurs, that may stop the rest of the images and you won't hear something. So everybody who is listening and whoever is telling the story is generating or allowing the images to erupt, to flow. Everybody participates in the world of images or imagination. The world of imagination is a very, very wonderful world with immediate rewards. You first experience it as a child. It is the child's world in the best sense. The images that come from a good scene in a story, a scene with a lot of dynamic stuff in it, are their own reward. It's like an inner art show that can be gone back to. "Wow, what was that when the wolves jumped up and tore that leg off of the horse when it went over the boundary? Wow, what is that? I can't understand it, but I've got this image of it!" It's a piece of imaginal territory that can be explored anytime anybody wants. Imagination is outside of time. Not that it doesn't have rhythm, but it is not dependent upon time. So it can be gone back to. You can mine images. You can go in there with a pick and a shovel and dig around, see what is in those images. And it turns out that there are, attached or associated with images, the emotions. They give us an emotional ground, or from the other point of view you could say, images of stories ground our emotion. Does that make sense?

To attain to the full its consoling propensities, its symbolic meanings, and, most of all, its interpersonal meanings, a fairy tale should be told rather than read. Telling is preferable to reading because it permits greater flexibility.

—Bruno Bettelheim

MEADE,
LANG AND
SIGNORELLI
RENEWING
OF THE FLESH

I: **When you are doing all these stories, isn't there a sense in which you are just beating around the bush? Can't you teach people by telling them about things? Why stories?**

MM: Well, we like to think we can be very direct in giving and receiving information, but I don't think that's the case. This image of beating around the bush is okay, depending on which bush. Now take the bush that Moses caused to burst into flames; I'm interested in beating around that bush. What is that story about, anyway? The imagination is intrigued with story—story is the movement of images, the flow of the imagination, the movement of the psyche and the movement of the emotions—and stories are the container in which we talk about soul. In some way, the soul starts to awaken if a story—a real story—is being told. It is heard with the soul.

I: **I was thinking about the story of "The Three Golden Hairs" this morning, and in that story the hero has to travel into the Underworld and get the answers in order to marry his bride. He also has to get three golden hairs from the head of the king of the Dark Region. The grandmother is there and she turns him into an ant, so the king won't devour him, and then she asks the questions for him. When the grandmother pulls a hair out she diverts the king's anger by saying she has a dream. Instantly, he says, "What is the dream?" It's that awakening of interest when we hear a bit of a story.**

MM: And what do we do when we get together? We tell stories—stories of ourselves and stories of other people. That's the business of people. The old stories are like carefully made containers; they are the careful putting together of images in such a way that there is no direct description, analysis, or understanding. Everybody who hears a good story—any story that has legitimate skeletal structure and has been handled by enough people for a long enough period of time—has his own interpretation of it. Take the story where the father strikes the son with an ax. You say, "How old was the son?" Someone says 7, 8, 14, 13, 17, 3, 2, 1. "Where was the blow?" In the head, in the shoulder, in the chest. Everybody had provided his own son. The story brings out all the inner characters of the psyche with their speeches and their little scripts that they have been working on in there, or the emotions that are attached. Their history, the actual history of the psyche, comes out. That's why the story works. It brings out all that stuff instantly and it does it almost against one's will. The story is moving too fast. It requires too much creativity to follow a story to control it. So what comes out is not what we expected. And that is the gift of the story.

I: So the story, then, really is a way to get into metaphor, to enter myth and to live in it.

MM: Absolutely.

I: In your work with men over the years, I think it is fair to say that you have earned the respect of many different men. How do you earn that respect? Where does it come from, and how does it grow and develop?

MM: Well, when you asked the question, I realized that if there is that respect, the respect is mutual. I can think of two places where it comes from for me. One of them is courage, and the other is depth. I am constantly awakened to the depth of other people by doing this work. It is not even smart to always be alert to that depth when walking up and down the street. It has to be done in a safe place. But when there is a sense of a safe place, a sense of trust, people are incredibly deep. So, at these men's conferences the depth gets seen and shared, and then the stories come out. This is where the courage comes in, because the stories are all grief and pain and suffering, and the fact that they can be told means that these things are conscious. So there is a conscious suffering, and when it comes out, when those stories are told, there is nothing to do but respect it. As a matter of fact that is what the word "respect" means—to "spect" means to see—respect means to see it again. So in sharing, in telling our own story—which is what we generally do—we also see it again. In seeing our own stories again in the story being told by the other person, we all of a sudden realize that we are in the story. The story leads to the

MEADE,
LANG AND
SIGNORELLI
RENEWING
OF THE FLESH

147

emotions and then there is the experience of being in an emotion. One of the key ones among men is grief, and it seems to me that a lot of the work that we have done is about being in that grief together. Part of our job is to bring our own grief to the place. Contrary to my upbringing, I've been learning to see grief not as a negative thing. I think being cheerful is okay—I enjoy it when I am cheerful—but I am now learning that grief is also okay. It is a strange thing to say, but I enjoy—enjoy is not quite the right word—I have become more comfortable in grief than I was before. And that is something that men seem to have the courage to do more readily with other men.

I: There is sort of a joy that follows behind it, in the wake of the grief, although you wouldn't say that while you are in it.

MM: Right, you go down in the feeling of grief and then if it is done very thoroughly and strongly, you come up. The feeling of joy, of course, is coming back up—free. Usually the ride back up is free. And that's why they call it joy. No charge. You paid on the way down.

I: You only pay once on the toll bridge.

MM: Round-trip. So once you have done that together, seen each other's grieving, you have to respect the grief in other people. There is something each of us has done to be alive at this point, and that is seen as something to respect. That's the business that happens when a trusting space is created or worked on.

IV
LIVING THE MALE ARCHETYPES

PATTERNS FROM THE COLLECTIVE UNCONSCIOUS

MUCH OF the men's movement—particularly that biggest part known as the mythopoetic branch, the one identified with poet Robert Bly—takes its inspiration from the work of Swiss psychologist Carl Jung and his successors. Jungian psychology (also known as "depth psychology" and "archetypal psychology") differs in some important respects from Sigmund Freud's theories. The major interpreters and developers of Jung's work for men's movement audiences in North America have been James Hillman, Robert Johnson, Eugene Monick, and Robert Moore. As readers have become familiar with the concepts and vocabulary of Jungians, more and more general-interest books on various aspects of male psychology from a Jungian perspective have been appearing.

One of the most basic concepts is that of archetypes. In their work, *King, Warrior, Magician, Lover: Rediscovering the Archetypes of the Mature Masculine*, Robert Moore and coauthor Douglas Gillette use a metaphor from computer "hard-wiring" to explain the innate blueprints, the "primordial images," the potentials for mature masculinity that all males are born with. They then relate the notion of archetypes to that of the "collective unconscious," Jung's term for the pool or source of these templates or patterns.

Jung and his successors have found that on the level of the deep unconscious the psyche of every person is grounded in the collective unconscious, made up of instinctual patterns and energy configurations probably inherited genetically through generations of our species. These archetypes provide the very foundations of our behaviors—our thinking, our feeling, and our characteristic human reactions. . . . Jung related them directly to the instincts in other animals.

Moore and Gillette go on to say, "There are archetypes that pattern the thoughts and feelings of women, and there are archetypes that pattern the thoughts and feelings and relationships of men. In addition, Jungians have found that in every man there is a feminine subpersonality called the Anima, made up of the feminine archetypes. And in every woman there is a masculine subpersonality called the Animus. All human beings can access the archetype, to a greater or lesser degree."

This basic premise of Jung's runs counter, on the surface at least, to politically correct contemporary thought. "Proper" thinkers minimize or deny the existence of inherent differences in the capabilities of men and women. While Jungians believe that certain qualities are inherent in males and others inherent in females, they don't make comparisons or value judgments as to which set of traits is better. Feminists, however, claim that bitter experience has taught them that in men's eyes any difference will inevitably lead to a judgment of relative superiority and that egocentric male chauvinism will always perceive masculine qualities as superior to feminine ones.

Psychological theories and political correctness might all seem inconsequentially academic if it weren't for the fact that Jungians also maintain that a man must become aware of the mature masculine archetypes if he is to complete his life mission of integrating his personality, or "individuating." To shore up areas

of weakness, temper excessive tendencies, or correct imbalances in his personality, a man must be in imaginative contact with whichever archetypes he needs to work on. Clearly, he must be aware of what the various male archetypes are if he is to judge how he is doing in any given area. If a man realizes he lacks qualities of the warrior, for example, he might read biographies of military heroes, take up a martial art, and play strategy board games.

Trying to apply archetypal theory to one's life may be difficult at first, but soon one begins to sense various kinds of archetypal energies in other people, in art works, even in one's own moods. Most men find that it is easier to access and explore their communal male heritage in the company of men than it is to work alone or in mixed company. While our society is moving toward thoroughly integrating both women and men in all areas of life, this inner work requires that we sort out these issues in single-sex groups before we come together in the common forum. The men's movement looks to other cultures, particularly primitive ones—which often had very clearly demarcated sex roles—for clues as to how men in other times and places resolved their male identity questions. ✍

IN QUEST OF ARCHETYPAL MASCULINITY

BY AARON R. KIPNIS, Ph.D.

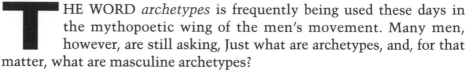

Aaron Kipnis's book *Knights without Armor: A Practical Guide for Men in Quest of Masculine Soul* (Jeremy P. Tarcher, 1991), from which this essay was adapted, discusses many aspects of archetypal masculinity and suggests a variety of means for both understanding and communing with the images of authentic, deep masculinity. ✒

THE WORD *archetypes* is frequently being used these days in the mythopoetic wing of the men's movement. Many men, however, are still asking, Just what are archetypes, and, for that matter, what are masculine archetypes?

According to the beliefs of analytical psychology, which began with the thinking of Carl Jung, archetypes are universal patterns within the collective psyche of all people. They are classic prototypes within our psyches that symbolize common life experiences which all humans share. These images occur in every culture and time. They represent eternal forms: the Wise Old Man, the Young Woman, the Soul, Death, Love, the Shadow, the Child, and so on.

Recently, the Jungian psychologist Robert Moore described the primary images of the mature, *male* psyche as Lover, Warrior, Magician, and King. As many men have begun to discover on their personal quests for soul, there are many other archetypal forms of authentic masculinity as well. Sam Keen is more interested in the Citizen, Robert Bly embraces the Wild Man. Others, like myself, have been captivated by images of the the Green Man, who is both Earth Father and Husband. There are countless other images of the masculine soul: Hunter, Sacred Clown, Sage, Tool Maker, Artist, Planter, Builder, Protector, and more.

In subtler forms archetypes may represent more abstract feelings, instincts, and other psychological tendencies, such as desire, envy, vengeance, grace, or wisdom. At still deeper levels they are the fundamental forces of nature itself. They precede and underlie human consciousness and exist independent of it.

Some thinkers, like the archetypal psychologist James Hillman, simply call archetypal images "the gods." They may be seen in the mythological images of all cultures, in literature, and in the arts. Some popular writers, such as Jean Bolen, have thoughtfully suggested that various gods and goddesses exist within the human psyche and that it is both possible and potentially beneficial to connect with these inner, archetypal forces. As we enter this mythological way of seeing, however, it is

important to remember that not only are the gods within us—we are, as it were, within them as well.

These archetypal forces are much bigger than our individual egos. In learning to work with archetypal energy, we must come to realize that to a significant degree we are all quite powerless. The forms of the gods are infinite in their variety and vast in their complexity. We cannot control them. Often we are possessed and can

even be destroyed by them. If we're lucky we may learn how to commune with the gods and receive an occasional gift through catching a glimpse into their mystery. Perhaps, through our attempts to know them, we will gain some insight into the myriad forces which move our lives from within and without us.

The gods may demand expression upon the stage of our individual lives. They make a claim upon us. If we ignore that claim we get possessed—driven. Learning how to host that claim—to welcome the expression of potent forces of transformation into our lives—is a large portion of our work together as men in quest of masculine soul.

Alcoholism, for example, is related to possession by the god of ecstasy—Dionysus. In our work together in my men's group we are attempting to learn how to commune with and honor this archetypal need for ecstasy and getting "loose" without entertaining addictive behaviors which can destroy our lives and the lives of others. This is one of the paths an authentic, mature male walks: learning how to approach and honor the

ancient gods of men. Through this work we may also learn about how to approach the Goddess without becoming devoured in the process.

Gods may lie at the core, or "root," of our individual psychological complexes. They are also the characters in the mythological stories which give rise to our religious beliefs. These myths, which we often tell at our gatherings of men, are like skeletons. They are the bones of the deep psyche upon which the flesh of our conscious lives is formed.

Our individual dreams link our modern lives to these ancient forms through the unconscious. We notice that our dreams often have elements in common with ancient myths. We are moved by images which have the power to disturb us—monsters, nightmares, angelic spirits, or gods.

In my men's group we often discuss our dreams during our weekly group meetings. We have discovered that they frequently have themes, stories, and symbols which mirror specific myths—recurring dramatic patterns we read about from many different epochs and cultures. For example, one man has recurring dreams about a man with wings on his head. We learned that one of the ancient gods of men is Hermes, a messenger from the gods who wore a winged helmet. Is this dream figure a messenger coming to teach us more about authentic masculinity? At times, as he tells us about these dreams and the radical transformations his life is going through, it seems so. For Hermes is a god of communication and transformation.

Another man, who is a Vietnam era veteran, still has occasional nightmares about the war. In several dreams he has seen a terrifying, angry figure with a sword or a lance in his hand. Is this Ares, the god of war? If so, why is he appearing now? What does he have to say? What claim has he made on this man's life? What does he want? we wonder. We address these dream figures with our intellectual curiosity and with our poetry, art, movement, and songs.

As we begin to bring our attention to the archetypal field of consciousness we may start to identify with and compare ourselves to these larger-than-life entities from mythology. At times, in our group, we have talked about ourselves as being like a particular god in various ways. In time, however, we have begun to understand these archetypal forces as autonomous—having a life of their own, independent of our imagination or will. The contemporary, post-Jungian perspective holds that our individual consciousness is actually composed of a number of distinct and separate archetypal identities in relationship with one another—a myth or story in progress. The characters and their relationships may change as our lives change, or vice versa. Through our relationship with the gods we affect them and are in turn changed by them.

Our consciousness actually may not even be a thing but rather a process, the result of the ongoing relationships of diverse psychic elements, like

an ongoing conversation in a play. We can imagine that we are not the individual characters, but the play itself. As we begin to think of ourselves in this way, we can look more critically at the voices which have dominated the play of our modern psyches and start to reach out toward ancient voices which have been silenced within men for a long, long time.

My other contribution to this book talks about a few ways to work with one specific masculine archetype—the Green Man. Some of the ideas there can be easily modified and applied to communing with many other archetypal forms. For example, if you want to know more about the Wild Man it is useful to spend time in the company of wild things and allow yourself to feel wildness moving through you in various ways. Through establishing relationships with these ancient images resonating in our modern psyches, we can deepen our experience of ourselves and of life around us. Through better understanding who we are in our depths, we can enrich life on the surface. Through coming to know the gods of men and honoring them in all their varied wonder and complexity, we can better know ourselves and the rich, psychic roots from which our consciousness springs.

BOOKS ON JUNGIAN PSYCHOLOGY FOR MEN

Robert A. Johnson, *He!: Understanding Masculine Psychology,* Revised Edition. New York: Harper & Row (Perennial Library), 1989. A classic text, this short book relates the various episodes in the Arthurian legend of Parsifal's quest for the Holy Grail to modern males' search for wholeness.

Robert Moore and Douglas Gillette, *King, Warrior, Magician, Lover: Rediscovering the Archetypes of the Mature Masculine.* San Francisco: HarperCollins, 1990. One of the essential texts of the men's movement, this book distinguishes between immature "boy psychology" forms from mature "man psychology" forms. This volume serves as an introduction to forthcoming separate books devoted to the King, the Warrior, the Magician, and the Lover.

Loren Pedersen, *Dark Hearts: The Unconscious Forces that Shape Men's Lives.* Boston; Shambhala, 1991. A Jungian analyst introduces depth psychology focusing on the anima (inner feminine) in men.

John A. Sanford and George Lough, *What Men Are Like.* New York: Paulist Press, 1988. This non-technical book blends anecdotes, case histories, and literary, cultural, and historical references to explain male psychology from a Jungian perspective. This excellent introduction to Jungian thought thoroughly illustrates concepts like "anima" and "individuation" through lively analysis of familiar stories like *Alice in Wonderland*.

RAJ AT THE BLUFFS

The king woke in a strange body.
He had been gone a long time.

It was no place he knew—
summer, a bluff above water, moist air.
Evening. Late swallows circled the sky.

His lungs reached deep and breathed.
How good to feel air again
and a human form.
He lifted a hand, dilated the chest,
twisted the supple waist first right then left,
and felt the power in belly and groin.

There was earth beneath his feet,
firm and alive.
Joy flashed up from it
and glowed from his face.

What was this?
Oh yes, command, clear command.
He was the king.
He remembered now.

How had he lost the sovereignty?
Pictures came dim at first, then clear:
an ill-conceived crusade
ransomed by lifetimes of self-forgetting.

That would not happen again.
From this waking on
he would be king without kingdom.
He did not miss the oversized horse,
the scepter, the obsequious crowds.
He would keep his disguise.

He walked.
He felt the power in his gait.
It was good.
The king had returned.

No one would know him.
It would be better than that.
When the king would look at them,
mirrored in his regal eyes
they would see a thing
most beautiful and strange.

They would remember who they are.

—ERIC KOLVIG

Only that is poetry which
cleanses and mans me.
—Ralph Waldo Emerson

A WALK WITH THE KING

BY GABRIEL HEILIG

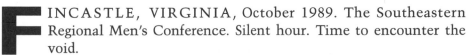

Archetypes can feel unreal and insubstantial if all we do is read about them. To feel them on our pulses, to sense them alive within us, requires that we summon them ... even if we have no clear idea about how to go about doing so. In the following evocative memoir, Gabriel Heilig recounts how he got in touch with the archetype of the King while spending some "alone time" in the woods. Heilig writes frequently on men's issues and is coauthor of a book called *Tenderness Is Strength: From Machismo to Manhood.*

FINCASTLE, VIRGINIA, October 1989. The Southeastern Regional Men's Conference. Silent hour. Time to encounter the void.

I walk up an old trail by myself. In five minutes I'm gone from the group of over a hundred men. Some men had mentioned a treehouse back up this trail, so I head off looking for it: some temporary North Star to orient the rowboat of my life.

As the trail leads me on, I feel my discomfort with the forest's silence, my anxiety at having no map, no agenda here. Yet I'm also beginning to feel at ease with the silence and hush of the woods. It smells good. The privacy is refreshing. For a surburban kid like myself who grew up without much in the way of either city street smarts or country wisdom, trails into the woods hold a sense of foreignness and fear. I keep expecting something to happen, something I won't bc able to handle.

Soon I find myself beginning to call out. At first, thc usual self-announcements. Banal stuff. My hellos to the trees. But as I do it a few more times, I begin feeling more comfortable with the sound of my own voice in the woods.

I begin shouting. It registers that I'm alone in that there are no other people, yet the woods are alive. I feel an ancient part of myself begin to reawaken: the hunter, reentering in his forest kingdom. I start getting into it. I shout more.

Before long, I'm bellowing. "I'M THE KING OF THIS FOREST." Wow! Where did *that* come from?

I listen to the echo of my own voice thundering unrestrained through the woods. Its tone has enough authority that I believe these words myself. I don't know where this king's been hiding, but he sounds real. My body feels fantastic as his presence rumbles through me.

I try it again—I'm into it now. No doubt about it: Kings definitely have more fun. I spot a sign: Treehouse this way. I head off the trail, bellowing out every few yards. This king . . . I like him.

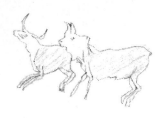

Snaps of twigs as I leave the trail, following a sign pointing toward the treehouse. After about 10 minutes of winding around, guessing at where the trail leads, I get to a clearing with two large treehouses. I climb a ladder into one of them. I find mattresses and a roomy space. A few minutes there and I know I'm in the woods for something else. So I clamber down the ladder and begin walking back the way I've come.

Tonight there'll be a poetry reading and I want to memorize a poem I'd written about my own "bucket work": my effort to get down into the dark psychic swamp where the Wild Man lives, his power chained, like mine often has felt.

I get back on the trail, slowing down now that there's no treehouse to find, no goal to reach. I start giving my poem to the woods, full throttle on the volume. What the hell—I'm king here.

"Muffled bubbled from below . . ."

As I begin, the tone of my voice downshifts to something I've never heard before in myself: a low growl, carrying the force of my words in a way I didn't hear even when I was writing them. I sound like a cement

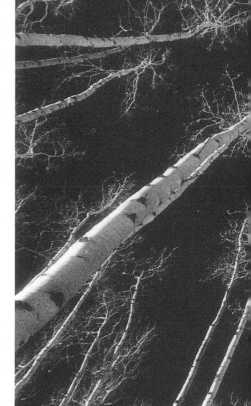

mixer or an old bull serenading the birds overhead. It dawns on me that I feel like a Shakespearean actor pounding out his soliloquy. And I feel old, at least 20 years older, like an actor playing Lear or some other aging king roaring his majesty across the forest stage.

I keep on giving the tone, loving it even more.

". . . like angry raindrops falling upward . . ."

I'm boiling with it. Probably I'm possessed by an archetype or some Jungian complex, but I could care less. I stand there for 15 minutes or so, booming out my lines, bringing my poem off the pages of memory and back into my body.

A question forms: Why don't I talk like this all the time? Not a bad question. But I'm not in the woods for self-analysis. I'm here for self-expansion. That much I can feel. An unexpected door down into an old castle room has suddenly blown open, and there's a king down there.

Is he my king? I don't know if he's mine or not, but he feels good to me. Yet

I have to ask: Where has he been all my life? Or, where have I been? Whatever the answer, he's here now.

I roar on, back down the trail toward the gathering of men and Robert and Michael, James and John, our teachers. As I come over the rise of the last hill before joining the road around the lake toward the lodge, I have another moment, another opening.

I'm not a large-bodied man, yet standing on that ridge, about to descend toward the lodge, suddenly I feel like Paul Bunyan. There's a flowing extension across my shoulders and a spacious warm feeling around my body. I feel like Ulysses home from the wine dark seas or a hunter back from the hunt. I feel *good*.

I stride into the hall where dinner's already being served. Suddenly, I feel an animal wildness filling me. Suddenly this gathering of men and the work of the past few days seem tame and forced, like we're trying too hard, trying to get underneath our *trying*. Yet, for this brief moment, I've gotten beneath it. I feel filled with something primal: animal, ancient, and unmistakably male.

HEILIG
A WALK
WITH THE KING

I make my way to the food tables. I don't want any silverware. I just want the food—and I don't want to be nice about it, either. I grab a plate, pile some food on it, and sit down. The man next to me tries not to look too startled as I bury my face straight down into the chow.

I munch away happily, like a famished horse. Who cares what I look like? I've been waiting 46 years to feel like this, unthinking of what others think of me.

All right, you Jungians and therapists. Probably I'm inflated, right? Probably my archetypes are having a royal feast on my ego state. But I'll tell you what—I don't give a sweet shit. These archetypes know how to have one helluva good time.

I spot Ed, one of my brothers from Washington, D.C. He smiles at me with a "go for it" wink. You got it, Ed. I'm gone.

Munching onward, I even get dessert down. It's good to know how the animals do it. Not bad, either. Lots of contact here.

Eventually, the mood evaporates. The room closes back in, and I shrink back to my normal identity. The question is: Which one is actually mine?

My feelings feel like they're stuck in a crowded elevator. No room to move their elbows or swing out. My ego casing is back, securely around me again.

And then I see it: Out there on the trail I met some presence who lives far from the suburbs where I was raised and taught to live. The work in the lodge with the men and our teachers was preparation, coaxing the ego to let go a bit, so I could move toward the dark voice that waits beneath my trained politeness.

I feel the same roaring tone a few nights later, when Michael gives a toast to our final night's feast. He raises his glass toward us; we raise ours toward him. His Irish blessing, "Sláinte," slices through the room like a thick spear of sound. Suddenly I feel like I'm in a medieval tavern with a band of soldiers about to ride off to war. The toasting rattling across the room is utterly male, without fear of death, and binding.

This is no longer a lodge in Virginia or a men's conference. These are *men*. Period.

Thinking back on my walk with the king, I know that for a moment's brilliant grace I released myself, initiating myself somehow on my own male ground. Some buried part of me rose up and claimed me. The tone in my voice touched it. My words carried it out of me, bucket by bucket, feeling by feeling. And the woods held me in it, spacious container.

Whatever did it, whoever was down there waiting for me—God bless you, you furious old soliloquizing bull-king sergeant-major.

You can sign me up.

THE BLESSINGS OF THE GREEN MAN

BY AARON R. KIPNIS, Ph.D.

In recent years, emphasis on Gaia, the Great Goddess, and Mother Nature has created the impression that traditionally nature has been conceived solely or primarily as female. Recently more studies have been appearing that convincingly chronicle the various appearances and disappearances in Western art and culture of a male counterpart to these female nature deities—the Green Man, consort, lover, and son of the Great Goddess. He persists in our popular culture in forms as varied as the Green Giant of frozen pea fame and Swamp Thing, the vegetable hero of the DC horror comic series. Aaron Kipnis suggests ways man can make the Green Man and his eco-masculinity (male involvement and concern for the environment) more present and real. 🖋

AS MEN in quest of masculine soul many of us are attempting to heal our lives and reconnect with our authentic, deep masculinity. Unfortunately, the male initiation process is, for the most part, lost in this culture. In the absence of male initiation, many men during the last few decades have sought reconnection to soul through the feminine. Femininity, however, is not the primary cure for masculine wounds.

Indeed, the trend to personify soul and the earth as feminine effectively perpetuates the divorce of the male psyche from its own fecund, inner-masculine, life-affirming nature. The modern envisioning of nature and soul as feminine has done the same injustice to men as monotheism did to women through exiling and degrading the sacred image of the Goddess.

Many of us have heard much about the Earth Mother. However, when we regard nature as *only* our mother, we risk remaining forever boys in her service, disconnected from the masculine power to heal, engender, and support life. If men cannot imagine a masculine connection to nature, if it is conceived of as being other than them, then their feelings of separation may breed alienation from life.

The pressing need of our time is for us to become more potent, generative, and embodied—powerful, mature men committed to life. For images of this masculine ideal some of us are turning toward the ancient *masculine* gods of the earth. One of these images is the Green Man. He is a masculine personification of nature—the Earth Father.

The new image of masculinity beginning to emerge from our quest is of a creative, fecund, nurturing, protective, and compassionate male, existing in harmony with the earth and the feminine, yet also erotic, free, wild, playful, energetic, and fierce. This image is a far cry from the patriarchal, hypermasculine, war-making hero or the feminized, deenergized, hypomasculine male who is subservient to the Goddess. Father Nature is beginning to reawaken as an equal partner alongside the resurgent Goddess.

Why is it valuable for modern men to embrace earth-based masculinity and to understand our archetypal nature as "green men"? To answer this practical query we must first consider that over the last few millennia only a few mythological images have served as our cultural foundations for masculinity: the youthful, invincible hero, like Hercules, the war-making gods like Ares, or the dominant elder male, like Moses, who rules in the name of an all-powerful god in the sky. This wrathful solar-sky god is known as Apollo, Zeus, Jove, Indra, Jehovah, Allah, and by many other names. The so-called patriarchy evolved from these images.

On the positive side, the solar image presents an ideal of warmth and light. It helps things grow. But problems arise when there is *too much* sun. That is the condition of many men today: too dry, too distant, too brittle—disconnected from their bodies and the earth. At this time, a masculine sort of moisture is needed to balance this global warming of the psyche and refresh the soul.

The Old Testament proposes that we are made in God's image. In depth psychology this belief is mirrored in the theory that our individual egos reflect archetypes—universal, recurring images. The development of men becomes unbalanced when they draw *only* from solar or sky archetypes for their inspiration.

The '"heavenly" model, taken alone, is dominating and oppressive. These heroic gods are often abstract and inaccessible to our imagination—the very images of remote or disembodied fathers. For centuries these sorts of images have served as our primary idea for masculinity. This ideal, however, does not feed us as men in quest of soul any more than does a cosmology of feminine images. So where do we turn for a new vision of masculinity?

The archetype of the Green Man reminds us of the ways in which a man is directly connected to, and representative of, the evocative beauty and power of nature. This life-generating, wild male is not merely the son, servant, or young lover of the Earth Mother as depicted in some writings. He's also a manifestation of the Earth Father—the cocreative, mature, masculine power of the earth deep in our mythological heritage and our bones. Our work ahead is to learn how to reclaim and reawaken this earthy, passionate, life-giving masculinity. It is important to remember the ways in which we are all men of deep emotions. These feelings make our lives rich.

The regreening of masculinity calls for us to learn to work and play in new ways which bring health to our lives, families, and communities. Green politics, which affirm the protection of nature as primary, call for impassioned, visionary men to revision our social and political institutions. A Green mind is a beginner's mind—a mind capable of embracing new ideas and fresh visions. When it comes to male mythopoeisis (the making of myth), most of us are "greenhorns"—revisioning as we go along rather than being "old hands" who uphold encrusted dogmas, dragging along dead carcasses of heroic masculinity. Male initiation for our time must come to us in this fresh way, as it has for every other culture, from our own dreams and visions. We lose this possibility when we dwell too much on the rites and symbols of other cultures.

The Green Man is immediately available to our imagination as soon as we begin to look at nature and soul with masculine eyes. He will speak to us if called upon. He offers us a deep source of wild magic and empowerment. The Green Man is connected to our creativity, our passion, and our capacity to generate and protect life.

How can we connect with the archetypal energy of the Green Man? There are many ways. Here are a few:

1. **Plant a tree**. Every New Year's Day some of the men in our community plant trees. It's enriching to be able to see them grow throughout the year and know we have begun the year by giving something back to the earth.

2. **Tend a garden**. Every man has a green thumb lurking inside him. Food from the garden refreshes the body and the spirit in ways food from the supermarket cannot match. The working of soil and tending of plants reconnects us to the earth, our bodies, and the natural order of things. Even if we are simply raising a tomato plant in a barrel on a condo's balcony, it feeds both body and soul.

3. **Enter the wilderness**. Go alone or with other men. Take the younger men with you. Hunt, fish, hike, raft, or simply be still, soaking in the nurturing strength of Father Nature and relishing the beauty of his lover, the Earth Mother. Something sleeping in the deep male psyche awakens when we allow ourselves to experience nature free from the numbing noise of urban life. The Earth Father welcomes us, challenging us to become stronger and deeper as men. We are at home in nature. Sitting around the fire we resonate with the generations of men who have come before us to wander, dream, hunt, play, tell stories, and simply be at peace in the green world. Where did we ever get the idea that nature was only our mother? In the home of my mother I, for one, as an adult man, never feel the same deep comfort and peace that I do in the deep, dark forests of the Great Father.

4. **Tie yourself to the top of a tree**. Feel the strength and ancient,

KIPNIS
THE BLESSINGS OF
THE GREEN MAN

163

deeply rooted power of the Green Man who dances, sways, and shudders with the wind. Of course, this is dangerous. So don't go up without proper training, safety equipment, and a buddy to secure you. Less terrifying but equally beneficial is sitting with a tree through the cycle of one tree-breath. This takes 24 hours. In this way we connect with masculine silence and the depth of soul in nature.

5. **Look at nature with masculine eyes**. With fresh eyes, wiped clean of a feminist perspective which claims nature as Goddess alone, seek the images of masculinity in nature. Those erect, thick, tall trees, do they remind us of mother or something else? What about

those mountain peaks that thunder at their summits and sometimes explode, covering the earth with rich, fertilizing ash? Are these the Earth Mother's breasts? How do they appear to you? In Africa, the name of the Earth Father in mountains is Obatala.

In other parts of the world he was known as Dumuzi, Iachus, Freyr, Karora, Ymir, or simply the Wilde Man. In Egypt he was Osiris, son of Earth Father, Geb, and Sky Mother, Nut. He represented the overflowing of the Nile River which deposited fresh alluvium each spring, fertilizing crops and regreening the world. Today, the glory of a male who nurtures the earth and his family is often ignored by our hero-worshiping culture. So, we must celebrate the Green Man in each other when we meet together.

6. **Commune with him**. Talk to him in your heart-mind. The archetypes of earth-based masculinity are sleeping in most modern men. Praying, writing him poems or stories, creating drawings,

paintings altars, masks, dances, chants, plays, and songs are ways to reawaken this image. Ask for his vital healing energy to come into your life.

7. **Dance**. In most cultures the Green Man is celebratory. One of the ancient, earthy male figures echoing in the psyche is Dionysus, a vegetation god of agricultural birth, growth, and death in ancient Greece. He loved to dance as an expression of his ecstatic aliveness. The Native American god Kokopeli, like our Johnny Appleseed, planted seeds wherever he went and was always dancing, playing music, and making love.

8. **Drum**. Drums are traditionally made from the body of the Green Man (a hollowed tree) and the skins of a bull, one of the most ancient symbols of earth-based masculinity. When we drum together, the Earth Father awakens. The Green Man comes alive and joins us in our celebrations when we drum and dance together.

9. **Carve an earth staff**. Select a piece of wood which draws you to it and carve a staff, walking stick, spear, talking stick, or phallus. Such objects were used in most Earth Father religions as symbols of the generative power of the masculine god in the earth. When we pass a talking stick around the circle during our discussions, it evokes the spirit of the life-generating Green Man in our speech.

10. **Make love in a meadow**. In England, carved into a meadow is the 180-foot-tall outline of an ancient Earth Father: the Cerne Giant. In the head of his 30-foot-long penis is a depression worn in the earth from couples copulating there over the centuries. When we make love on the earth, we connect with an ancient tune still sung within our bodies. The Green Man awakens in us in such circumstances. But watch out for poison oak, forest rangers, and startled bears.

Osiris

The Green Man is the Earth Mother's partner, neither dominating nor dominated by the feminine principle. His forests, with their erect trees, passionately embrace and encircle the earth. The dance of archetypal masculinity and femininity intertwining is ever present in each moment. Through returning masculine, green energy to the male psyche perhaps we can better nurture the seeds of the new male which are beginning to break through the hardened, sun-baked ground of our culture.

Several chapters in my book *Knights Without Armor: A Practical Guide for Men in Quest of Masculine Soul* explore other images of Father Nature in his many different guises throughout the ages. These ancient images, like the Green Man, forgotten or forbidden since the rise of monotheistic cultures around the world, have much to teach us as contemporary men who, like ancient Osiris, are committed to the regreening of masculinity and the world in which we live.

FOR MY BROTHERS

Some days ago
I saw the wild men.
The men without a shave, or a haircut,
or two bits.
They were sitting on the sidewalk
down-town where people don't sit
(unless they're having heart attacks)
by the open door of a garage.
They were men of the bush
in camouflage clothes, which stand
out in the city.
A tame man drove by
in his Mercedes. He had a
silk noose around his throat tightly
so that he could not chant.
And pointy slippery shoes
so that he could not dance
but only flit from place to place.
He was on his way to the
Crystal Tower, from where he would fly.
As he drove by he saw the
shaggy ones who pick through
his garbage like raccoons.
They sat, "menacingly," at the
level of his tires and his
eyes said, Bums!

—WALTON STANLEY

Poetry is language that tells us, though a more or less emotional reaction, something that cannot be said.

—Edwin Arlington Robinson

The images of the War-
rior and the Wild Man
have alarmed many people
outside the movement,
who have come away with
the erroneous impression
that men's work is about
imitating Rambo, Conan,
and mad-dog killers. In
this article, which originally appeared in *Changing
Men*, Christopher Burant
distinguishes these two
archetypes and puts them
in a scholarly context. ✒

OF WILD MEN AND WARRIORS

By Christopher X. Burant

IT'S NO secret that men are responsible for wreaking much of the havoc that besets the world today. Men! Men! Men! In armies terror- izing populations, in the streets hounding women, in homes brutal- izing women and children. What are we to make, then, of Robert Bly's call for men to find the "wild man" within? Isn't that what we've got now? Men on a wild rampage, filling hearts everywhere with fear? Haven't men's minds gone wild with inventions of torture and mass destruction? Do we really need more, stronger, or better wild men?

In fact there is a difference between men who are uncontrollable in a murderous and destructive frenzy, those "gone wild" in the usual sense, and a Wild Man. Written as a single word or more often as two capital- ized words, the Wild Man refers to a specific mythological being with a long and illustrious history, most elaborately defined during the Middle Ages. This Wild Man was a symbol of the conflict between civilized men and "natural" man. He was comparable to the unicorn or the phoenix; that is, an image with psychological potency for medieval European society. The Wild Man was a mixture of projected and repressed qualities in the human personality, lost as cities and civiliza- tion developed. Often visualized as a hairy, unclothed, mute hulk, he lived in the forests and deserts surrounding cities.

WHY THE WILD MAN?

Why has Bly brought this creature to our attention at this time? In the early seventies he spoke and taught on the nature of women's energies. At his Conferences on the Great Mother he shared his understanding of the goddesses, and the importance of female modes of being. Through his interactions with scores of men in these workshops, he sensed that many men had incorporated a deep respect for the feminine but now for their further development needed to look into the depths of their own

psyches, where the Wild Man lurks. In 1982, he shared this insight: "Young men today are nurturing and gentle and life-preserving but not exactly life-giving. There's no energy in them."

Bly uncovered his model for the next step in male development from an old Grimm's fairy tale called "Iron Hans." A huge hairy man has been found submerged at the bottom of a lagoon in a forest. When resurrected and caged in the center of town, he becomes instrumental in furthering the development of a young hero. On the episodes of this tale, Bly hangs his observations about the devalued state of masculinity and the need for men to take the next step—uncovering the "deep male" within themselves, getting "in touch" with the Wild Man.

But here we must be careful. This Wild Man image is powerful but potentially confusing and easily abused. For example, in some Wild Man–type workshops being offered to men across the country, what is being marketed as "wildness" is often nothing more than thinly disguised anger at women, a militaristic attitude, and familiar patriarchal roles. Men who have made the decision to fight sexist stereotypes and who have sought, like Bly, to "contact the 'feminine' within" wonder if Bly is reacting against the demands of feminism and provoking a surge of antiwoman sentiment. Many have suffered from even "shallow" masculine behaviors. Why then should we embrace a vision that encourages men to get in deeper touch with masculinity? Might that only bring forth more of essentially the same kind of savage and oppressive masculine behaviors, only entrenched more deeply than before?

In fact Bly understands this and has promised another article distinguishing the Wild Man from the angry savage. Confusing this destructive savage energy with what is more correctly understood as an aspect of the Warrior than of the Wild Man is a common misunderstanding. Warrior energy is a highly cultured and civilized form of human effort requiring great control and refinement. Wild Man and Warrior, however, are two distinct modes of male energy. They have different images and different kinds of feeling attached to them. To use Wild Man and Warrior interchangeably demonstrates a confusion about the nature of the Wild Man and how such images function in the psyche. Since ours is an extroverted culture, our experience of inner beings is foggy and indistinct. When we hear a deep voice booming loudly, we imagine a horde of thundering soldiers full of death and destruction. Perhaps this is so because we have few living examples of forceful and energetic men who also are inwardly rich and outwardly compassionate. Let us look, then, at the nature of the Wild Man, and distinguish him from the energies, attitudes, and mores of the Warrior, both life affirming and destructive.

NATURAL HISTORY OF THE WILD MAN

Who is this hairy creature of the wilds? Originally, the Wild Man was a personification of the raw forces of nature. He was at home in impenetrable forests filled with wolves, bears, and cougars. Like the animals he lived with, he was covered from head to toe with hair, except for his hands and face. He was the absolute terribleness of nature: arcane, uncommunicative, thundering, storming, and flooding at will. He ate human beings raw. He was the "abominable snowman," an uncouth ogre who could jerk trees out by their roots and use them to club back the armor-clad swordsmen of the Middle Ages.

The Wild Man is said to have come from the mating of a satyr with a woman. He watched over the animals and delighted in foul weather. When it thundered and rained, it is said that the Wild Man smiled. He slept in the crevices formed by rocky outcroppings or tree stumps. He did not know how to fashion tools and had to find food using his massive strength.

While most times wandering alone through the forest, he occasionally found a mate, a Wild Woman, with whom he lived in innocent harmony. He had no rationalizing intelligence and remained unconscious of the ideas of sin. He was neither corrupt nor evil like a devil because he was innocent. His sexuality was wanton until he satisfied himself, and then he forgot about it. In some versions of the myth he had no fathering instinct and would leave his children, once born, out in the forest to fend for themselves. He had no civilizing moralities and sought only instantaneous fulfillment of his desires. He would gorge himself on food one day and starve the next.

Perhaps, a millennium ago, the Wild Man was suppressed to facilitate the development of civilization. In certain regions of Germany an annual festival was held during Whitsuntide, called "The Expulsion of the Wild Man." In this ritual a youth from the village, covered with leaves, moss, and furs, hid in the forest. The townspeople chased, captured, chained, and symbolically killed him. The next day a stretcher with an effigy of the Wild Man was carried in a procession to a lake, where the executioner threw it into the water. For them the Wild Man had become the universal scapegoat for the uncivilized extremes in nature. Onto him also were projected the baser parts of the human personality. "If we can kill the crude mean brute, then we can go on learning to read and write and develop our fine table manners."

THE TENDERNESS OF THE WILD MAN

But another side of the Wild Man is banished when his uncouth side is repressed: the original Stone Age man in harmony with nature. He is the

Since 1974, the American artist, William E. Parker, has been defining images of the male in photographs upon which he paints and draws. Early images of the nude symbolized a renascence of the male body as associated with the earth archetypes and his most recent grand-scale portraits of men explore psychological expressions configured by the masculine persona.

His recent Der wilde Mann (The Wild Man) series, features grand-scale black and white silver prints defining male portrait-heads handcolored with oil, aquamedia, wax crayon, pastel, and graphite. This series of portraits identifies varied aspects of human temperament expressed by the faces of men. Founded on historical studies about physiognomy and expression as a measure of psychological type and character, Parker's portraits of men identify varied aspects of temperament—such as the choleric, melancholic, sanguine, phlegmatic, demoniacal, contemplative, heroic—that in premodern periods were associated with ritualistic and sacred psychic states.

From Der wilde Mann Series/1985: The Temperaments (Melancholia II), Handcol, black and white silver print (oil, aquamedia, wax crayons, graphite on Kod Type N polyfiber paper. Frame size: 49"h x 45"w; Image size: 44"h x 40"w). Scholder Collection, Scottsdale, Arizona.

enlightened being who has sidestepped the stifling conventions of civilized society to live in ecological equilibrium with his environment and his animal instincts. He uses branches and grapevines to set the broken leg of a deer and tenderly pulls the thorn from the paw of a lynx. He is true to himself and himself alone. A kind of god to hermits and nature lovers, he was honored for his knowledge of trees and herbs. Alone in the woods, content with a pine needle mattress and a cave for a home, he is paragon of elegant simplicity.

Anecdotes about the Wild Man from the Middle Ages give us some clues to his psychological nature. An old tradition in the time of knight-errantry held that if a knight loved a noble damsel enough, he would long for her so deeply and passionately that if he were rejected by the lady of his dreams, he would rip off his clothes and run off to the forest in a state of deep anguish. Gradually he would grow out a coat of hair and forget how to speak, eventually turning into a Wild Man himself. A man whose spirit is crushed by unrequited love turns into a Wild Man. During his time alone in the woods he could heal his wounds and reestablish contact with his own natural instincts.

Robert Bly has fashioned a contemporary understanding of the nature of the Wild Man. In his view the Wild Man possesses spontaneity, the presence of a developed female side, and the embodiment of a positive male sexuality. If we go back to the story "Iron Hans" we find that in the end Wild Man returns as a King himself. This means that the Wild Man was an enchanted King, the inverse of a King. Like a forlorn King Lear, the Wild Man owns nothing, commands no one, and lives in the storming elements. Since the hidden nature of the Wild Man is kingliness, it may be more likely that one could find his lost Wild Man if he could conjur up his own enchanted inner King.

What has happened to this hairy, unclothed Wild Man who has lain for centuries submerged in the murky ooze of a forest lagoon? Wild Man has probably grieved for the thousands of obliterated ecological niches and the disappearance of hundreds of delicate and unique species of plants and animals. His tears, so numerous, fill the forest with lagoons and swampy places. In his watery prison he has had to rely upon his free-running dream life to create and animate the myriad species of his soul. His lush imagination will not stay cramped beneath city sidewalks for long.

THE WARRIOR SPIRIT

In our culture, the culture of the Warrior, the Wild Man is often misunderstood and misrepresented as the Warrior, especially the Warrior as soldier. Most men receive their training in handling and developing their masculine strengths through sports activities or military duty. Through

these rigorous, though incomplete, "initiation" procedures, the Warrior qualities of discipline, courage, loyalty, service to a higher ideal, and willingness to endure pain are instilled. During his training, the Warrior develops a skill and becomes so adept at a technique—be it martial arts or engine repair—that he can "do it in his sleep."

Much has been written about the need for men to experience an initiation. Indeed, men have a longing to experience an emotionally intense symbolic and spiritual rebirth. Unfortunately, our culture has lost much of this instinctive cultural knowledge during its passage through the Industrial Revolution. This is the situation in which we find ourselves now: hundreds of thousands of young men partially developed by a haphazard athletics-style initiation that has little awareness of the mythological world.

Once the Warrior spirit is activated in men's psyches, they are available to have their newly mined resources of courage, skill, and self-discipline used not for themselves but to further the aims of the initiating group. Consequently, they are dragged along by the striding colossus of military might. Their human energies are released by forms of initiation ritual which lack depth of content. Once evoked, the Warrior spirit is an amoral force like the wind that carries human beings along with it. For the lone soul caught in its swirl, this is an exhilarating experience.

INFLATED WARRIORSHIP

However, the glories of this exhilarated state are not without their pitfalls. One of these is the tendency toward pretentious heroism. Warriors and heroes are closely linked by their mutual willingness to engage in self-sacrifice for a higher ideal. In the hero the tendency is self-conscious and exaggerated: The hero will perform some brave and noble deed but he will want to be noticed for his achievement. This is a primitive and adolescent manifestation of Warrior energies. True Warriors do not seek to be heroes.

Another struggle in the soul of a human devoted to Warrior spirit lies in the inherent tension between the Warrior and the Lover. A man who spends time and energy developing the skills and disciplines of Warriorship has less available for developing and refining the ability to appreciate things as they are. Lover energies, with their emphasis on tenderness, personal relationship, and pleasure, are antagonistic to Warrior energies. The Warrior doesn't want to be so much in love that he won't fight. The soldier-warrior brushes off the weeping wife as he goes off to war. Personal relationships take second place to the cause, the fight. The Warrior cannot allow himself to be seduced by the feminine. Sex is not an experience of relationship for him, rather simply a means of relaxation. Compulsive behavior types and workaholics are possessed by the image of the Warrior. The achievements and successes that accompany sublimated sexuality are intoxicating rewards for the loss of pleasure. As a person leaps into the tasks of life, of civilizing society and of cultivating the wilds of one's nature, tremendous stores of energy are released.

Central to a successful mission is the Warrior's willingness to use destructive force. Admittedly, "destructive energies" are necessary in everyday life. The ability to say no to the myriad distractions that would otherwise prevent us from completing even the most rudimentary tasks of living is analogous to brandishing the Warrior's sword. We all regularly "cut" ourselves free of unhealthy people, places, and habits.

But Warriors get especially good at this, and in their quest for mastery of a technique they can come to relish and take delight in destruction for its own sake. In its most dangerous manifestations the Warrior pursues the massacre and obliteration of beauty, especially feminine beauty. Of course, most Warriors don't have the opportunity to indulge themselves in these depths, but we are not lacking in historical examples of such behavior.

Warrior spirit is not to be found only in the realm of soldiery. The knack for tying together the Warrior qualities of self-discipline, service to a higher ideal, and mastery of a technique to the Lover qualities of appreciation, delight, and empathy is the special providence of the artist. Warrior spirit is also the spirit behind the self-sacrifice necessary for spiritual life and religious and social justice movements in general. Catholic Worker movements and the Salvation Army are examples. The saints of Christendom, and holy persons everywhere, glorified for their struggles against their own sensual desires, are Warriors just as much as the fiercest karate expert or Special Forces assault trooper. An important difference is in the technology these saints master—prayer and meditation—and what they serve, divinity and compassion.

Foremost in the mind of the Warrior, religious or military, is the consciousness of death. It is through the contemplation of their own death that soldiers develop courage and monks develop nonattachment.

OTHER VISIONS OF WARRIORSHIP

Finally, two other recent mythologies of Warriorship put forth recently deserve mention. In *Tales of Power*, Carlos Castaneda reports don Juan, the Yaqui Indian sorcerer, saying, "The basic difference between an ordinary man and a warrior is that a warrior takes everything as a challenge while the ordinary man takes everything either as a blessing or as a curse." This potent insight sums up a major quality of Warrior spirit. To become don Juan's Warrior, the massive energies of Warriorship are focused into a quest of personal quasimystical powers. Don Juan's vision of a Warrior has more qualities associated with shamanism than those typically linked to the Warrior. Don Juan teaches esoteric knowledge, the understanding of sacred places, admittance to higher planes of knowledge and the value of long periods of solitude. These qualities are developed in a long slow initiation under the tutelage of a master. Castaneda's writings are a depiction of initiation into the shamanic-magic realm.

The second, an ancient theory recently laid down by Chogyam Trungpa in his book, *Shambhala, the Sacred Path of the Warrior*, deep-

ens the connection between the Warrior and the saint. His vision of the Warrior is grounded in a radically gentle Buddhist worldview. "In the Shambhala traditions," he says, "fearlessness comes from working with the softness of the human heart. You no longer feel shy or embarrassed about being gentle. . . . Your softness begins to become passionate. . . . You would like to extend yourself to others and communicate with them." The first principle of this warrior is "being without self-deception." His bravery comes from not being afraid of who he is. His absolute self-acceptance is possible because he believes in the basic goodness of self and others. Such goodness is uncovered by the primary discipline of the Shambala warrior: sitting meditation.

To a person moved by compassion for the sufferings on the planet, very little goodness is evident. Our Western landscape is littered with the broken victims of sexism, racism, and the thundering dominance of an inhumane technology. Striding with relentless precision through this maze is the specter of gleaming weapons of ultimate destruction. This, indeed, is the triumph of the age of the Warrior.

THE COMING OF THE WILD MAN

The image of the Wild Man exists in almost direct contradiction to the Warrior. Wild Man was most alive in the imaginations of people during the same age as the gallant knights of yore. Two modes of being so opposite can scarcely be found: one, clad in armor on a bridled horse with metal weapons and the structures of an entire society behind him; the other, unclothed, speechless, holding on to the antlers of a stag as he gallops with a tree stump in his hand through his forest domain. Warrior has from the beginning hunted down Wild Man, chased him into the darker reaches of the forest.

The Wild Man is not a Warrior gone berserk, not another deranged muscleman with a cache of automatic weapons. He also is not another highly skilled technician with no tender human relationship to another person. Rather, he is a deep, soulful being, close to animals and forest life, whom we repressed long ago in our movement toward refined city life.

The differences between the Warrior and the Wild Man are dramatic and stark. Where a Warrior exhibits courage in facing fears, the Wild Man exhibits deep empathy for other forms of life. Where the Warrior is heroic and useful to himself and society, the Wild Man because of his untamable wildness cannot be appropriated for any social cause. Where the Warrior lives with consciousness of death as the ultimate doom, the Wild Man lives with a sense of the naturalness of the flow of life into death. The Warrior tests himself repeatedly against concrete challenges in the world while the Wild Man floats in the vague netherworld of dreams. The Warrior sees sadness, melancholy, and regret as foolish self-indulgences; the Wild Man sees grief and deep sorrow as a door to a magical world. The Warrior is an almost exaggerated type of civilized man while the Wild Man has no use for the conventions of society. The Warrior is a man of rationality, the Wild Man is a man of soul.

The Warrior through self-control, fearlessness, and risk taking masters the natural world, while the Wild Man uses tenderness and sensitivity with animals and nature. Warriors tend to see sexuality as a block to self-control; Wild Men welcome their sexuality with its passions and messy commitments. The Warrior works well in a group, the Wild Man tends toward solitude. Warrior believes in some principle or person outside of himself; Wild Man experiences the inner beings of his own psyche and cultivates a relationship with them. The Warrior strives to live with chaste purity; the Wild Man embraces religious ecstasy. The War-

To the extent that a man is wild, he is also unowned, unmanipulated, unbowed, unbeholden, undomesticated, unapologetic, and unashamed. Unfortunately, we see very few men so free. And yet we yearn deeply for such wildness. Our literature and cinema are filled with Wildman fantasies: Tarzan, Robinson Crusoe, Lonely Are the Brave, Grizzly Adams, The Rainmaker, Iceman, Crocodile Dundee, The Emerald Forest, Jeremiah Johnson or Dances With Wolves, to name a few. The Bible, too, is full of Wildman stories with plenty to teach about the way this archetype connects men to God: the narratives of Adam, Ishmael, Esau, Samson, Amos, John the Baptist, and especially Jesus. Nowhere in Scripture, however, does the Wildman archetype appear more powerfully and vividly than in the legends of Elijah.

—Patrick M. Arnold,
Wildmen, Warriors
and Kings

rior provides clarity, decisiveness, and cleanliness to men; the Wild Man provides access to the moist, fertile ground of the imagination.

Warrior disciplines deserve honor and regard. They are necessary and valuable energies, certainly for confronting and overcoming the real threats to one's personhood in our technological civilization. And they may also be necessary for finding the Wild Man at all. In the "Iron Hans" fairy tale the Wild Man in the forest lagoon is refound and emptied by a lone brave man with a dog. Is the man a Warrior? Certainly he was brave in setting aside his fears of the dark forest. He went in without weapons, he went in with his vulnerability and labored long and hard to scoop the water out of the pond.

Western civilization has tried to drown the Wild Man. He has lain at the bottom of the forest lagoon, at some forgotten place in our consciousness, for centuries now. Boeing 747s, autobahns, World Wars, life insurance policies, and computers have taken over our world in his absence. This one-sided madness has now increased to the point where it does not require much imagination to foresee our total destruction. The resurrection of the Wild Man, like the coming of a hairy and sexual Christ figure, may provide a way for men to transform themselves into lush, tender, profound, and passionate beings.

REFERENCES

R. Bemheimer, *Wild Men in the Middle Ages*. Cambridge, MA: Harvard University Press, 1952.

Robert Bly, *A Little Book on the Human Shadow*. Raccoon Books, 1986.

Robert Bly, "What Men Really Want." *New Age* (May 1982).

C. M. Castaneda, *Tales of Power*. Simon and Schuster, 1974.

J. E. Cirlot, *A Dictionary of Symbols*. Routledge and Kegan Paul, 1962.

E. Dudley and M. Novak, *The Wild Man Within*. Pittsburgh: University of Pittsburgh Press, 1973.

George Leonard, "The Warrior." *Esquire* (July 1986).

Robert Moore, "Lectures on Male Archetypes." February 1987.

C. Trungpa, *Shambhala: The Sacred Path of the Warrior.* Shambhala Publications, 1984.

SPIRITUAL WARRIOR
AN INTERVIEW WITH JOSEPH JASTRAB

Talking about the archetype of the warrior is like wielding a double-edged sword. Many men are attracted to the immense power of the image and become fascinated with the warrior's destructive shadow side as manifested in films like *The Terminator*. Others have such a total horror of war and bloodshed that they look on the image of the warrior with distaste, forgetting that a warrior can fiercely pursue and protect. Joseph Jastrab, in this self-interview which first appeared in *Wingspan™*, explores the somewhat oxymoronic term "spiritual warrior."

Joseph Jastrab is a psychotherapist with a background in psychosynthesis and Native American medicine ways. He is the director of Earth Rise Foundation, where he guides wilderness vision quests and workshops exploring the nature-self relationship. Since 1982, he has been guiding the Men's Quest, an annual nine-day wilderness rite of passage in the Adirondack Mountains. He and Ron Schaumburg are collaborating on a book about his Quest experiences. ✍

*T*HE WORLD needs a man's heart ..." The words echoed down through the desert canyon walls, dropping like so many pebbles into the quiet pools of my evening's meditation. I was fully engaged that Summer Solstice eve with a group of datura in full bloom. Their trumpeting, ghostly white blossoms seemed to be enjoying a secret courtship with the moon rising in her fullness. I had come to these plants, to the moon, to seek counsel, intent on learning more of the ways of the Earth Mother. I had come with a wounded heart disguised in the question, "How might I better serve the planet?" Again and again, just the echoing words, "The world needs a man's heart." My first reaction was to try to whisk the words away as one would attempt to blow out a burning ember. Of course, the harder one blows, the brighter the ember. At the time, such counsel seemed out of place, as I was expecting an initiation of another sort. Like many wounded and searching men of my generation, I believed that my personal and planetary salvation lay entirely within the cultivation of the inner feminine. The Earth, in her compassionate wisdom, threw me back on myself that night. "If you wish to serve me, forgive ... forgive your heart to me ... your man's heart. It all starts with forgiveness."

—From Joseph's journal

Wingspan: *Joseph, can you give us some of the context of this experience? Were you questing alone, or with a group?*

Joseph: I was a member of a group of about 35 men and women who responded to a call put out by Elizabeth Cogburn. Elizabeth is the chief choreographer, shaman, and vision keeper of the New Song Ceremonial Community. We had come together in the canyonlands of Utah for two weeks during the summer solstice of 1981 to participate in the New Song Sun Dance Ceremonial. Part of our time together was devoted to separate men's and women's lodges, where we worked to understand and embody male energy and female energy and sought to create life-affirming ways to bring these energies together in balance. I honor Elizabeth

for creating a context which encouraged a radically new look at what it means to be a man, what it means to be a woman, and what it means to be in a relationship with a fully-empowered other.

The experience from the journal excerpt happened one night when I left our camp to sit alone. It was such a setup! I was surrounded by images of the feminine; the full moon, night-blooming datura, the womblike canyon, a powerful woman as our community leader.

Wingspan: *It almost sounds like your deeper masculine side was evoked to meet the feminine energies present.*

Joseph: It was either that or choose to remain a little boy in relation to a powerful mom—a relatively secure position, but very boring after a while, for both parties. Basically, I was put on notice that it was time for me to grow up. I use the term "Earth Mother" advisedly in that description. That's who I was seeking at the time, and for an early phase of development, that's fine. Now I heard the earth saying, "Please, haven't we had enough of this 'mother' business?"

If I relate to the earth as "Mother Earth," then the highest relationship I can have is to be a "good little boy," and I am blind to the possibilities of relating to the Goddess. As a Goddess energy is awakened in a man, the deeper aspects of his masculine side, or God nature, are likewise stimulated.

Wingspan: *I am aware that you credit that canyon experience with being the origin of the Men's Quest. How did you bring this experience home, and how did it relate to the work you do now with men?*

Joseph: Well, walking in the everyday, business-as-usual world with the seed of new vision is rarely easy. And this certainly was a case in point. I returned home with great enthusiasm but few words. My trying to rationally understand or verbally communicate the experience always seemed to trivialize it. I brought the vision to the personal therapy I was engaged in. There was an initial stirring of energy that promised germination, but that soon fizzled, and once again I was left carrying just a seed of possibility.

I spoke with individual friends most receptive to processing the inner life—mostly women at the time. I received much encouragement from each of them but still felt incomplete. I kept asking myself the question, How do I nurture this seed? It seems so obvious to me now, but at the time, I was a man blind to the most natural source of support for my quest. It eventually dawned within me that the encouragement of the potential of my canyon vision required a larger context, a group context. But not just any group: a group of men. And I thought, God help me!

At that time, I had little regard for men as cotravelers, except in the realms of sport and idea polishing. Women seemed to be the ones who could draw the best out of me. I was involved, along with many of my

brothers, in trying to open my heart by cutting off my balls (or at least pretending they weren't there).

But what a revelation, to consider for the first time the possibility that men, indeed the masculine principle, might carry a healing, nurturing aspect of its own! I opened to the possibility that my search for wholeness as a man had led me into a box canyon which allowed only the narrow vision that all of the evil in the world was due to masculine qualities of perception and action. You know, the all-too-familiar notion that men create war, men create poverty, men create pollution, et cetera and the distorted indictment of the entire masculine principle that grows from that. I realized that, while many men and women were looking to the Great Mother for salvation, nobody I knew was seeking to embody the Great Father. In fact, at that time, I hadn't ever heard of such a thing as the Great Father. Imagine what that means to a 31-year-old man in our culture. We all seemed to be reacting against the terrible father, the one who fathers reason cut off from love, truth hardened into static form, law and order void of compassion.

Wingspan: *Wasn't it the role of the elder males in traditional cultures to introduce the younger males to the positive ways of manhood?*

Joseph: It certainly was, and still is in some parts of the world. Yet, for most men of our culture and generation, such initiation is haphazard at best. The father is away from home much of the time; the mother is the predominant force in our lives. Men can't get very far by using their mothers as role models, except to attempt to be not like them. It's difficult to grow up with a positive self-image when all you have to go on is a sense of who you can't be like. That's like trying to get somewhere by backing away from what you don't want. No wonder we stumble!

Occasionally we turn around, face forward, and in the absence of adequate male role models, we face nothing; that's scary. Every so often, into that vacuum comes crashing a figure like Rambo. The young boys of today are so hungry for a male role model. With Dad gone, you can't blame them for latching on to figures like Rambo.

Wingspan: *Getting back to the process of creating the Men's Quest, after you opened to the value of being together with men, what moved you to act on that?*

Joseph: The most important single event was Keith Thompson's *New Age* magazine interview with Robert Bly entitled "What Men Really Want" in May of 1982. I read it, and the world stopped for a moment. It was more than just reading an article; Bly put words to the instinctual call to a truly heroic and vital manhood that was seeded in me the summer before. It was as if Bly had written a personal letter to me. But this, of course, is the gift of the poet: to give voice to the pulse beat of creation in such a way that we hear our own voice speaking as we read the

poem. Something came through Bly's words that provided the act of confirmation for my vision seed. It was as if all the elder males in my tribe encircled me, gave of their blood for me to drink, and said, "Go for it!" And feeling the ground confirmed beneath my feet, I was encouraged to take my next step in growing my vision.

Wingspan: *Which was . . . ?*

Joseph: At the time, I was guiding Vision Quests for mixed groups of men and women. It was a natural step to then put out the call for an all-male Quest. I remember the mix of enthusiasm and terror that accompanied that act. It was clear that the only way I could "guide" a men's Vision Quest would be as a full participant. I would be coming with as much ignorance about what it meant to be a man as anyone else. And none of us had any idea of where this thing was headed. We all stood pretty naked, gawking at each other. Yet, I trusted that there was fertile soil for our questions and stories that longed to take root.

Wingspan: *What happened in those early Men's Quests that you remember now as significant?*

Joseph: I remember an early perception that each man came to the Quest as a "seed," a seed carrying medicine that could heal both itself and the planet. And I remember being shocked at the depth of suffering within men. The most censored, most ignored story of our times is the story of men's suffering. Until that story is fully told by men and heard by both men and women, the medicine contained within a man's "seed" will be forever impotent. But it is precisely the tears released as the story is told and witnessed that moisten the hard seed coat, initiating that rooting into the earth; that is an act of love, an act of courage.

We began to open our hearts to both our joy and our suffering, and further, to the beauty and suffering of our planet. And through this, we began to understand what courage was really about. Gaia [the earth] is calling for her spiritual warriors now, perhaps more now than ever. She is calling for warriors who are courageous lovers as well as courageous hunters. I find that men who are open to their suffering make better warriors. And better lovers. That is where the strong counsel on forgiveness from my canyon vision comes in.

I noticed during the early Quests that most men were attracted to the warrior image and came with an inner list of criteria for being a warrior. These lists generally included such qualities as commitment, courage, strength, discipline, etc. The warrior archetype awakens me to a more fully embodied life of service and action. It helps to focus strong, primal male energy toward service to one's people. And one thing is for certain: To follow the warrior's path necessarily means that one will repeatedly fall flat on one's face, short of the ideal.

For me, the warrior's way is about doing whatever it takes to live life at the highest level of integrity. There has always been risk involved in that, and likely there always will be. Without forgiveness, the high ideals of the warrior's way remain ideals at best and severe reminders of one's inadequacies at worst. We men must come to forgive those aspects of ourselves, our brothers, fathers, grandfathers, generations of grandfathers that have fearfully denied life. This forgiving is the giveaway of renewed life. And this renewal must begin at home before it can expand to embrace the earth. I see this beginning to happen.

Wingspan: *Tell us about your use of the term "warrior."*

Joseph: I use the term "warrior," or even "spiritual warrior," and I know many men feel both a strong "Yes!" response and a strong "No!" response. Some feel there is something regressive and barbaric about the image of the warrior that might keep us stuck in an old story that isn't working. Well, there certainly have been men who have called themselves "warriors" whom I would consider barbaric. But let's

explore those two responses. Where does that strong yes come from? What in us resonates positively with the term "warrior"? Perhaps it's the excitement, the adventure of the warrior that we're drawn to, that part of us that feels fully alive when we have a mission in life, a sense of purpose and commitment.

And what in us says no to identification with the warrior? Perhaps we react to images of destruction, blood lust, war, and violence that arise. We fear that the use of the term "warrior" might somehow tend to validate these images.

Let me say at the outset that I am not encouraging wholesale acceptance of the warrior identification for men of service and action. I use the term "warrior" because it is a transformer for me, now. It reveals to me those aspects of myself that are destructive and warlike. So this play with the spiritual warrior image has catalyzed an awareness of the war that goes inside me between, let's say, subpersonalities engaged in a win-loss conflict. For example, I have a couple of inner characters I call Striver and Layback. Striver says "Go, go, go!" and Layback's motto is "Mañana, tomorrow." Needless to say, these two are often at odds with each other. They each feel that their freedom can be met by wiping out the other. They create a win-loss game built around fear and distrust,

JASTRAB
SPIRITUAL
WARRIOR

181

which is essentially war. I find close parallels between tensions of these two inner beings and the tensions between world superpowers. I don't think war would be the most popular world game if it were not the most popular inner game as well.

So, I can personally relate to anyone's yes-no reaction to the warrior image, knowing that both sides live within me. It's helped me to come clean with myself to acknowledge that war is not just somebody else's problem.

Wingspan: *What would you say is the difference between what you call the "new warrior" or the "spiritual warrior" and the warrior of the past?*

Joseph: I would say that both share qualities of aliveness, courage, and committed action, but they are dedicated to different purposes. The old warrior still believes in the win-loss game, and he dedicates himself to protecting the life and values of a particular ideology or nation. The new warrior's allegiance is to the whole planet and to the whole self. And I imagine that the battleground of the self is a well-traveled territory for the new warrior. I think another important aspect in our imaging the new warrior is this: The new warrior has a very inclusive definition of his or her "people." This warrior's people include, as the Lakota would say, the "flying people, swimming people, tall-standing tree people, four-leggeds" and the rest of creation, as well as the "two-leggeds."

There is a world war going on at this present moment that rarely gets recognized as such. It's the imperialistic violence of us two-leggeds against the other peoples of the earth. I see the new warrior as one whose heart grieves for this loss of life and takes inward and outward action to show a way to peace. The spiritual warrior, I would say, is one who is not willing to substitute the kind of action that simply buffers one's heart against the suffering of the planet.

I'm thinking now of my many political protest acts during the sixties. On the surface, they appear, at least to me, to be acts of healing service. But not far below the surface there was desperation, and now I see that may of those acts were done to resolve the tension and discomfort I felt when I really opened up to the suffering of Vietnam. My grief tolerance level was very low then, so many of my acts were a defense against feeling. And I think men generally have a more difficult time than women with simply being with suffering. When I hear, "The world needs a man's heart," I sense that there is a healing that takes place for both men and the earth simply by keeping our hearts open to the grief that pervades our planet now—just that. And our tendency to do, do, do all the time cuts us off, and the earth off, from the nurturing presence of the male heart. Of course, it's not that doing is wrong. Yet, if action covers up or denies feeling, then the action has little potency.

I love the image Chogyam Trungpa offers of the warrior in his book

Shambhala. He speaks of the "sad and tender heart of the warrior." You cannot be a warrior without a sad and tender heart, he says. That's beautiful; there's strength in that. Trungpa says that without the sad and tender heart, one's bravery is brittle like a china cup. You drop it and it shatters.

We're to call on the tenderness, the courage, that allows us to hold the earth in our hearts—the whole earth, not just the "nice" parts. Can you feel the compassion that arises from carrying the whole earth in your heart? It's a compassion that is enduring enough to inform all of our actions, so that everything we do becomes "earth-healing work."

BOOKS ON MALE SPIRITUALITY

Patrick M. Arnold, *Wildmen, Warriors, and Kings: Masculine Spirituality and the Bible.* New York: Crossroad, 1991. This book by a Jesuit priest deftly blends mythopoetic archetypal analysis with careful study of New and Old Testaments. Robert Bly, who wrote the introduction to the work, calls Arnold's chapter on Jonah as a Trickster figure "brilliant." The study has a strong male-positive, life-affirming quality that will appeal to both Christians and Jews.

Harry Brod, ed. *A Mensch Among Men: Explorations in Jewish Masculinity.* Freedom, CA: Crossing Press, 1988. This anthology of twenty-one articles and essays, which evince a strong pro-feminist, gay-affirmative, social activist slant, includes "Learning Talmud from Dad, Though Dad Knew No Talmud" and "How to Deal with a Jewish Issue: Circumcision."

John Carmody, *Toward A Male Spirituality*. Mystic, CT; Twenty-Third Publications, 1989 (203) 536-2611. Using his personal experiences as well as a wide variety of theological sources, Carmody suggests ways men can find their own paths to life-enhancing Christian spirituality. The slim volume contains some good, but sympathetic commentary on other contemporary books on male spirituality.

Changing Men: Issues in Gender, Sex and Politics. Issue 23, Fall/Winter 1991. This special issue examines men's spirituality from a pro-feminist, gay-affirmative perspective. Articles include "Politics and Spirituality—Allies, Not Enemies" and "Where Are the Ethics in Men's Spirituality?"

James Nelson, *The Intimate Connection: Male Sexuality, Masculine Spirituality.* Philadelphia: Westminster Press, 1988. A Professor of Christian Ethics displays his ultrasensitivity to the situation of women and gays in a book which consists largely of the author's summary and paraphrase of other writers' work. This feminist study includes a discussion of "Jesus as Sexual Man and Man of Power."

Martin Pable, OFM, *A Man and His God.* Notre Dame: Ave Maria, 1988. Conventional Catholic doctrine served up for male readers.

Richard Rohr and Joseph Martos, *The Wild Man's Journey: Reflections on Male Spirituality.* Cincinnati: St. Anthony Messenger, 1992. Thirty short chapters based on the popular audiotapes by Franciscan priest Rohr.

R. J. Stewart, *Celebrating the Male Mysteries.* Bath, UK: Arcania, 1991. This practical guide to reviving male mysteries and adapting them to our current understanding of archetypes contains many vivid guided meditations and visualizations on spiritual empowerment for men.

WARRIOR IMAGES

BY GREGORY J. SCAMMELL

The reality of being a soldier in battle is very different from both the images of the sanitized heroes glorified in World War II movies and of the dehumanized baby-killers despised by war protesters. In combat men feel a strange exhilaration and humility, an intensity that nothing in peacetime seems to equal. Many veterans regard wartime feelings for comrades-in-arms as the closest and fiercest of their lives, even surpassing their love for their wives and children—though they rarely articulate these sentiments. Vietnam veteran Gregory Scammell is one of the exceptions, as he demonstrates in this meditation on the range of a warrior's relationships, first printed in *Wingspan*. ✍

I RECEIVED MY first images of warriors while growing up as a young boy in rural America in the 1950s. I can still hear and smell my toy cap guns, recall the feel of my plastic toy soldiers ordered from my Blackhawk comic books, smell my father's army gear, and remember playing with my frogmen, which were propelled with baking soda.

My first exposure to communities of men was in Cub Scouts, and later Boy Scouts. The Scouts gave me hints about warriors and their habits. We busied ourselves with tying knots, learning survival skills, and gaining ranks, medals, honors, and badges. I enjoyed and thrived in the company and camaraderie of males, and learned much about the world outdoors. I wanted to be a true Boy Scout—one who is trustworthy, loyal, helpful, friendly, courteous, kind, obedient, cheerful, thrifty, brave, clean, and reverent. I pledged to do my best to God and my country.

I moved into adolescence, where new images of warriors filled my young, hot brain. My father admonished me to heed my country's call for warriors, should it ever come. To ignore the call was not an option. Such an act was to fail to become a man. If I became a coward, it was worse that death itself. To answer the call of God, duty, and country was a rite of passage, at least for the poor man. Televised World War II and Korean War movies showed me what a real war was like and how other boys had become warriors and men. Superman teased my struggling feelings of adolescent omnipotence. Past deeds of warriors had led America and its perfect television families to the ultimate. We were good and we were right. The only God was on our side.

Graduation from two years of college brought a change in my draft status and an opportunity for me to answer a call for warriors. I was frightened and exhilarated. It didn't seem odd to me that I could be drafted and forced to go to war, but was not old enough to vote. Neither did it seem unusual to me that only the young boys were made to go. I felt pride that my gender could withstand the punishment. I felt the collective shame of deserving it simply because I was a man.

Basic training provided my passage from American civilian to American warrior. The American civilian's rights are cherished and upheld by laws. The American warrior's rights fall under the Uniform Code of Military Justice, a separate legal system. I felt pain and pride in the transformation from civilian person to military warrior. The loss of my individuality seemed to pale beside the gain of my group warrior identity. I was reborn.

After my basic training rite of passage, I was finally ready to go to war and become a warrior. Although we had passed many grueling tests and trials, we had not passed the final exam and ultimate test of manhood—combat with and against other real warriors. My years of preparation in mental and physical survival, starting with Blackhawk comic books and Scouts, could now be put to use. My potential as an instrument could now be realized.

Very little of the above prepared me for the actual experience of being a warrior. There is the traditional side of warriors that we often see in the movies. This traditional showing rarely deals with the wide range of feelings and emotions actually experienced by the warrior. War is living in a constant state of fear and being unable to know what feelings to trust. This horrible side provides a backdrop and is a culture for very unusual experiences for men.

I never met anyone who wasn't against war. Even Hitler and Mussolini were, according to themselves.
—David Low
The New York Times

There just isn't a single war story that can capture all that it means to be a warrior. Once in war, my memories and images no longer follow in a logical sequence, a story with a beginning and an end. Instead, my mind is filled with random images that are my own and other men's. These images are sacred to me and I hope that through sharing them with you, that there will be a deeper appreciation for warriors as they were in Vietnam. Warriors in Vietnam interacted on multiple levels with other warriors, and Vietnamese men, women, and children, with the environment, and with the deepest part of our young souls and selves.

WARRIORS INTERACTING WITH OTHER WARRIORS

Learning how to be a buddy and how to have a buddy was one of the first steps in Vietnam. We genuinely smiled and laughed together, our arms tightly hugging each other's strong shoulders. Men comfortable holding and hugging one another. Men waltzing and doing the watusi together. Men sharing the most special times men can have. Men doing this sharing regularly and taking sustenance from it. Men sitting together on sandbags watching the Day-Glo pink-orange sunsets, and talking about their families and loved ones. Men willing to put their lives on the line for food, water, and the safety of their buddies. Men cooperating, being resourceful, and not demanding individual credit for group efforts.

Men not afraid to be strong, brave, compassionate, and decisive leaders. Men loving, trusting, and feeling safe with each other. Men, in the

SCAMMELL
WARRIOR
IMAGES

face of death, living life with each other. Men being sweet with other men. Men free to feel and feeling free to bare their souls to other men. Men often courteous, friendly, and respectful of other men's feelings and experiences.

WARRIORS INTERACTING WITH INDIGENOUS MEN

A wizened Montagnard man with betel nut–stained teeth, loincloth, and water buffalo stands alone at the fork in the trail deep in the jungle. He points in a direction with his hand. Is he pointing in the direction of safety or danger? I do not have the language to know.

Sharing marijuana, but not language and culture, with the local village shaman. The barber who shaved your neck yesterday is caught in the concertina wire in an attack that evening. Feeling the men's fear of you, but lacking the language to calm them. Feeling sad at the inability to share what is most in common, being a man.

WARRIORS INTERACTING WITH WOMEN

Check any freshly cleaned clothes for razor blades before putting them on in the morning. Men freely smiling at and flirting with women, without being self-conscious. Feeling the disgrace of paying someone to touch you. Learning about bartering packets of American Swiss Miss for joints of Cambodian Red. Feeling the sharp edge between smiles and fear of danger.

Smelling Emeraude and hearing nylons rubbing together. Realizing that there are no women anywhere near. Unadulterated fantasy.

WARRIORS INTERACTING WITH CHILDREN

Men laughing, smiling, and playing with little boys and girls. Men loving the children and feeling very protective toward them. Feeling the sadness when seeing little boys who look up to you because their own father is gone. Feeling the sadness of knowing that you can only be with them until the end of your tour.

WARRIORS INTERACTING WITH THE ENVIRONMENT

Adopting and nurturing mice, dogs, poisonous snakes, mongeese, parakeets, monkeys, and other small animals. Holding and cradling a small monkey, while it gazes directly into your eyes and reaches up to touch your face with its human hands. Feeling tenderly in touch and in love with all living creatures when this happens. From coaxing your bitch through labor, in the heat of the day, to providing euthanasia, burial rites, and services for the puppy who was born without hips to walk. Taking pictures of your lovely bitch having her puppies.

Famous Korean War photo of one soldier comforting another whose buddy has just been killed

Lying alone, for nights, in the dark, on the deep jungle floor. No dark corners anywhere, and everywhere. Telling myself that I am not afraid of the jungle that never sleeps. Hearing the jungle breathe at night. Snakes at night, without faces and names. Only the knick-knocking of the bamboo trunks to mark the passage of the dark.

Life as a warrior is, as they often say today, in the here and now. Death hangs in the next breath on patrol, while your life can depend on what you are doing with this very breath now. As Michael Meade has

said, "You are being initiated into life, if you survive, or into death, if you don't." Sensory experiences, naturally heightened with adrenaline, give new meaning to the phrase . . . a beautiful life.

An ever-ready supply of nicotine, caffeine, sugar, alcohol, opium, pills, heroin, marijuana, speed, and LSD. Some men resisting, some not even tempted, some selecting their favorite option, and some simply opting. All trying to deal with the relentless pain of war. Searching for freedom from an emotional life that is too intense to live.

WARRIORS INTERACTING WITH
THEIR SELVES AND SOULS

A warrior in touch with his power can afford to be extra sweet and tender. Men are free to show their gentle side on the battlefield. Men in touch with endurance and bravery. A warrior pushes his face into the winds. He puts aside the life of his ego and physical body. To become a warrior requires a transcendence of the self.

Feeling your most inner guts violated and ripped open by the disgust of war. Resisting the violent intrusion is as harmful as allowing it to penetrate. Stress fractures deep in the mind. Why? Your god isn't sure anymore, their god laughs, and my god weeps.

One day the beauty and the violence stopped. The privileges accorded to me as a warrior stopped. When I returned home I realized that, not only had my privileges been revoked, but now to be a warrior was shameful. I naively believed that you would accept me and love me more if I agreed to sacrifice my life for your highest ideals. I learned what betrayal meant. I felt raped.

I met other throwaway warriors in the Vietnam Veterans Against the War. We continued to work together, as we had in the past. It felt powerful to be in the presence of men's endurance again. It was sustaining to be in the company and comfort of men again.

Many things have changed. These warrior images are now two decades old. Forget being a warrior? Put it behind me? Not on your life! I am still understanding that my warrior in me was misguided and misled by faux leaders who had never been in touch with the true warrior within themselves. I am learning that my warrior experiences cannot be stolen from me and manipulated by the well meaning but unknowing. My growth from trauma continues.

I continue my journey as a warrior pushing my face into the winds. I am proud of and blessed by the warrior within me. I am in the process of making the warrior within me my friend.

THE TRICKSTER ARCHETYPE
POTENTIAL AND PATHOLOGY
BY ROBERT MOORE

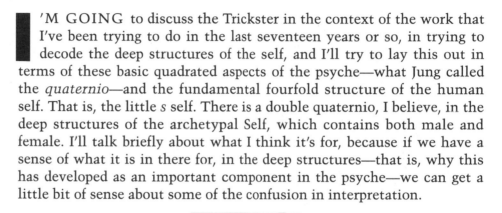

The following excerpts come from a series of audiotapes recorded during a seminar given at the C.G. Jung Institute of Chicago on July 28, 1990. Here the prominent Jungian analyst Dr. Robert Moore explores an immature form of the Magician archetype: the Trickster. This figure appears in virtually all cultures. Among Native Americans he was almost always a male figure known as Coyote or Raven. Hermes from Greek mythology and Nasrudin from the Sufi tradition are other important manifestations. This mischievous character is behind Br'er Rabbit and Batman's foe, the Joker.

I'M GOING to discuss the Trickster in the context of the work that I've been trying to do in the last seventeen years or so, in trying to decode the deep structures of the self, and I'll try to lay this out in terms of these basic quadrated aspects of the psyche—what Jung called the *quaternio*—and the fundamental fourfold structure of the human self. That is, the little *s* self. There is a double quaternio, I believe, in the deep structures of the archetypal Self, which contains both male and female. I'll talk briefly about what I think it's for, because if we have a sense of what it is in there for, in the deep structures—that is, why this has developed as an important component in the psyche—we can get a little bit of sense about some of the confusion in interpretation.

I've come to believe that is enormously important for you to have the Trickster, working for you in your psyche. Because if you do not have the Trickster really accepted in your psyche and working well, you are going to overidealize too many people. You're going to be too reverent, hyperidealizing of all sorts of people. It's not that you don't need appropriate idealizing transferences—you do. But if you feel weak and impotent, I will guarantee you the Trickster is not functioning well enough in a positive way in your psyche, because you're giving away your power in idealizations, in idealizing projections, in idealizing transferences.

And there's another side to the pathology of the Trickster, when he's on full automatic. If you tend to have a little problem with self-esteem, it may also be that the Trickster is deidealizing, but it is deidealizing you yourself right out of existence. The only appropriate target for the Trickster's firepower is grandiosity, pathological, infantile grandiosity. And when it starts getting into good muscle and good structure, you need to turn it off.

Most of the Trickster adventures throughout the world tend to be cast in oppositional terms. Whenever he is deploying his powers, he is aggressively trying to attain some individually desired goal, or he is aligning

himself with the small animals in a team effort against powerful opposition. That's a key thing. He's willing to cheat to get what he needs. When he sets out alone against a powerful adversary, he employs deception, disguise. There's the camouflage aspect of the Magician archetype, you can see it clearly there. He has the ability for self-transformation, to be a form changer, shapeshifter. This is behind the Wizard of Oz. It even includes the power to change sexes. So, if you've had a little problem with gender identity, you probably have Trickster stuff going on. Another motif, which the scholars have said is practically universal, is defiance of natural restraints. Do you have a problem being defiant? Your Trickster stuff is not adequate. It's also interesting that his physiological needs are often enormous and insatiable, and he's often characterized as having aggressive, very self-serving sexuality and wanderlust. There are widespread accounts of the enormous size and maneuverability of his penis. And there are also many many tales about the painful discoveries that he has to make about the limits of his magical powers and his native abilities. Even if you have the most wonderful dick in the world, there are some things it can't do. That's one of the things that is always a problem for the Trickster.

This Coyote mask was created by Tom Daly

There's much Trickster stuff in the mythology of Krishna, especially the child Krishna. A lot of Krishna's sneaking around and having sex with everybody else's wives—these are Trickster phenomena. You also see this clearly in the Native American character Coyote, who is always going around putting his penis everywhere. He sees this pretty princess over on the other side of a lake and he extends his penis under the water. "Got her!"

In Hindu and Indian culture, there is a tremendous amount of this energy that is available. There's so much of a sense of play. The whole idea in Hindu mythology of a god who is represented with *lila*, play, who's not all that serious—that is this sector operating. The sense is that somehow there's something divine about irreverence. Now, Christians don't like this too much. In the Christian tradition, the Trickster gets seen as, who else? Judas, Satan, but also, Christ the fool.

The Trickster has boundless energy, seems to be totally self-centered. He seems to be fascinated and involved in all sorts of clumsy experiments with his body and his body's capacities. He's always turned on by how fascinating his anus is. His anus does all sorts of things. He'll get his anus into all sorts of trouble. He just puts it over here, and it gets burned up, and then he's always trying to find it. Have you ever heard of that? Getting your ass into all sorts of trouble? Somebody who can't find it with both hands? Well, this is Trickster.

But the anus is just endlessly fascinating for him, and he has no sense of revulsion for feces. In fact, one of the things that he thinks is wonderful about feces is how you can smear it on everybody's temples, and on their sacred objects. And there are many stories about Trickster taking a shit and just wiping it all over all the most sacred precincts. Does that remind you of any dreams of Jung's? Trickster has an amusing kind of ignorance about the ways of the world, and they say that this conveys something of an awkward and aggressive curiosity in which he moves brazenly from one exploit to the next. In short, he plays all the time.

Freudian scholars tend to interpret Trickster phenomena as very archaic and regressive, childish, undeveloped, having no ego structures— in classical terms, *id* phenomena. The Trickster is the id. And you can see why they might say that, because he's unabashed, he's not ashamed. He's going to do what he wants to do and get into what he wants to get into and he's not going to be too upset. Let's say he doesn't have a particularly strong superego. And the Freudians tend to interpret him in that way as a regressive phenomenon.

Some Jungians see him differently. There's an interesting essay by Jung in Paul Raden's volume on the Trickster. Jung talks about the Trickster as relating a lot to the shadow. He sees it as an expression of shadow dynamics for most people. And certainly I think that is true. But you know, there are a lot of people for whom it's an expression of persona dynamics.

A Trickster type may tend to use a lot of pornography and masturbate a lot. This is the detachment motif. He tends to go off on his own and be private; he tends to do his private thing and sneak his sex in. He's got a sense of his own body, but he cannot consolidate it. He can't really fully occupy this space, because if he could fully occupy this space, he would be very visible. If you have a shame issue, you've got to be able to really get into this space fully to heal your shame issue. You've got to be able

The Trickster enables you to deconstruct all those things that make you pompous, that keep you from cooperating with other human beings for a common task.

—Robert Moore

If you have a compulsive tendency to blush and be embarrassed, you probably need to work on integrating your Trickster more, because he doesn't get so embarrassed so easily.

—Robert Moore

WINGSPAN
INSIDE THE MEN'S
MOVEMENT

to appear, you've got to be able to get naked and stand in front of your
full-length mirror and say, yeah, you're wonderful. Try that.

———————————

I like to say to groups of men in not so polite company that the Trickster
is your "bullshit indicator." If you have trouble being able to see through
the Jim Joneses of your environment—and if you find a guru who's got
all the answers and has come up with all the right mythological perspectives, the new Theosophy, the new truth, the four quadrants—see, you
need your bullshit indicator to say, "I just don't get this shit." Fine, your
Trickster is working.

    Fundamentalisms are very dangerous in our world today and they are
getting very strong. In other words, if we don't support the Trickster
worldwide now in a constructive way, we're going to have a terrible
impasse like the one we have in Jerusalem as the fundamentalist Christians and Jews and the fundamentalist Muslims get more and more heavily armed and less and less tolerant of each other.

    If you don't have a lot of Coyote energy in the world, pretty soon
we're going to likely have some nuclear shoot-outs between fundies of
different persuasions. It's true in nationalism, but the place where we're
seeing it in the world is a resurgence of militant religious fundamental-
ism of all kinds. And it's not just limited to us people of the Book, you
know, the Jews and the Muslims and the Christians. You run into the
fundamentalist Buddhists and the fundamentalist Hindus, even fundamentalist Native American types. And you'll run into the people who
have had their initiation from such and such a mescalero shaman and
now they're going to give you the vision quest, the right one, and you will
be enlightened, and they'll take you down to the sun dance and whatever.

———————————

You have to ask yourself, Where do I tend to be credulous? Where do I
tend to overidealize systems of thought, psychologies, schools of psychology? All the psychoanalytic schools of thought tend not to have
enough Trickster when it comes to themselves. And they tend to be
overappreciative of the uniqueness and once-and-for-allness of their contribution. In your religious life it's pretty important to take a pulse on
this. There are a lot of people who, because of a credulous commitment
to their religious system, really cause themselves enormous difficulties
in living. So that would be one place to take a pulse: Does the Trickster
enable me to have appropriate constructive irreverence? And that's true
of cultural forms, theories, ideologies, religions, political commitments,
even your social justice commitments. You've got to be careful about
credulous mythologizing of your own particular ideological social justice
favorite issue, because it may be the place of a very hard to see inflation,
and one that needs to be balanced in some way by some good totally
selfish egotistical hell-raising.

You can almost always tell a person for whom the Trickster is on full automatic, because they make a lot of starts, but they can't get very far before the ground they were trying to stand on disintegrates, and then they will start again on something else, and that will disintegrate, and they'll start on something else. And it could be relationships, it can be jobs, it can be careers, it can be religious commitments. You know, somebody whose Trickster is on full automatic may serially debunk 14 fundamentalist cults.

If you have a friend who is a very, very cynical individual, his Trickster is on automatic. And you can ask him to tell you about the men he admires. And if he cannot list his masculine saints who function for him in his life as an important resource of masculine self-objects, then his

Trickster is on pretty full automatic, because he cannot admire men. You show me a man who has no men he admires, I'll show you a man whose Trickster is running over all the time.

You need a pantheon that represents what Jung would call the *pleroma*. We need feminine and masculine sets of saints, but I'm talking now especially in terms of your own gender identity . . . about forming up your mature masculine self, or your mature feminine self. It's very important to have figures that you bring in to solidify your gender identity. And for a guy who has got a lot of overloaded Trickster stuff, a lot of the time he's been so abused by men that he cannot imagine admiring a man. They're all sadistic killers. They're all abusers. And you have to help that type of man work on understanding that not all men are sadistic abusers. Some men are very vulnerable to sadistic abusers. A man who has been abused a lot by men will have a hard time idealizing or admiring any men.

Jung points out that the Trickster and the Shaman are very closely related, and in some ways may be the same. But a lot of other scholars say that the Trickster may have been in opposition to Shaman Priest, who was serving the God of Order. The Shaman Priest will try to be powerful through placating the High God, by obeying or doing rituals or sacrifices to it, whereas the Trickster will figure out how to get what he wants without placating the High God.

—Robert Moore

ROGER KOSE

VISUAL POEMS OF THE DREAMTIME

BY TOM DE MERS

S HAPED BY different continents, cultures, and religions, and assembled in the dreamtime of his imagination, Roger Kose's photographs are best seen in light of the

borders he has crossed and the divisions he encompasses within himself.

The son of missionary parents, Kose spent the first 18 years of his life in India, returning to the United States to attend college. Men's

Excerpted from the *Men's Council Journal* 11, November 1991.

WINGSPAN
INSIDE THE MEN'S
MOVEMENT

councils and ritual, drawn from many traditions, became part of his experience in Boulder, Colorado, many worlds away from his Asian childhood. These geographic and cultural realities come together in his work, giving it a distinct otherworldly character that is not there by accident, or is perhaps the accident by which his photos find their particular distinction.

Take the hooded figures as one example. "The robed figures come from my childhood," he says. "Indian men dress in shawls, not all Indian men but the farmers and peasants who live close to the land. They are solid men— at least that's how I see them—simple men who are kind and gracious and long suffering."

Kose remembers these men from his boarding school days in the Himalayas. They embody a shamanic quality, the deep wisdom of men who have acquired and share spiritual gifts. In his pictures they appear as initiators or as contemplative elements in a natural setting.

Like the robed figures, the simplicity of earth appeals to Kose. "I don't see my photos as archetypes but as being about the elements: earth, air, fire, and water. Earth is what you see the most because that is my element; trees, stone, mud, that is where I am."

While he insists the photos are made without a viewer in mind, he also sees them as "cracks into the dreamtime," openings through which people can grasp the essence of men and men's ritual. The images thus aspire beyond the visual to an experience the viewer is invited to have with the ritual moment—the "inscape" of the male soul, to borrow a term from poetry.

"The audience is getting a look into the space we access when we are dancing or doing men's ritual," he says, "a place that is preverbal, a place where definition and ideas are meaningless. A place where we

DE MERS
ROGER KOSE

195

know. A crack opens and a blinding light flares up. That is a place of knowing and being. That is the mystical experience, a place of absolute gnosis and complete connection. Such a place exists for me in the middle of the ceremony when it's not words anymore."

DE MERS
ROGER KOSE

The vision of man in nature, in meditation, or in ecstasy is for Kose a unity binding the multicoastal shifts of his experience. It is at once Calcutta and Lakota, mystical and technological, Christian and Hindu, for himself alone and for the viewer's mysterious tumble into the unknown. In all, a unity contoured by the significant fractures it overlays.

V

CEREMONIES
Body and Soul Work

SACRED CEREMONY
OR "GOOFY CIRCUS"?

For some men who have only heard about the movement but not actually experienced it, one of the most off-putting aspects is the notion that participation involves getting involved with strange rites and ceremonies. For starters, the vast majority of men's events consist entirely of a bunch of guys sitting around and talking. But the media prefers to concentrate on those few activities that will shock Middle America. Reactions to all-male ceremonies range from politically correct indignation ("No reason is good enough to justify excluding women from any activity in our society!") to derision ("You won't catch me painting my body blue and running naked through the woods!").

Like most misconceptions, suspicion of men's rites is based on lack of information. In contrast to the women's movement, which has been eager to air grievances and get the media's attention, the men's movement is only reluctantly being coaxed into the public eye. Except for the "Wild Man weekends" led by Marvin Allen, who has been eager for publicity, most men's groups absolutely ban the presence of the television cameras and are ambivalent about allowing male reporters to write about their events.

The reasons for this desire for privacy are many. In order to create the safe container necessary to invite men to speak from the heart, the participants must feel sure that the strictest confidentiality will be observed. The phenomenal success of 12-step programs like Alcoholics Anonymous depends on this guarantee of confidentiality. The presence of a member of the press or the whiff of suspicion that a man's painful secrets will end up in the paper or just spread around the office is enough to keep most men shut clam tight.

At an even deeper level, men's work involves the sacred. Many people who have no real feeling for or concept of the sacred perceive some men's activities as "crazy" or "funny." These outsiders don't take seriously participants' willingness to explore and learn from unfamiliar spiritual traditions and ideas.

Critics of the men's movement use the sketchy information they glean about men's rites to mock ceremonies as "contrived" or pointlessly mimicking long outmoded behaviors. They see all this ceremony mania as merely a sign of nostalgia for primordial perfection and vitality that never was, or a reaction against the suit-and-tie constraints of civilization.

Critics of men's exploration of primitive rituals overlook the possibility that there is power and efficacy in these ceremonies. One of the reasons some Native Americans disapprove of untrained white men's simulations of their ceremonies is that these men actually endanger themselves physically, psychically, and spiritually by monkeying with forces that they don't comprehend.

Many of us are surprised at the hostility with which the press derides our good-natured, well-intentioned exploration of ritual. *Time* magazine's Lance Morrow lashed out in a profile of Robert Bly in its August 19, 1991 issue.

> Bly may not be alive to certain absurdities in the men's movement that others see. Ask him about the drumming, for example, which strikes some as a silly, self-conscious attempt at manly authenticity, almost a satire of the hairy chested, and he pours forth a thoughtful but technical answer: 'The drum honors the body as opposed to the mind, and that is helpful. It heats up the space where we are.' As a spiritual showman (shaman), Bly seeks to produce certain effects. He is good at them. He could not begin to see the men's movement, and his place in it, as a depthless happening in the goofy circus of America. It is odd that Bly is not more put off by the earnest vulgarity of the enterprise.

Maverick philosopher and *L.A. Weekly* columnist Michael Ventura admitted to *Time* that "some of it may look silly, but if you're afraid of looking silly, everything stops right there. In our society, men have to be contained and sure of themselves. Well, fuck that. That's not the way we feel. The male mystery is the part of us that wants to explore, that isn't afraid of the dark, that lights a fire and dances around it."

Dr. John Weir Perry commented on this subject in an interview conducted by Forrest Craver for *Wingspan*™. "It's easy and cheap to poke fun at ritual process involving drumming, chanting, etc. But the point is to break out of the common, conventional, anesthetizing mode of life where the culture is putting us to sleep for its own purposes and to regulate our behavior. To break out and do something wholly different carries us back to the archaic man inside us."

This exploration of "liminal space," says Perry, "however innocent or even ineffectual, always looks dangerous to conventional people. Or silly because it is not wedded to the status quo. Or even feared because it carries within itself the seeds of change and revolutionary thought. The dominant group in any culture wants to preserve everything as it is and will caricature and make comic anything coming from outside the cultural mainstream."

Reading the accounts of the rituals and the body and soul work in this section should allay doubts about the nature of these activities and possibly whet the appetite to participate in them. *

RITUAL IN MEN'S GROUPS

BY BILL KAUTH

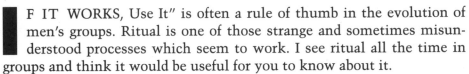

Some men who in their youth felt alienated from the rituals in their church or temple hesitate to incorporate rituals in their regular men's work, feeling that ceremony is artificial, empty, or too formal for the brotherly tone they seek to evoke in their gatherings. Actually, conscious ritual is one of the speediest and simplest ways of bringing men together. The following chapter from *A Circle of Men* (St. Martin's Press, 1992), the most comprehensive handbook on creating and sustaining a men's support group, outlines the basic concepts.

Kauth is a cofounder of the highly popular New Warrior Training Adventure Weekend and associated programs. He may be contacted at:

New Warrior, Inc.
4913 North Newhall St.
Milwaukee, WI 53217
(414) 964-6656. ✍

"IF IT WORKS, Use It" is often a rule of thumb in the evolution of men's groups. Ritual is one of those strange and sometimes misunderstood processes which seem to work. I see ritual all the time in groups and think it would be useful for you to know about it.

What is a ritual?: The briefest definition I've heard is, Ritual is anything that worked once and got repeated. Our lives are full of rituals that we do day in and day out. Sometimes they are functional. In other cases, if we asked, we would be hard pressed to say why we do them.

A more formal definition: Ritual is any repetitive practice or procedure done as a rite. Rites are ceremonial, formal acts or procedures prescribed by custom. Most of what we do every day is prescribed by, and an enactment of, the mythology of some social, religious, or family custom. Shopping is rooted in the myth of consumerism. What time we get up, brush our teeth, have coffee in the morning, what we eat for breakfast, whether we pray before the meal, read the paper, hug (or not) the kids, kiss (or not) our wife good-bye, they all once served some function based on some belief or mythology.

Ritual is everywhere. One of which we as men will all be aware is the social rite of courtship. We all know about the carefully prescribed dating steps and procedures we have been dealing with since we were in high school. Warren Farrell in his 1986 book *Why Men Are the Way They Are* talks about the unspoken ritualized process of taking sexual initiative with women. He points out that we men "risk rejection about 150 times between eye contact and sexual contact." Why we take all the risk is rooted in myths about men and women; your group may want to talk about them sometime. Meanwhile let's consider types of rituals.

Social Ritual

They are, as suggested by the examples above, functional. There is something comforting about everyday rituals. They do not have to be thought about or re-created each time. There is a sense of belonging built into some social rituals, a feeling of identification with the culture, religion, or family from which the ritual evolved. Other social rituals form a code of behavior which, although unspoken, provides safety for people who are strangers to each other.

Ceremonial Ritual

Formal rituals serve as transformers for powerful archetypal energy. This is the energy of transformation, of changing consciousness from one state of being to another. The most obvious in our men's work is the transition from boyhood to manhood. Historically, most groups or tribes had awareness of such a process and honored it through some ritual, a rite of passage.

The ceremony (ritual) was a safe space in which the transformation could happen. I think it is important to note for my fellow linear-thinking men that I'm talking about intuitive process here. We "know" it and honor it, whether it makes logical sense or not.

These ideas are rooted in C. G. Jung's concept of the 2-million-year-old man who lives in each of us. It is the energy we share just by being human males. It is accessible to us through our genetic coding and/or our connection to the "collective unconscious." Jungian analyst Robert Moore has suggested that the archetypal energy is so powerful that to attempt to access it without going through the ritual transformer would be like plugging a toaster directly into a nuclear power plant. So let us use this energy with awareness and all due respect.

PURPOSE OF RITUALS IN MEN'S GROUPS

We use ceremonial ritual to bring us together with shared intention and focus, to mutually create the safety necessary for change to happen, to enact a certain mythology and sometimes to create an altered state of consciousness. You may notice that rituals are connected with one or more of our senses, which grounds them in our physical reality. Some examples:

1. **Opening:** A repetitive process which offers consistency, group focus, and bonding.
2. **Smudging:** The use of smudge sticks (sage and cedar bound together) burned in a symbolic cleansing. It is a ritual washing away the cares of the day, the negative energies. This is borrowed from our Native American brothers. It is excellent nonlinear thought preparation for being together.
3. **Chanting:** The blending of voices in a sound (*om, aum, ram*), a phrase, or a song (we found doing the old hymn "Amen" with an emphasis on the "men" part of it is great fun in men's groups). This brings the energies of the men together. Chanting, by the nature of

Traditions of the Royal Navy? I'll give you traditions of the Navy: rum, buggery, and the lash!
—Winston Churchill

the vibrations it creates, can also alter consciousness. There is an inner peacefulness that often accompanies the process of vibrating in harmony with others.

4. **Spirit chair:** A symbolic honoring and modeling of men who live in our awareness. In the New Warrior groups we sometimes bring in the "spirit" of a Warrior. He is a (now dead) man deeply committed to something worthwhile, whom we admired. In my own group of executives we bring in a King spirit. He then sits with us (sometime in a separate "empty" chair) during the meeting as a presence we can emulate. We gratefully send him back when we are done. The "bringing the spirit in" part of the ritual involves standing in a close circle with our right hands in the air and starting with a loud sound which becomes soft as we bring our hands down together in the middle of the group. Implying, he is here with us now.

Smudging ceremony

The "sending him back" ritual is the reverse. Hands down in middle, soft sound building and exploding out loudly as we throw our hands skyward, implying that he has gone back. It's a great way to end each meeting. (Some examples of men whose spirits we have invited to sit with us have included Gandhi, Abraham Lincoln, John Lennon, and Martin Luther King.)

5. **Drumming:** It seems that many groups across North America are using the ancient ritual of drumming to create the desired sacred space in which to do their work. Drumming can be used to open the group, close it, or both. The vibrations of this ritual are so powerful that you and your group might want to invest time in making your own drums or money in buying some fine-quality drums. You might also seek out a man to teach you some drumming techniques.

Please appreciate the ancient power of drumming.

6. **Talking Stick**: The stick itself,

often decorated with feathers and fur, is a ritual object with specific meaning. Borrowed from our Native American brothers, the talking stick represents respecting a man speaking from his heart. All listen to the man holding the stick. Sometimes a man takes the stick when he feels moved to speak, in order to be sure he is heard. At other times it is ceremonially passed around the circle.

7. **Closing ritual:** This could be gathering the group in a circle arm in arm, chanting, hugging, or reading a passage from which everyone takes inspiration. Whatever your group creates as its closing ritual, it is repeated consistently and signifies the end of that meeting.

8. **Make up your own**: Once you get a sense of needing a ritual for a specific purpose, make a suggestion about what might work or, better yet, ask your group for ideas about a ritual to serve the purpose. When the group is in consensus, try it out. If it worked once it may work again. Then, by trying innovations that may work even better, you can let your rituals evolve.

Some ritual men's groups exist with mythology as their primary focus. These are known as ritual groups and they take on the challenge of creating their own spiritual experiences. As your group matures, you may want to do more transformational ritual processes. If your group is ready and/or interested, I recommend Wayne Liebman's book, *Tending the Fire: The Ritual Men's Group* (Ally Press, 1991).

THE VOICE OF THE DRUM

BY GEORGE A. PARKS

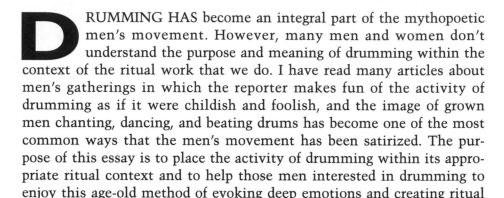

BOYS LIKE NOISE. That's a simple explanation of why so many of our men's events incorporate drumming, the most basic link we have with males of all other cultures and all other times. Little boys love to wallop pots and pans. Chimps in the Budongo Forest in Africa make and beat clay drums for long nighttime sessions.

We men often begin drumming somewhat reluctantly, and then only because all the other guys are doing it, but soon we discover how slapping those skins is a wonderful community builder, a form of prayer and poetry, an inhibition-loosener and blood-rouser that gets all our hearts beating in sync. ✒

DRUMMING HAS become an integral part of the mythopoetic men's movement. However, many men and women don't understand the purpose and meaning of drumming within the context of the ritual work that we do. I have read many articles about men's gatherings in which the reporter makes fun of the activity of drumming as if it were childish and foolish, and the image of grown men chanting, dancing, and beating drums has become one of the most common ways that the men's movement has been satirized. The purpose of this essay is to place the activity of drumming within its appropriate ritual context and to help those men interested in drumming to enjoy this age-old method of evoking deep emotions and creating ritual time and space through the pulsing rhythms of a community of drums.

My first experience with drumming at a men's gathering occurred about six years ago when the men attending the Men's Wisdom Council of Seattle asked Robert A. Carlson and me if they could start bringing drums to our meetings. The Men's Wisdom Council of Seattle is a monthly gathering of men that Robert and I started in April of 1986. At first we had presenters who spoke to a group, with some questions and discussion following the talks, but we soon learned that the statements from the hearts of the men in the "audience" were far more powerful and honest than the prepared presentations of the speakers.

Gradually, our meetings evolved into a talking circle or council in which men simply spoke about a specific theme we had agreed to explore that day. These meetings were inspiring and meaningful, but when we began to drum, the energy of our gatherings increased and the quality of the personal statements seemed to deepen. The drumming also seemed to create a sense of brotherhood and community that made men feel more at home and members of the same tribe.

Soon, drumming was a routine event which opened every gathering. It was a gradual evolution of ritual process that occurred without specific direction from the facilitators or in response to any mode of how to do it. However, it appears that our experience is far from unique, as drumming has become a key element in almost every gathering of men across the United States. As Tom Daly writes in the spring 1991 edition of *Wingspan*, "In my own lodge nothing brings us together faster and more effectively than drumming. The drum is like having a magical being among us. When used by council brothers for sacred ritual, the drum takes us out of the cultural trance and connects us with the earth, our communities and our own hearts and souls."

As the number of men attending the wisdom council grew from about 40 to over 100, and is now approaching 300, the strength and power of the drumming has increased. More and more men are bringing conga drums, hand drums, snare drums, rattles, sticks, pots and pans, anything that can be used to make music together. We have never had any instruction in how to drum nor have we ever discussed why we drum. And yet, over time I have noticed how the drumming is a threshold forming a bridge between the ordinary space and time of the world outside of our gathering and the ritual space and time we seek to create for our sacred talking.

Even without instruction, as we begin to drum, the uneven sounds start to synchronize and within a few minutes it sounds like a group of musicians who are playing a communal composition that no one person is conducting and that everyone feels a part of. The feedback that Robert Carlson, Roj Easterbrooks, and I are receiving as facilitators of the council is that men enjoy the drumming more and more as time goes on and for some of us, it has an amazing power to transport us into states of feeling that would be impossible without the vehicle of the drum. Of course, not every man drums and not every man appreciates or even likes the drumming, but most of us feel it is an essential part of our meetings.

As time passed, we in the Northwest were exposed to our first day for men featuring Michael Meade and Robert Bly and my experience with drumming took on a whole new dimension. The event was held in December of 1987 in a large auditorium on the Seattle University campus. As I approached the building, I could hear the drums from a hundred yards away. It felt exciting and maybe even a little scary to hear the rhythmic pounding of drums as I registered for the event. I was directed to enter the auditorium through a door located to the left near the stage. The doorway was covered with evergreen tree boughs and in order to enter the room, I had to bend down and almost crawl. As I raised up to walk upright again, I was greeted by the sound of at least 25 conga drums being played by men who were seated on both sides of me forming a channel which extended the portal of tree boughs into the room. Several men had already arrived and were standing in front of their seats clapping their hands, swaying to the drum beat, or standing there, a little stiff, as if they might have been thinking, What the hell is this drumming all about?

Me, I was exhilarated! The beat was intense and the men who were drumming looked so confident and some of them seemed entranced by the rhythm and the shared experience of drumming. I watched as hundreds of men entered the room as I had done to the welcoming, even enticing sounds of the drumming. Before long there were over 700 of us facing the stage, which was also decorated with tree boughs, some of which had masks hanging in the branches. It was a primal feeling of excitement, high energy, and a deep sense of community with my brothers that I had never felt before.

Soon, both Michael Meade and Robert Bly entered the room in the same way as others had done. Robert took a seat among the drummers and began to play while Michael hit some Ago go bells with a stick, creating a counterpoint to the deep rhythm of the conga drums. After a few more minutes of drumming, Michael hit the bells to signal the drumming to stop and the men in the room responded with a loud and spontaneous cheer which broke into appreciative applause when Robert Bly said, "Let's thank the drummers!"

After the intensity of the drumming, I felt alert and alive and ready for the program ahead. I looked around the room and the community of men gathered there seemed particularly together, joyful, and eager to experience the activities that Michael and Robert had planned for us.

Michael was seated next to Robert on the stage and had a drum in front of him which resembled the congas, but which I later learned from its maker, Brad Davis, was called a "tacked head storytelling drum." It was somewhat shorter than the congas and instead of a metal rim around the head with bolts which are used to adjust the tone, the head was tacked to the drum barrel with nails and its tone was dependent on temperature and moisture. Michael Meade explained that he was going to tell a story accompanying himself with the drum. He told us a tale about a hunter and his son which he said originated in Africa. Michael is a master drummer and storyteller as well as a mythologist well versed in the mythic traditions of a variety of cultures. As he began to drum and to tell the story, the attention in the room was focused on his every word. Hundreds of men were transfixed by the rhythms of the drumming and the evocative images and plot of the story of a hunter, his son, and the conflict created between them. Eventually, the story came to an end with the dilemma of the son, which was given to every man in the audience: to choose between loyalty to the father and loyalty to the king.

I had heard the drum used in this way before. I was so taken with the story accompanied by the drumming that the boundary between imagination and reality began to melt. It seemed to me that nearly every man there was moved as much as I was by the power of the drum and the images in the story to take us to the realms of consciousness beyond those that could be realized without the power of the drumming.

Mickey Hart in his publication *Drumming at the Edge of Magic: A Journey into the Spirit of Percussion*, describes the ability of the drum to induce trancelike states as "entrainment." Hart discusses how the repetitive sounds of drumming create rhythms which profoundly affect the body, especially the brain, to create altered states of consciousness. He says, "If the rhythm is right, you feel it with all your senses; it's in your mind, your body, in both places. Get a group of musicians vibrating harmoniously together and you have one of the most powerful emotional experiences on the planet, one that would be impossible if we hadn't evolved the conscious ability to entrain ourselves rhythmically." Drumming as an accompaniment to storytelling or drumming in a community of men seems to have this power to entrain, to connect us with deeper rhythms in our bodies and souls, and to create a certain musical magic that men seem to enjoy.

In the winter following this day for men the first Northwest Conference for Men was held. Michael Meade and Robert Bly were the teachers for this gathering, which was held north of Seattle in the woods near a small lake. It was at this event that I had my first instruction in drumming, where I first experienced the power and beauty of a South American musical form called the samba. Michael Meade taught each clan of men within the conference to create a full spectrum of harmonious rhythms by combining three different beats with several men drumming in an organized, structured way. This was very different from the almost random drumming I was used to at the Men's Wisdom Council which always eventually settled into a synchronized rhythm. In the samba, each group of men plays a specific beat and when you combine these beats on time, the result is music.

The first beat of the samba forming the foundation of the rhythm is the grandfather beat, which consists of two strikes on a drum with bass tones. Michael asked us to imagine old men walking slowly down a path to keep this beat slow and steady. The second beat of the samba is more complex, involving several strikes of the hand on a conga drum with middle tones. Michael asked us to imagine a group of mature men who are working for the community. The last beat of the samba is the most complex of all, with more and faster strikes of the hand on a drum with high tones, creating the lead of the samba. Michael asked us to imagine a group of youths in exuberant play. When a group of men play all three beats in the right timing, the rich and moving sound of the samba is created. Michael was an exceptional teacher, giving clear instructions and having the patience to practice it again and again until we were all amazed at our ability to make music together.

The purpose of learning to drum the samba was to provide the music for an event called Carnival, which occurred on the last night of the conference. We made costumes and wore masks and the atmosphere was

The most persistent sound which reverberates through men's history is the beating of war drums.

—Arthur Koestler, *Janus*

similar to the festival of Mardi Gras. Groups of men took turns playing the samba as the rest of us listened or danced to the rhythm. It created a great sense of joy and revelry in our community. Sometimes, one group of men would play intensely for 20 minutes or more and it was really fun whether you were drumming, listening, or dancing.

The drums we used in the samba are usually called conga drums, but I have learned that the conga is actually just one of a group of cone-shaped drums called tumba doras. There are three drums in the tumba dora family: the tumba, the conga, and the quinto. The tumba holds the bottom beat and has the largest head and the lowest pitch; the conga is in the middle and is the most common drum I have seen at gatherings of men except maybe various types of hand drums; the quinto is the lead drum, with the smallest head diameter and the highest pitch. I'm surprised how many men own drums of this type, because they are relatively expensive, but they are powerful and a good investment if you want to drum on a long-term basis. Many men also own hand drums, which vary from the Arabic dumbek, which is usually made of clay with a goatskin head, to the Moroccan bandir hoop drum made of wood with a goatskin head, to various round or octagonal drums often inspired by Native American designs and made of wood with cowhide or deerskin heads. I personally own an octagonal hand drum made of cedar with a deerskin

Congas at various stages of completion

head and a beautiful design of the Eagle painted by Olin Lonning, a Tlingit artist from Alaska. Whatever type of drum you choose, nothing deepens one's relationship to drumming like owning your own drum and developing a relationship with one of these percussion instruments.

Brad Davis, a craftsman of fine handmade drums, lives here in the Northwest on Vashon Island. Brad owns a business called B. D. Drums and he sells his drums at men's events. He has been hand making drums for about five years. Brad is intrigued by the rhythms, the pulse, and the heartbeat that the drum can create. He calls his creations, "My idol towers of passion" and he puts his passion and his skill as a craftsman into every drum he makes. He feels that drumming shifts awareness from rational head to intuitive gut, and the pulsations of the drum are in concert with the vibrations of the human body.

I visited Brad at his Vashon Island workshop and saw the process of drum making first-hand. Brad selects the finest wood available and then decides what type of drum to make. After milling the staves down to the appropriate size, the staves are steamed for an hour and then clamped into a form to dry. The staves are trimmed to precisely the correct width and angle necessary to be fitted together to form the barrel of the drum. Then, 24 carefully selected staves are glued together with three coats of glue each and are assembled in a compression-type press to assure a tight joining of the wood.

Twenty-four carefully selected staves receive three coats of glue each. They are assembled in a compression-type press to assure a tight joining of the wood

Brad Davis, who provided the pictures on conga-making, may be contacted at:

B. D. Drums
P.O. Box 211
Vashon, WA 98070
1-800-767-6120.

PARKS
THE VOICE OF
THE DRUM

The drum shell is removed from the press and both ends are trimmed to achieve an absolute parallel between the head of the drum and the foot. This process is done with a specially designed lathe Brad acquired from Benny Sotelo, who made drums called "fat congas" in the 1970s and who Brad consulted during the design phase of his drum making. After the staves are joined and the drum shell is trimmed and sanded, the drum shell is covered with four coats of nontoxic finish outside and one on the inside, and the bottom of the drum is epoxied against moisture and impact. A cowhide drum head is then either tacked to the top of the drum shell or fitted with a metal rim and bolts, making it a tunable head.

Distant drum, sweet music.

—Turkish proverb

Brad Davis told me that "in drumming, a part of me is waking up and in that waking up I discovered my passion and that passion is the world because drumming has the power of connectedness both between people and among parts of ourselves." Brad says that it was the healing power and captivating force of the drum which pulled him through the trial and error of developing the prototype for today's B. D. Drums. My own experience with the drum and drumming has convinced me that whether you buy a drum or make one of your own at a drum-making workshop, get a drum somehow and join us in the community of drummers. As African drummer Babatunde Olatunji said in a *Seattle Times* article, "The evocative power of the drums can be compared to the Trinity; the drum's frame comes from the trunk of a tree, and that tree has a spirit. It is not dead wood. There is also spirit in the animal skin; if there wasn't, it would not produce sound. Those, plus the spirit of the person playing become an irresistible force."

The force of drumming is an important ritual tool for men's gatherings and the voice of the drum is a universal language that we in this culture are just learning to speak and to hear.

DESCENT INTO DRUM TIME
WITH THE SONS OF ORPHEUS

BY BRUCE SILVERMAN

The Sons of Orpheus is a healing community of some 40 men directed by Bruce Silverman. Practicing the arts of drumming and chanting, poetry, dance, and storytelling, the group meets weekly, works on a variety of psycho-spiritual issues, and offers some of its work to the community as a performing troupe of drummer-ritualists. They have appeared at men's gatherings, concert halls, religious ordinations, rain forest demonstrations, and healing conferences, as well as at parades (winning second place in music at the San Francisco "Carnaval"), weddings, and rituals.

Bruce Silverman founded the group in 1987, one and a half years after the birth-death of his first child—a stillborn son named Jacob. Bruce is a drummer-psychotherapist-ritualist who lives in Pleasant Hill, California, with his wife, Audrey, and two daughters, Elana and Naomi.

DARKNESS HAS just begun to descend, and encloses the alcove where three men commence with their task of unloading the drums from the car. On the street directly above them one hears commuters and large trucks; at times the pavement rumbles as though the earth might split open and suck them in.

Yet, even in this formerly industrial cement enclosure, what sounds like crickets or Caribbean tree frogs can be heard chirping a staggered rhythm, as if to announce the onset of a totally different reality—one of darkness and sound, feeling and rhythm, the music of man's grief.

Afro-Brazilian surdo drums—huge metal cylinders—the gourded and colorfully bowed berimbau, bells, shakers, candles, and conga drums get loaded onto the old service elevator, whose single bulb has been burned out for months. The elevator key turns, and for a moment there is complete stillness, followed by the sound of metal grinding and a low groan. Total darkness immerses the men who descend.

An hour later the members begin to arrive. You can see the fear in the darting eyes of the first-timers as they watch the regulars greet and hug each other, chat, and exchange jokes, hellos, fliers, and small talk.

The men gravitate toward the candlelit room, which seems too small for the 20-odd bodies assembling, one wall solid brick, the enclosure bedecked with all of the percussion instruments. The sound of a train smothers the nervous conversation in the room and a single conga drum rhythm is emanating from the group leader:

Doon-doon—doon doon—ke-doon-doon-doon-doon!

A theme and variation on the human heartbeat continues while a circle is formed. Other men set up conga drums and join the leader's rhythm, known as "Samba Caboclo," a traditional Brazilian form which mixes African and Indian elements. As the participants enter the room, now swaying with the sound of four congas, bells, and shakers, hips and shoulders begin to awaken and gyrate, and impromptu dances emerge. The drum has begun to fulfill its age-old task as the medium which transports human beings from one world to another. In this case, the

213

world of work, freeways, and competition gives way to a reality of
ancient sounds, dance, and camaraderie.

Suddenly, the sound stops—the silence evokes a cheer from the
group—they have all arrived—descended into a different time—the
"drum time."

The leader continues—now by himself—a slow, earthy, and respectful cadence which leaves plenty of space for the spoken word. In staccato
fashion, various men "check in": "I'm excited"... "I'm scared"... "I felt
terrible all week, I'm really glad I'm here"... "I got laid last weekend"...
"I've been missing my father, who died four years ago." This man's eyes
get misty but he is not yet ready to release the feelings. Suddenly a body
leaps into the center of the circle and screams! The drum negotiates a
clean break. A few eyes widen but the now undulating circle of men
seem to just swallow up his anger.

The conga drum changes its cadence to a more percussive beat—a
syncopated Haitian riff with more space and an abrupt resolution. The
rhythm evokes the spontaneous grunts and clatters of men at work on
the docks of San Francisco, Marseilles, Lagos, and Cape Town. The bodies mimic the motions of men digging; they grunt in unison to the beat
of the drum as they mime, their shovels tossing their loads into the
"hole" in the center. The leader asks, "What do you want to get rid of?"
Someone yells, "Taxes!" The faces of the new men start to release their
suspicion. A large, jovial-looking man chortles, "My ex-wife." Everyone
laughs. The room has now become transformed into a circular, almost
mechanical work crew that has broken into a spontaneous dance in
order to ease the burden of its labor.

The conga drumbeat is relentless. It presses against the chests of
each man as he takes his turn verbally "unloading." And as the rhythm
and movement blend into a singular entity, one senses a change in the
room; there is a shift in the "material" being thrown into the hole in the
center. What began as complaints about life's externals—taxes, freeways,
and bosses—now moves toward the affairs of men's hearts: betraying
lovers, broken families, estranged children, friends with AIDS, mothers
and fathers facing death, and eventually on to the men's personal striv-
ings and shortcomings, fears and failures.

The mechanical 60-legged monster in the room now has many smiling eyes that reflect the play and excitement present, and many misty
eyes that are touching the grief and pain. The room is hot and moist;
sweat begins to drip; there is a fluidity to the movement as the drum
reaches a new crescendo. Two men break into a spontaneous jig, another
just growls fiercely. The "new" men no longer scan the room self-con-
sciously.

The actual time since the group formed has been less than 30 minutes. But the men have entered a different time, not linear, not horizon-

tal, but circular and vertical, like Alice tumbling downward through a hole in reality. Twenty men—bankers, cooks, carpenters, artists, salesmen, computer programmers—have all begun to traverse the inner jungles and deserts beyond the upper world, where men must perform, work, make money, support their family, and contain and even deny feelings, toward a different reality. These moments have acted as a portal to a lower world, the animal world, the instinctual realm where spirits and ancestors roam, where Orpheus sought Eurydice, his lost love. And on this journey the men carry only drums, shakers, their fear, and the commitment to take risks.

For a couple of hours each Wednesday night in Emeryville, California, barely out of earshot of the waters of the San Francisco Bay, these men become the Sons of Orpheus. Black and white, Asian, Anglo, and Hispanic, Christian and Jew, old and young, gay and straight, married and single, they all become the sons of the Greek hero who sang his grief to both gods and men with such power that the "trees crowded round him" and the rocks were "softened by his notes [and] the very ghosts shed tears."

These men all yearn for the camaraderie and magic which we all for-

merly knew as the fire circle, the male lodge, the elders discussing the Talmud, the whirling dervishes, or the Brazilian Capoeria clubs. For many of these groups, the vehicle of transformation has been the drum.

The conga drum of West Africa, the Native American water drum, the Middle Eastern dumbek, the Afro-Brazilian surdo: the drum which marks time. We enter the magical world—the drum time—where past, present, and future tense no longer lock the arms and hearts of men into a tense and constricted and lonely world. The drum is the ancient unconscious rattle of the bones of our ancestors, who beseech and beckon us with the stories of the hunt, of crossing the great seas on ships, and of their gods and heroes. And yet, drum time is not simply allegorical; its sound is the almost imperceptible rumble which cultures the world over have stumbled upon as a doorway to the psyche.

As Peter Hamel points out in his book *Through Music to the Self*, "This frequency . . . between 1 and 30 Hz . . . is all but inaudible . . . yet the properties and effects of these undertones penetrate right into the unconscious."

Lei Kung—Buddhist God of Thunder

So as we focus upon the transformative components of the acoustics of the drum, we cross into the realm of brain waves, frequencies, and a subject more traditionally associated with psychic transformation: the dreamtime. Here, too, the separateness of the tenses dissolves and the barriers within men (and women) and between men often disappear. The similarity is striking between the so-called drum time, the dream time, and also the "drama time," which are all modes of entry into worlds beyond the normal. It is within this context that we find Jungian and archetypal psychology, mythological exploration, drumming, poetry, and storytelling at the heart of the "mythopoetic men's movement," so called by Dr. Shepherd Bliss, professor of psychology and men's studies at John F. Kennedy University in Orinda, California.

The three words—drum, dream, and drama—raise the question of their etymology. Robert Hoffstein's inquiry into the mystical construction of our language, *The English Alphabet*, tells us that the letter *d* is derived from the Hebrew letter *daleth*, which means door. (The *d* also suggests male qualities: dada for dad and doer, the one moving forward.) The *r* is from the Hebrew *resh* meaning the front of the head, or will. (Hence words like rash and rush, which suggest impulsive movement and heat.) The *r* is used to amplify as in *br-r-r-r* and *gr-r-r-r*. The *m* from the Hebrew *mem* (mom) means water. (A series of *m*'s suggests the hieroglyph for water.) This refers to all waters, the seas and the waters of the womb, where we begin and perhaps return. Consequently, the inner work or soul work of the Sons of Orpheus revolves around this *d-r-m* nexus. The drum time, the dream time, and the drama time all become components of trusting through the new doors of "being" (*d*) moving through the medium of sound and creating heat and alchemical fusion (*r*) and returning to the waters of the primal source, the great mother (*m*). Each of these words is a secret vessel carrying the encoded message which describes the "hero's journey" of mythologist Joseph Campbell. Campbell's hero moves out of his safe world into strange environments (d) with supernatural forces at work. A struggle or heat ensues (*r*), a decisive victory is won and the hero returns home (*m*).

The work of the Sons of Orpheus reflects the role of the drum itself. Since the Industrial Revolution, the sounds and feelings emanating from the "male lodges" of the world have been disrupted. The city, the factory, and the office have pulled men out of the family and apart from each other. The drum has the capacity to puncture the modern work-womb in all of its loneliness and isolation and rebuild the circular male womb which affirms manliness as strength and tenderness—maleness as both pushing out and receiving with open arms. The male womb contains movement as well as firmness of stature, music as well as silence, humor as well as grief, and rhythmic play as well as the cadence of work. Like Orpheus, we can best undertake this journey singing and playing our joy and grief.

The noise of the drum drives out thought; for that very reason, it is the most military of instruments.

—Joseph Joubert, 1842

SILVERMAN
DESCENT INTO
DRUM TIME WITH
THE SONS OF
ORPHEUS

217

EVERY MAN'S STORY, EVERY MAN'S TRUTH

BY JOSEPH JASTRAB

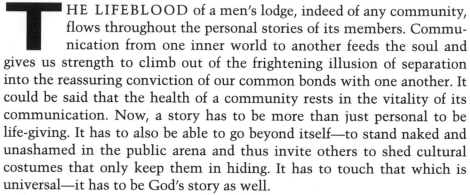

What differentiates a men's council from a bull session? For one thing, the respect and attention men accord whoever is speaking at the moment in the circle. Not only must he strive to speak from his heart, but the others must strive to listen with theirs. In many situations, the natural masculine brand of humor can be an energizing boost to a conversation, but certain deliberations like a talking staff council require that men restrain themselves from cheap shots and easy laughs or even sympathetic expressions of encouragement so as to ensure a safe and sacred container for the man who has the floor. Joseph Jastrab carefully examines the context of the deceptively simple format of the talking stick/staff council in this article, which first appeared in *Wingspan™*.

Joseph Jastrab describes himself as a "facilitator of the inevitable." He can be reached at:

70 Mountain Rest Road
New Paltz, NY 12561
(914) 255-5177

THE LIFEBLOOD of a men's lodge, indeed of any community, flows throughout the personal stories of its members. Communication from one inner world to another feeds the soul and gives us strength to climb out of the frightening illusion of separation into the reassuring conviction of our common bonds with one another. It could be said that the health of a community rests in the vitality of its communication. Now, a story has to be more than just personal to be life-giving. It has to also be able to go beyond itself—to stand naked and unashamed in the public arena and thus invite others to shed cultural costumes that only keep them in hiding. It has to touch that which is universal—it has to be God's story as well.

Many of you have likely participated in groups where the personal sharing rarely went beyond itself. It can be a frustrating and deadening experience and typically the prime cause of premature group dissolution. Information is shared, but it lacks transformational power. The stories go in circles, serving only to reconfirm tellers in well-worn identities. The flame of spirit is smothered, and enthusiasm dies. But let's face it: Most of us were taught to fear our nakedness, our truth. And most of us need support in allowing the God who we are to speak.

And so, societies dedicated to the art of transformational communication will have a form, forum, or ritual container designed to support their members in going beyond themselves, beyond fear, into the naked truth of who they are. The talking staff council is one such form that has arisen in our time from the old root stock of the heart's longing for truth.

ORIGINS OF THE TALKING STAFF

I was introduced to the talking staff way at a 1979 midwinter ceremonial led by Elizabeth and Bob Cogburn. The story of the origins of that staff serves as the best introduction I know to the ways and means of this process. In an article written for the *New Song Village Journal* (Dec. 1985) Bob Cogburn tells of a dispute that arose among himself, Elizabeth, and a friend, Tom. These three had set off to locate a tree that would serve as center pole for a ceremonial scheduled to begin the following day.

"Within minutes after parking our old VW bus in the forest each of us had found the perfect and correct tree to go to the dance. Naturally they were three different trees. While Elizabeth and Tom were debating the merits of their choices I got out the axe and headed off to the tree that I had chosen. But I never got there because Elizabeth and Tom, seeing me walking into the trees with the axe, came running and asked me just what the hell I thought I was doing. We now had a three way disagreement which went on for some time and got rather heated . . . It wasn't only a matter of finding the right tree: somehow we had to get beyond our feelings of resentment, hurt, anger and distrust that all the miscommunication was generating. . . . As I wondered what to do I remembered the opening scene in the 'Anger of Achilles,' Robert Graves's great translation/revisioning of the *Iliad*, which I was reading at the time. It opens with a council of war of the tribes . . . gathered together to try to break the power of the Trojans. There was much disagreement, and a bitter dispute broke out between Achilles, the god-man, and Agamemnon, the king. The dispute was not settled at that council. Nevertheless I remembered a compelling image of the talking staff, a ceremonial staff representing the right to speak and to be heard without interruption."

The passage that Bob refers to is this:

> *By this dry wand no more to sprout*
> *Or put green twigs and foliage out*
> *Since once the hatchet, swinging free,*
> *Cross-chopped it from a mountain tree,*
> *Then trimmed away both leaves and bark—*
> *By this same wand, which men who mark*
> *Ancient traditions praised by Zeus*
> *Have set to honorable use*
> *In ruling their debates: I vow*
> *That all you Greeks assembled now*
> *Before me—mark these words . . .*

"Casting about, I found a dry cedar limb and tied my bandanna to one end. As I started back I saw three fine blue jay feathers and felt they appropriately represented the three of us in our squabbling, so I inserted them in a crack at the top of the staff. Thus I returned with the first talking staff of our new tradition. . . ." Bob goes on to relate that after several rounds of passing the staff there was an opening that occurred that allowed each of them to speak from a position beyond identification with the personal ego. This, in turn, fostered a consensus that emerged from the richness of the conflict, delivering each member of this particular council to a more inclusive level of integrity than before. Unity was served, but not at the expense of diversity.

WHAT IT IS

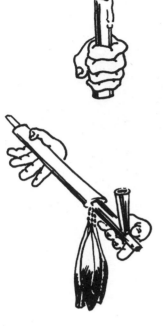

I have experienced talking staff councils successfully woven together with sticks, medicine pipes, rattles, drums, bowls of water, lit candles, eggs, feathers, swords, and stones. The "staff" itself can be any object that can be held and passed from one to another. The only requirement beyond this is that the staff carry transformational significance for the group. By this I mean that it serves as an invitation and encouragement to speak from the most undefended place in the self. The process of carefully choosing a staff prepares the ground that will support the council. Recognize that this is a birthing process that takes time—and is well worth the wait.

A ritual inauguration of the staff before it is used helps to awaken it to the group's resolve and empowers the staff to return authority to where it belongs. "This staff is to be used for _____ ." "May it help us to remember _____ ."

HOW IT CAN BE USED

The following guidelines are some of the bones of this practice. You will undoubtedly discover more as you work with it. The images and practical suggestions are intentionally kept sketchy. Let them engage your creative imagination and presence.

1. It is helpful to designate a council guide(s) who will offer an opening, a closing, and care-take the ritual form. Begin by reminding yourself of your community with all life. Put yourself in good relation with a living cosmos, with the animal, plant, and mineral people of your place. Invite those who have gone before. Feel yourself rooted in a tradition that is older and wiser than your local particular time and space. Feel how old you really are (15 billion to 20 billion years by last estimate). You are about to journey out to sea; the mind is not capable of navigating such a voyage.

2. Remind yourself of the authority and intentions that your group has invested in the talking staff.

3. Present the topic or question that will serve as center pole for the council. Consider that the fundamental question behind them all is, Will you share with yourself, with us, what is in your heart now?

4. Pass the staff around the circle, stating the council question each time the staff is passed. In this way the questions are as important

as the responses. Consider Rilke's counsel "to love the questions and perhaps then we may live into the answers." One pass may be enough, yet there may be times that warrant many passes, or yet further—the commitment to remain in council until there are no more words to speak. Another variation, often called "popcorn style," is to return the staff to center after you speak and allow whoever is ready to burst forth to take up the staff next to continue.

5. You are asked to speak from the heart to the issue that is before the council and to trust that you don't have to say it all at once. Your sharing is medicine ("that which heals") and endless detail dilutes it. Keep it potent by continually returning to, speaking from, the heart. When you receive the staff allow it to carry you beyond reason—let yourself be surprised by what you have to say. One way to facilitate this is to drop the use of the word "I." Let your story begin, and continue, with "He" or "A man who" or perhaps "There is one in this circle who feels." As you speak you can imagine viewing yourself from the perspective of the gods describing what lives within that person. Know also that your "story" may be shared in words, in song, in dance, or in silence—whatever is true for you in the moment that you hold the staff.

6. The one holding the staff is the only one empowered to speak. The rest of the circle is then empowered to listen. At the beginning, the guide may have to quietly remind the group of the commitment to no interruption. Use whatever gesture works. A common exception to this rule is to allow for simple utterings of assent by those who are moved by someone's story, such as, "Ho!," "Amen!," or some other hearty grunt. If the speaker cannot be heard from across the circle, a hand held up to the ear alerts his attention to this.

7. The listeners, or witnesses, are essential to the process. The talking staff council allows us to practice presence in listening. You will experience many reflections of the "other-yourself" as you give yourself over to the council—some of whom you may experience creating a safe world for you, others who seem to create an unsafe world for you. The practice here is not to give yourself over to your reactions, but also not to deny your reactions. Rather, you watch them and take responsibility for them. Sometimes sitting as witness in a talking staff council is an extended practice of hauling in one projection after another. You may find someone carrying your brilliance for you. If so, note what you have given him and look for it inside—take it back. You may find others carrying your darkness for you. If so, note that and take the darkness back as yours. The one holding the staff is your guide into the Mystery. Stalk him, let him take you beyond the borders of comfort and knowing. Let his words and images inhabit your body—and just keep listening. Good luck.

JASTRAB
EVERY MAN'S
STORY, EVERY
MAN'S TRUTH

8. Consider closing the council by honoring the qualities present that helped each man bare his soul, bear his truth. Honor this truth saying as medicine. Dedicate this medicine to serve beyond the immediate circle. Give it away.

TO MEDIATE CONFLICT

The origin story above illustrates how a talking staff can be used to help us navigate through conflict to discover the creativity that waits within. A conflict arises between you and another within the group, and a call is put out for a council wherein each man takes his place in the circle. Each takes a moment to ground himself, remembering that the earth gives equal authority to everyone in the circle. The staff is passed to you. Allowing yourself to feel the commitment to truth embodied in the staff you gaze across the way to the other voices of yourself present—those in accord, those in disagreement. You reflect on your stance: To what degree am I now in fear's counsel, armed against the enemy? To what degree am I willing to walk undefended into what fear describes as a battleground? You see yourself across the circle and speak to him, first honoring the unfulfilled need that brings him into conflict with life (you) and then you speak what is in your heart.

TO REVEAL THE NEW STORY

Times of cultural and personal transition are times when the mythological soil is being turned over. The images, stories, beliefs we have lived are breaking and being turned under. The heart's experience of the pain of all this, when shared in tears, in song, in dance, enters the mythological soil as compost. No grieving the loss of the old? Then dead soil.

The new story is always a garden of great diversity. And the stories of our hopes, dreams, and visions are the seeds that slowly grow this garden. To the extent that these seeds come from who we are emerging, as opposed to who we should be, the new story will be vital enough to guide us with respect and wisdom.

The talking staff council way holds the heart and the creative imagination as honored guests. Each man is respected for his unique contribution to the work in the garden, and as seed bearer. Again and again I find myself returning to recognize that the "real work" of the men's movement is done in the telling of our stories. And forms that honor each man as storyteller, or seed bearer, are essential to this process.

May the talking staff help you remember who you are.

BOXING: A PATH WITH HEART

BY KEN ALBRIGHT

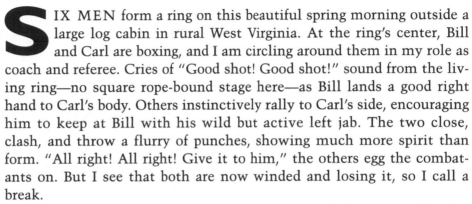

Men yearn to test themselves, and whatever a man's achievements in other areas, he can't help occasionally wondering how he'd fare in a good old one-on-one slugfest. No matter how firmly he believes that fighting is wrong and "proves nothing," every American man has been subjected to so much propaganda that he can't avoid equating, on some level, physical prowess with masculinity. Gestalt therapist Ken Albright has used his own ambiguous feelings about fighting, particularly the "manly art" of boxing, to develop a workshop called The Warrior's Fierceness. It invites men to don gloves and use ritual combat to discover how and why they fight.

Ken Albright can be reached at:

1520 Shughart Road
Carlisle, PA 17013
(717) 243-1882

SIX MEN form a ring on this beautiful spring morning outside a large log cabin in rural West Virginia. At the ring's center, Bill and Carl are boxing, and I am circling around them in my role as coach and referee. Cries of "Good shot! Good shot!" sound from the living ring—no square rope-bound stage here—as Bill lands a good right hand to Carl's body. Others instinctively rally to Carl's side, encouraging him to keep at Bill with his wild but active left jab. The two close, clash, and throw a flurry of punches, showing much more spirit than form. "All right! All right! Give it to him," the others egg the combatants on. But I see that both are now winded and losing it, so I call a break.

In fact, we have been going at it for a good while now on this hot morning, pair after pair trying their stuff at the group's center. We were able to advance more quickly than I had expected on the morning of this first full day of a weekend workshop on The Warrior's Fierceness. We began with some stretching and movement to music, broke spontaneously into some very fierce nose-to-nose growling matches, and then put in about 30 minutes of practice throwing jabs and right crosses to the heavy bag. After that it took only a couple of light rounds of instructional sparring, with me as the punching bag, and the guys were ready to get in the ring with each other. At this beginning level we were punching to the body only and using body protectors that are normally worn by lacrosse goalies. These safeguards helped the men to exchange punches at full force without too much limiting fear of either getting injured or of injuring someone else.

The eight participants at this workshop ranged in age from late twenties to late forties, but there was one old warrior, or elder, in attendance who was 60. It was a diverse group—black and white, straight and gay—of men from varying personal backgrounds. Our elder was a retired military man, and we had a lawyer, a barber, two guys in the computer field, two writers, and a veterinarian. The identity we shared, then, was that of being law-abiding middle-class citizens. Some of the men were

clients of mine (I am a psychotherapist); others I had met through my involvement in the Men's Council of Greater Washington, D.C.

Boxing can be—*is*—scary. We began this workshop Friday evening by talking about our fears of the boxing to come and also about how fears can hold us back in our work and love lives. As for the boxing, there were fears both of getting hit and of hurting someone by hitting him. Interestingly, fears of being overmatched and humiliated predominated over fears of being physically hurt. The workshop created a situation not only in which a man faced an opponent but also in which his performance was observed: This was a performance in a radically masculine mode. In our group discussion and later while talking in pairs, stories emerged of being beaten up as a kid or teenager, of being cowed by intimidation or threats, and of being embarrassed or shamed in front of others in a way that one's masculinity, or masculine pride, was felt to be compromised and damaged. At the same

time, early on, men used ideas and images of themselves as warriors to express hope, confidence, and excitement. They would heal their places of hurt pride and enlarge their self-respect. They would resume the development of the fierce side of themselves, which they had repressed in the interest of being "good boys" and seeking parental and social approval.

I too brought my own sets of fears into this workshop. I had some misgivings about being responsible for bringing a couple of urban middle-class black guys out into "redneck" territory. I had fears about my ability in this workshop: a departure for me away from a strictly therapeutic focus and into a broader venue of men's issues, men's consciousness, male ritual. I didn't want to flop in front of my clients, and I was anxious to make a positive impression on the D.C. Council men, whom I saw as potential friends and allies. On top of all this, I was putting major weight on the boxing, which I had

never before used so extensively or in a
group format. Would it work? Would there be a major division in the group between guys who were really into the boxing and ones who were not?

On the other side, confidence came from knowing that I always get the jitters before a workshop. And I wasn't going completely out on a limb because I had been using boxing as an adjunct to psychotherapy with my male clients for several years, so a few of the workshop participants had already been initiated into the sport. My experience so far had shown me that boxing can be a very powerful experience for men whose path has been that of mental work; they are eager to give it a try and do well with it once they are given an invitation and presented with the equipment.

There is magic in simply putting on a pair of boxing gloves. It is a miniritual in itself, and it takes two to do it. You need a helper to pull the gloves on all the way and to lace them up and tie them for you. There is a good firm feel to the tightly fitting glove whose curled shape forces your hand to form itself toward a fist. Then there is the rich smell of the glove leather—and the atavistic smell of the coming combat.

I enjoy watching what happens when a man puts on the gloves for the first time, or for the first time in a very long time. There is a momentary shy hesitancy and flicker of fear, but by the time the gloves are securely on this reticence is quickly transformed into eagerness. I step back from tying the laces and already the guy is taking his stance, throwing a few tentative jabs, and then the footwork comes automatically into play. Most of us men are boxers: inside our heads, in front of mirrors, against shadows and imaginary opponents.

I am now 48, and I began boxing at age 22 at the YMCA. I had grown up in the country on a farm, and upon graduating from college I moved into Baltimore. There I got in touch with fears of being attacked by another man, or men, on the unfamiliar city streets at night. Such hauntings led me to seek boxing instruction at the nearby Y. The teacher there, Lee Halfpenny—a short, stocky, flattened-nosed old battler—gave us a 5-minute lesson on the basics, worked us out hard for 20 minutes to tire us out some (he didn't want anybody to get knocked out), then paired us off for sparring matches. What I remember clearly to this day is how invigorated, relaxed, and good-tired I felt after these evening boxing

TOP TEN BOXING MOVIES

1. **Body and Soul** (1947) *The definitive boxing film starring John Garfield—even the camera angles are knock-outs.*
2. **The Champ** (1931) *Three-hanky tearjerker about a washed-up prizefighter and his adoring son.*
3. **Gentleman Jim** (1942) *Reportedly Errol Flynn's favorite role—Gentleman Jim Corbett.*
4. **Movie, Movie** (1978) *"Dynamite Hands" segment is a glorious spoof of all boxing pictures.*
5. **On the Waterfront** (1954) *"I could'a been a contenda!"*
6. **Penitentiary** (1979) *Best of three "Penitentiary" films about a young black man boxing his way to respect in prison.*
7. **Raging Bull** (1980) *Robert De Niro achieved an amazing physical transformation to play Jake La Motta.*
8. **Rocky** (1976) *The first and still the best of the five Rocky pictures.*
9. **The Set-Up** (1949) *The only fight film based on a narrative poem!*
10. **Somebody Up There Likes Me** (1956) *Paul Newman plays a not-so-bright Rocky Graziano.*

workouts and how comfortable I would feel on the city streets as I walked back to my apartment. My confidence came not from feeling that I could beat someone up if I needed to, but simply from being thoroughly grounded in my body and in my senses. The boxing helped me to feel and own my power. More than that it gave me a sense of sanity which put me magnificently at ease.

Boxing went out of my life in the 1970s, in the decade of the sensitive male. But then in 1984 I met a teacher who ripped away my peacenik mask and revealed to me my more genuine warrior self lurking beneath. As a man entering middle age I took up boxing again and began using it with my clients.

Most of my clients come to me after having put in a day at the office. My basement work space is casual, and I ask them to come dressed so they can do some form of body and/or breath work as needed. More and more, body work has come to include boxing. At first, I will ask a client to work out on the heavy bag so he can connect with his body and get some earthy energy flowing. Part of this workout includes instruction on how to throw punches properly. This exercise quickly enables him to connect with whatever feelings of frustration and anger he may be carrying, and to ventilate these feelings. Part of the workout includes connecting breathing rhythm, sounds, and words to the punches. This approach usually helps a client to quickly cut through a lot of cerebralizing and get to the core of what he needs to work on. Five minutes of hitting and vocalizing can easily be worth half a session of sitting and talking. The hitting also helps men to move beneath their anger to the more guarded feelings of sadness, fear, and pain.

Sometimes I do move from work on the bag into sparring with a client. This encounter can help us to loosen up with each other both physically and effectively. I use the sparring to work directly on fears of conflict, on being stuck in a "nice guy" persona, and on wounds inflicted by other men in the client's life. At the start, this boxing is controlled. I limit the punching to the body, take a defensive role myself, and continue some level of verbal exchange.

As the client gets cooking on his issue, we may well put on protective body and headgear and go at it full tilt for a while. I may take on the antagonistic role of the client's parent, or shadow, or his worst nemesis in life. After a few minutes of fierce boxing we are both drenched in sweat, grounded in our bodies and in our breathing, and opened up to each other in a special way. My sense of this connection is that our energy fields have expanded, touched, and combined to form a sphere that includes us both. It's like that moment at the end of a professional fight when the boxers embrace each other. Suddenly our barriers are down, and we wonder why we keep bothering to put them back up.

Boxing is a celebration of the lost religion of masculinity, all the more trenchant for its being lost.

—Joyce Carol Oates, *Newsweek*

ALBRIGHT
BOXING: A PATH
WITH HEART

But unlike these fighters, we maintain our connection, and our conversation is on target and makes enormous sense. Instead of getting elaborate stories with a lot of the punch left out, I get satisfyingly clear, crisp statements: "I'm mad," "I'm afraid to be honest with my boss," "So this is what it is like to feel alive," "I spend half my life walking around in circles," "When I leave here I'm going to just pick up the phone and call my father," "You seem really human, not so distant; I feel like I can trust you."

Boxing is not by any means the only way to penetrate defenses, but it is one such way and one that seems to have special power and potential for men. Personally, I just like to box. I think that boxing is a great and sadly neglected amateur sport, particularly for white-collar men. But for me, boxing is more than a sport. It is a *path with heart* for me precisely because I do get scared as I take it on more. At times I notice myself resisting using boxing in a session when it seems called for and avoiding opportunities to arrange sparring sessions with friends. In the moment I have a rationalization or good excuse, but later my wisdom tells me that I have avoided touching or stirring something deep, something having to do with rage . . . or is it grief? . . . or is it some great joy? . . . A mystery there. Something I keep circling around, getting closer to.

My trust is that my connection with the Men's Council and with the men's movement will take me where I need to go, with boxing, ritual combat, conflict somehow at the center of it all for me. I experience the process as extraordinarily beautiful. Feeling the support of the Men's Council to begin with, I began to turn some of the guys on to boxing. The response has been very positive. The Warrior's Fierceness workshop went very well. So now I have some sparring partners and a growing list of men who want to learn. This interest pushes me to become a better teacher, work on my conditioning, and ultimately to face my own deeper resistances and conflicts. I feel myself now centered on that journey by which the Wild Man frees himself from his entrapment and isolation, leaves the forest, and becomes a mature warrior, fighting and working out there in the King's realm, side by side with his brother warriors.

VI

CHALLENGES

FRIENDLY FIRE

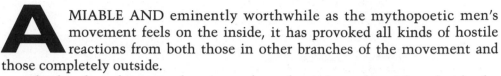

AMIABLE AND eminently worthwhile as the mythopoetic men's movement feels on the inside, it has provoked all kinds of hostile reactions from both those in other branches of the movement and those completely outside.

The harshest language has come from feminists who either deride the movement as regressive and childish or warn that it is a reactionary backlash by frightened men who are intimidated by the progress that powerful women have made in the last 20 years. Robin Morgan, editor in chief of *Ms.*, told *USA Today*, "This movement is at best irrelevant, even hilarious, and at worst an unsettling new form of male bonding." Betty Friedan, author of *The Feminine Mystique*, commented to the *Washington Post*, "Oh God, sick. If I've ever heard a demonstration of threatened macho—this Wild Man thing—I mean, honestly. I'd hoped by now men were strong enough to accept their vulnerability and to be authentic without aping Neanderthal cavemen."

Friedan's reaction is somewhat understandable given that virtually all she has to go on in assessing the men's movement are media accounts that sensationalize and misreport "Wild Man Gatherings," misrepresenting what Bly was talking about in *Iron John*. Lately, feminist celebrities have been refusing to give the press the juicy slams of the men's movement that the media feel are needed for "balanced" coverage.

Men in other branches of the men's movement can be equally critical as women, and their taunts can have more sting because unlike female critics they are likely to have attended mythopoetic events and know what they are talking about. One major criticism of the mythopoetic camp seems to unite the profeminist/gay affirmative men and father's rights/men's rights men, who otherwise disagree on everything else: The mythopoetic movement is self-indulgent, rich white boys playing at cowboys and Indians, wasting time and money that would be much more productively spent advancing either of their (opposing) political and legislative agendas. Male feminists deplore the celebration of traditional masculinity because it runs counter to their campaign to get men to surrender their male power and privilege.

Few such critics understand that retreats allow men time and space to straighten out their thinking and recharge themselves with a sense of mission. Then they are able to go out into the world and get involved with social change. However, unlike their estranged brothers in the two political camps, mythopoetic men do not feel the need to agree with each other or anyone else on what constitutes "enlightened" action; each man finds his own truth.

Mythopoetic men spend a lot of time studying and imitating the spiritual practices of primitive peoples because they have become disenchanted with organized religion. Scholars from traditional churches, however, charge that mythopoets are floundering around, delighted by half-understood exotic traditions and scornful of the faith of their fathers.

Leon J. Podles in a review of *Iron John* for *Crisis: A Journal of Catholic Lay Opinion* praised Bly for this "useful contribution to the analysis of the mythic dimension of maleness." But he went on to deplore: "Unfortunately, his distaste for Christianity prevents him from pursuing the deepest implications of his insights. The Christian can see with the believer in myths that the male is destined by his maleness for bloody sacrifice. From the male animal victims of the Old Testament to the heroic tales of all societies (Gilgamesh, Beowulf, Odysseus), the destiny of the male is to be wounded or slain."

Podles goes on to relate Christ's death to the archetypal journey of the hero who confronts death and conquers it, bringing back a wisdom that enables him to be King. He then faults Bly for not adopting the Christian view that Jesus was a historical being who actually fulfilled what was prefigured in all the myths of other cultures. "Every myth of a dying god, of the warrior hero who faces monsters, of the king who dies to save his people, is fulfilled. . . .

There is really, in history and in eternity, a God-Hero. It is a pity that because of his prejudices Bly cannot follow the golden thread of myth all the way. If followed to the end, it will lead home."

Whether or not Podles is being fair or accurate in his assertions about what Bly's religious beliefs are, it is at least apparent that the discussion of myth and the fate of males is one that calls up an impassioned response from Podles. Some people take myths very seriously.

The selections in this final section are not derogatory or spiteful. Rather, these challenges are issued from clearly identified camps, and their thoughtful objections are not easy to explain away or dismiss. In general, men in the movement are quick to learn and quick to make amends, if they feel that's necessary. We welcome—and need—intelligent, heartfelt criticism. 🖉

THE MYTHOPOETIC MEN'S MOVEMENT
A POLITICAL CRITIQUE
BY HARRY BROD

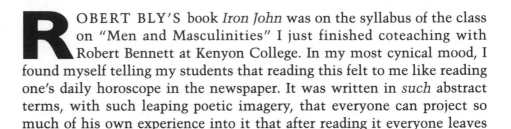

Spokespersons for the profeminist men's movement like Harry Brod, director of the Women's and Gender Studies Program at Kenyon College, disagree with many of the basic tenets of the mythopoetic men's movement and see a remedy for men's malaise in disengaging from the patriarchy.

The following is an excerpt from the opening keynote address at the Sixteenth National Conference on Men and Masculinity, sponsored by the National Organization for Men Against Sexism (NOMAS) and the Tucson Men's Cooperative in Tucson, Arizona, June 6–9, 1991. 🖋

ROBERT BLY'S book *Iron John* was on the syllabus of the class on "Men and Masculinities" I just finished coteaching with Robert Bennett at Kenyon College. In my most cynical mood, I found myself telling my students that reading this felt to me like reading one's daily horoscope in the newspaper. It was written in *such* abstract terms, with such leaping poetic imagery, that everyone can project so much of his own experience into it that after reading it everyone leaves with the feeling "My God, this is talking *exactly* about me."

I know this is unfair to Bly. I am both by professional training and personal temperament a philosopher, and what you may be hearing is simply another enactment of the age-old quarrel between the philosopher and the poet, with me playing Plato to Bly's Homer, the philosopher wanting everything spelled out in neat linear arguments, and the poet resisting this demand. I do want to say that I find much of value in his work. Men are responding to him so enthusiastically because he is talking about things men feel a crying need to talk about, but which no one else is discussing, at least not in a way most men can relate to, and which the culture has not wanted to discuss. He is answering real needs for men to reach out across generations, for men to honor their fathers (though I confess I find myself nostalgic for the biblical formulation, which at least told us to honor our fathers *and mothers*), to have a positive, assertive sense of self, to heal men's grief. I wonder: Who is the audience for this? One segment which seems to be responding to the warrior imagery in the 1990s seems to consist of white, middle-class men who overdosed on sensitivity training in the previous decades. If these men have stopped contemplating their navels and have now reached down to their hairy feet, we may hope that eventually they will reach the ground, and cease being "flying boys," as our mythopoets put it. This does seem to me a positive step. On a similarly positive note, I remind those of you who've been around this movement for a while, and who might be skeptical whether we ever make real progress, that if I had given a talk like this a number of years ago, I would have had to define our right wing by reference to the men's rights movement. Today, they are no longer part of our discourse, they have passed beyond the pale. I am much happier to have mythopoetic groups define our right wing than men's rights groups. The Bly wing does represent progress. He is someone we can wrestle with.

To understand Bly's appeal we need to look more closely at the issue of class. I have a speculation, a gut feeling, for which I have no empirical evidence whatsoever, that he attracts not only middle-class men but, more specifically, a high proportion of middle-class sons of working-class fathers.[1]

Upward mobility in these capitalist United States requires that we turn our backs on our roots, that we psychically disown our families of origin and the work of our fathers. I wonder how much of the quest for the mythic father is fueled by guilt over this venal betrayal of our real fathers, the banishing from sight, sound, and sense of their work and sacrifices, their accents and their smells, in order for the next generation to "make it" and "pass" in these WASP, nonclass-conscious United States. And the elder Minnesota farmer named Robert Bly understands in his gut what these "young, urban professionals" are missing from their lives, and he takes them on weekend camping trips into the woods.

This is not the first time we have seen such a response from men who feel themselves under siege by what they perceive as an increasing and increasingly threatening feminization of their world. Michael Kimmel has analyzed what he calls the masculinist or promale response to feminism a century ago in the United States. Men flocked to fraternal organizations: lodges, fraternities clubs, and the Boy Scouts when it was founded after the turn of the century. I quote from Kimmel: "The reassertion of traditional masculinity resonated with antiurbanism and the reactivated martial ideal that characterized a strain of antimodernist sensibility at the turn of the century."[2] Sometimes one really does get the feeling that there is very little new under the sun.

To move on, there are specific points of mythopoetic practice I would like to address. We are told that the key issue is the lack of personal initiation rites into masculinity. Other older and wiser cultures had such initiations but we lack them. Hence, our problems. A number of things must be said about this. First, we need to look at history through a different lens than the one Bly offers. The history of masculinities, the history of men in families, at work, with each other, must be

[1] This has since been partially confirmed for me in a local study by Michael L. Schwalbe of the Sociology Department at North Carolina State University.
[2] Michael Kimmel, "Men's Responses to Feminism at the Turn of the Century," *Gender & Society* 1:3 (September 1987), 270–271.

told as the history of patriarchy, or it is not truly being told at all. Without that perspective, we are in the presence of myths as falsehood, rather than myth as deep truth. I find an awareness of patriarchy utterly lacking in the story of our past which the mythopoetic movement tells us.

Yes, industrialization separated men from their families. And yes, we miss them. But industrialization was part of another process as well, the process of the institutionalization of patriarchy. In preindustrial societies, patriarchs are men who hold and embody in their own person political, legal, social, economic, and religious power over the other members of their families. But with the shift from preindustrial or precapitalist to capitalist patriarchy, this power is taken out of scattered individual male hands and centralized into more controllable and controlling collective institutions: the state, the market, the military, and so on. Theorists have developed various ways of describing this shift—some speak of it as a transition from private to public patriarchy.[3] I have elsewhere suggested that in referring to this more advanced phase of patriarchy we might speak not of patriarchy as the rule of the fathers, but of fratriarchy, the rule of the brothers, whose sibling rivalry is a form of competitive bonding that still keeps things all in the family of man.[4] So why do men no longer receive personal initiations into manhood in modern societies, and why will there never be such rituals in modern societies no matter how many devotees of mythopoetic practices clamor for them? Because individual manhood is no longer the fundamental site of the exercise of male power. Initiation is always initiation into authority. Today, the most important game in town, the club worth joining, is the depersonalized, institutional recognition of one's manhood. So I say to those who feel a lack of personal empowerment, and who are looking for a rite of male initiation to bestow it, that I have another solution to offer. Join a political movement to overthrow the capitalist patriarchal state, which is taking your power from you only to use it against you, and become empowered.

Something else follows from this analysis of the institutionalization and depersonalization of male power under modern patriarchy, something very relevant to themes I addressed earlier about the importance of listening to men. We need to understand that when we approach men with our theme of "what you need to realize is that you are a powerful patriarch" and they respond with "well, then how come I sure don't feel

---

[3] Carol Brown, "Mothers, Fathers, and Children: From Private to Public Patriarchy," in Lydia Sargent, ed., *Women and Revolution: A Discussion of the Unhappy Marriage of Marxism and Feminism* (South End Press, 1981).

[4] See my "Pornography and the Alienation of Male Sexuality," *Social Theory and Practice* 14:3 (Fall 1988), 265–284. Reprint in Alan Soble, ed., *Philosophy and Sex*, Second Edition (Rowman and Littlefield, 1991), 281–99.

like one? How come I don't seem to have this authority over my own life, let alone anyone else's, that you're telling me I have?"—we need to understand that there's something profoundly right in what they're trying to tell us, something many of us usually don't hear. Given the classical, preindustrial image most people have of the authority real patriarchs had, where a man is the king of his castle, these men are right—they *aren't* personally patriarchs in that sense, though patriarchy and male power as institutions remain just as powerful as ever. But there *is* today a disjunction in men's experience, a contradiction, between the very real facts of their power, which we as a movement are aware of but which are often not visible to men, and the feelings that men *are* aware of, acute feelings of personal disempowerment. We serve no one, we advance no just causes, if the only message we bring to these men is that they're just wrong about their experience of power, or that they're not being honest, or that they suffer false consciousness, or any of the standard arrogant elitist responses those who think they're more enlightened make to those they think less enlightened. Our job is to explain the connection between how men experience their powerlessness but don't experience their power under advanced capitalist patriarchy, and thereby enlist their help in overthrowing this system.

And we need to eliminate the class bias by which we experience other men. Stereotypes of who are the *really* sexist men target working-class men, while middle- and upper-class men appear more "sensitive." But the reality is that working-class people have only their personal power, so they manifest their prejudices personally. But those who hold institutional power let the institutions do it for them. So those who often appear personally "kinder and gentler" are often those who in reality are exercising greater patriarchal power.

The abuse of history by mythopoets becomes even more acute as we move further back into the past, and ancient tribal rituals are invoked as models. First of all, not all imitation is flattery. I have reservations about, for example, the appropriateness of appropriating Native Ameri-

235

can religious ceremonies for purposes quite foreign to their native use. Second, historical and anthropological evidence is invoked in a highly selective fashion. The brutality of many of these initiations, the way they demote women to secondary status, and the way many involve homosexuality, are all ignored. Finally, a more theoretical consideration. My general interpretive framework for understanding the nature of gender is referred to in academic circles as a social constructionist view of gender. It tells me that gender itself is artificial. The process by which we all become engendered is a process of manufactured difference being imposed on us. So any theory which tells us the solution lies either in a new, improved masculinity, or in the recovery of some real or essential manhood, cannot solve the problem, because that theory itself is part of the problem. It solidifies an idea of gender which needs to be dissolved. The question is not *how* we are to be men. Rather, the fundamental violation and violence done to all of us lies in the notion that we must *be* masculine, that masculinity is a goal to be attained.

Mr. Brod sent Robert Bly a copy of his speech. Bly wrote back:

Dear Harry,

Thank you very much for sending me a copy of your speech at the recent Conference on Men and Masculinity. I don't think there are any enormous differences between us, and I certainly wasn't offended by anything you said. Everything needs to be qualified. I thought one point that you brought up was particularly interesting, namely that when culture shifts from precapitalist to capitalist patriarchy, individual men— initiated or not—no longer have personal power. You mention that Carol Brown referred to this as the change from private to public patriarchy. Those are very good phrases.

I have somewhat different images for the same thing, although I developed them after Iron John. I think that the disappearance of the father really means that patriarchy is dead; however that high-altitude multinational corporate system that moves 10,000 feet up into the atmosphere is still alive and well.

You say rightly that initiated men today are not and will not be in a position of power in this multinational airstream. I agree with you. To me that doesn't mean that one should abandon the study of initiation, nor abandon the effort to be initiated in our private lives. Your solution—that we should immediately join a political movement to overthrow the capitalistic patriarchal state—to me is highly naive. It belongs with the other habits of the naive male, such as the belief in Walt Disney game parks.

I don't admire Stoltenberg as much as you do. But I have thought it was probably brave of you in that situation to set down your doubts about him. I certainly agree with you that we don't need one theory of masculinity but several or hundreds.

With good wishes,
Robert Bly

RAPACIOUS NORMALITY

THE WAR BETWEEN THE SEXES

BY SAM KEEN

Sam Keen's ambitious psychological analysis, *Fire in the Belly*, which traced the role of men throughout history, was an impressive success on the best-seller list. In this excerpt from another of his books, *The Face of the Enemy*, he unsparingly attacks the glamour of the warrior archetype.

RAPE IS a necessary part of the ritual of warfare. Whether it happens seldom or often, no war is symbolically won until the enemy is humiliated by the abuse of "his" women. Psychologically speaking, the sexual territory of the enemy must be occupied and possessed. Men will understand neither themselves nor the nature of warfare until the psychological dynamics of *Homo hostilis* are seen clearly.

Let me begin with some statements that may at first seem preposterous. In large measure, war is a form of sexual perversion. The continuing battle between the sexes is abnormal even if practiced by a majority. The violence we regularly visit on the enemy is related to the systematic violence we have first committed on ourselves. The neglected truth, and therefore neglected hope, in a psychological rather than purely political understanding of war will emerge only if we look long and hard at some obvious but ignored elements of the war system.

First. War is a man's game. With very few exceptions, women have never organized or taken part in systematic violence. They have so seldom been warriors that without fear of rebuke we can use the masculine pronoun in discussing the history of war. Women have traditionally been pictured as supporting and nurturing their warriors, and they have entered into the romance of war by considering a man in uniform as especially masculine and desirable. But to the best of our knowledge there have been no matriarchical societies in which women organized mass violence against other societies.

Second. For roughly the last 10,000 to 13,000 years, the male has been socialized and informed primarily by the imperative to become a warrior. During this time we have cultivated reason, inquiry, artistic sensibilities, political skills, technological abilities, and many other capacities. But all the while, in the majority of societies, the male has been conditioned to be willing to kill or to die to defend the tribe or nation against its enemies. The single greatest difference between men and women, other than the obvious biological differences, is that the male

must win the title of "man" by becoming a potential killer, while women retain the luxury of innocence. Almost universally the rites of passage for the male involve some painful ordeal—beatings, hazing, circumcision, fasting, killing an enemy or wild animal—in which the elders teach the young that men must be able to suffer in silence, fight, and be brave. Battle itself is seen as the baptism of fire, a wound as "the red badge of courage." Any man who fails to acquire the martial virtues is considered less than masculine. Phillip Caputo, speaking of the first "firefight" his platoon had in Vietnam, says,

As I moved from one man to the next, I became aware of a subtle difference among them, and I might not have noticed it if I had not known them so intimately. They had taken part in their first action, though a minor one that had lasted only ninety minutes. But their company had killed during those ninety minutes; they had seen violent death for the first time and something of the cruelty combat arouses in men. Before the fire-fight, those marines fit both definitions of the word *infantry*, which means either a "body of soldiers equipped for service on foot," or "infants, boys, youths collectively." The difference was that the second definition could no longer be applied to them. Having received that primary sacrament of war, baptism of fire, their boyhoods were behind them. Neither they nor I thought of it in those terms at the time. We didn't say to ourselves, we've been under fire, we've shed blood, now we're men. We were simply aware, in a way we could not express, that something significant had happened to us.

Third. The warrior psyche is created by a systematic destruction in the male of all "feminine" characteristics. In order to be a good warrior, a man must learn not to cry not to yield to the body's demand for comfort and sensual enjoyment. To fight we must gird up our loins, toughen ourselves, feel no pain, no fear, disregard the will to live, and sacrifice life for the higher good of the tribe. Drill instructors in the marines are following an ancient military tradition when they insult recruits by calling them "sissies," "pussies," or "cunts," in order to try to get them to become good soldiers. Some African tribes surgically remove men's nipples to exorcise all traces of femininity from those who were destined to become warriors. And Gilbert Herdt notes,

The Sambia of New Guinea are typical of warrior societies in their suspicions and repression of the feminine: "A society of warriors tends to

regard women as unkindly, and Sambia attitudes have carried this emphasis to its furthest recess. . . . The rhetoric and ritual of men represents women as polluting inferiors a man should distrust throughout his life. Men hold themselves to be the superiors of women in physique, personality, and social position. Indeed, survival for individual and community alike demands hard, disciplined men as unlike the softness of women as possible. It forms the bedrock on which economics, production, and religious life are based. . . . Men idiomatically refer to women as a distinctively inferior and "darker" species than themselves.

In the patriarchal tradition, which has created the warrior psyche, both the female and the feminine virtues have been degraded. Women and all things feminine must be kept in control. As Nietzsche said, "When you go to a woman do not forget the whip."

Fourth. The sexuality of the warrior is a blend of repressed homosexuality and phallic assertion. A boy is made into a warrior by removing him (usually between the ages 9 and 12) from the influence of women and placing his care and training in the hands of men. Among the Sambia, explicit homosexual rituals are involved. An initiate can become a warrior only by years of ritual fellatio, swallowing the seed of older warriors. Although most groups do not make the homosexual elements of war so obvious, it is just as present. To become a soldier, a man must submit to a superior officer, sacrifice his individuality, be broken in some equivalent of boot camp, identify with the history of military heroes. Within the context of battle, men grow to love each other and often sacrifice themselves to their love. Seemingly, it is only the matrix of violence

ANTIWAR MOVIES

1. **Apocalyse Now** (1979) Nightmarish updating of *The Heart of Darkness* to Vietnam War.
2. **Alice's Restaurant** (1969) Pacifist Arlo Guthrie bumbles through draft physical.
3. **All Quiet on the Western Front** (1930) Early talkie about young German soldiers in WWI.
4. **Born on the Fourth of July** (1989) Gung-ho Marine comes home paralyzed and becomes an antiwar activist.
5. **Casualties of War** (1989) GIs as bad guys, raping and murdering Vietnamese woman.
6. **Catch-22** (1970) At times gory US Air Force farce demolishes the notion of heroism.
7. **Full Metal Jacket** (1987) Dehumanization of basic training and combat conditions.
8. **Grand Illusion** (1937) French classic about French prisoners in WWI German POW camp.
9. **The Killing Fields** (1984) Harrowing depiction of the genocide in Cambodia.
10. **Paths of Glory** (1957) Stanley Kubrick depicts senseless waste of life at Battle of Verdun.

Whatever they may be in public life, whatever their relations with other men, in their relations with women, all men are rapists, and that's all they are. They rape us with their eyes, their laws, and their code.

—Marilyn French,
The Women's Room

that allows the emergence of tenderness in the warrior psyche. John Wayne can cradle a dying man in his arms, even shed a fugitive tear, but cannot touch another man in tenderness without raising the specter of being "queer." So threatening is any overt homosexuality that in 1984 the U.S. military discarded 1,796 homosexuals on whom they had spent $22.5 million to recruit and train. One of the ways in which the warrior covers up his unconscious hostility toward the feminine and his latent homosexuality is by phallic aggression. His penis, instead of being a potential means of expressing tenderness, becomes a tool, a rod, a gun. To have sex with a woman is to "bang her." Gang rape becomes a "gang bang," a ritual of latent homosexual warriors who prove to themselves that they are "real" men by degrading a woman.

Homo hostilis can never be at peace because both the traditional warrior's psyche and the woman's psyche, artificially informed by the myth of war, are socially constructed in such a way as to make intrapsychic conflict and conflict between the sexes inevitable. When society molds men into warriors, it creates a systematic antagonism between the conscious ego ideal and the unconscious or repressed potentialities of both men and women, and artificially polarizes the sexes.

The psychological structure of the traditional warrior and the woman that have thus far been created by the habit of warfare may be summarized as follows:

In the degree that women have recently entered into the public world of business and government and have begun to define themselves as competitors and executives, they have started to take on many of the personality characteristics (and diseases of stress) of the warrior.

But to date, they have remained innocent of the single most important defining activity of the warrior—the systematic education in violence and the willingness to kill. Short of entering fully into the power-violence-killing game, women will not gain equal political and economic power with men and the traditional psychological structures will remain.

The conclusion seems inevitable. Once men have destroyed their own "femininity" in order to mold themselves into warriors, they will inevitably perceive women as a subspecies of the enemy, a threat to their integrity, and will live with civil war within the self, the war between the sexes, and political war between nations. Those who live by the sword perceive all reality, inner and outer, through the metaphor of war.

Recorded human history roughly coincides with the era of *Homo hostilis*. From this we may conclude that human beings are innately hostile, territorial animals. Or we may, after studying the intricate social process necessary to create and sustain the warrior psyche, conclude that we do not yet know very much about the man's psyche. What would the male psyche be like if it were not systematically desensitized, subjected to a taboo on tenderness? What would the female psyche be like if it were not forbidden overt aggression? What kind of psyche would we create by raising children in an atmosphere in which the warfare between sexes was absent? If we ceased to consider the rapacious psyche normal, a new type of man and woman might emerge and for the first time we might know what we were when we were not separated by gender-related, psychic, and political conflict.

THE WARRIOR		THE WOMAN	
EGO IDEAL	SHADOW	EGO IDEAL	SHADOW
Consciously: He is expected to protect, to suffer, to kill, and to die. His body and character are hardened to allow him to fight.	Unconsciously: He is fragile and terrified of his tenderness and mortality.	Consciously: She is expected to inspire, to nurture, to heal. Her body and character are softened to allow her to care.	Unconsciously: She is tough and terrified of her power.
His psyche centers in reason, will. He is spirit, mind.	Moody, lacking skill in dealing with emotion.	Her psyche centers in emotion and sensation. She is nature, body.	Opinionated, lacking skill in disciplined thinking.
He is dominant, cruel, sadistic.	Covertly submissive and passive.	She is submissive, obedient, masochistic.	Covertly manipulative and cruel.
His defining virtue is power.	His controlling fear is impotence.	Her defining virtue is warmth.	Her controlling fear is frigidity.
He strives for independence, self-definition.	He is unconsciously controlled by dependency needs, surrenders to and obeys authority.	She strives for relationship, belonging.	She is unconsciously controlled by rebellious emotions and fears of self-definition and freedom.
He is allowed anger but no tears.	Grief and melancholy cause his depression.	She is allowed tears but no anger.	Resentment and rage cause her depression.
He is supposed to be brave, bold, aggressive.	He represses his fear and shyness.	She is supposed to be fearful, shy, passive.	She represses her boldness and aggression.
His sphere of action is public, political.	He has abandoned the familiar and domestic.	Her sphere of action is private, domestic.	She has abandoned the worldly and political.
He is extroverted, practical, focused, linear, goal oriented; at worst, obsessive and rigid.	He fears feeling, nature, woman, death, all that evades his efforts to control.	She is introverted, intutive, un-focused, cyclical, process oriented; at worst, hysterical and atomic.	She fears abstraction, history, man, power, politics, all that evade the logic of her heart.
As actor he assumes super responsibility and Promethean guilt.	Arrogance and pride shadow his life.	As reactor she becomes victim, blamer, martyr.	Timidity and low self-esteem shadow her life.

MASCULINITY AND SENSE OF COMMUNITY
AN INTERVIEW WITH JAMES HILLMAN
BY FORREST CRAVER

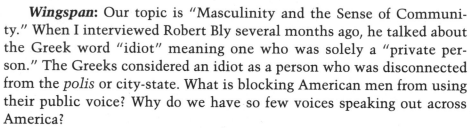

James Hillman is recognized as one of the world's foremost psychologists. Trained as a Jungian analyst in Zurich, Switzerland, he remained there for 10 years as director of studies at the Jung Institute. He is the author of many books, including *Revisioning Psychology, Healing Fiction,* and *Blue Fire.* For the last six years, Hillman has been a leader at national men's conferences, coteaching with Robert Bly, Michael Meade, and others. Bly has described Hillmaan as "the most important psychologist in the world today."

Hillman was interviewed at his home by Forrest Craver, convenor of the North American Masculine Mysteries School and collaborator with Dr. Robert Moore on a series of audio- and videocassettes about the challenges of grassroots masculine leadership in the 1990s. 🖎

The Greek "polis" has come to mean a "sense of community" and is the root of words like police, policy, politics, polity, and metropolis.

Wingspan: Our topic is "Masculinity and the Sense of Community." When I interviewed Robert Bly several months ago, he talked about the Greek word "idiot" meaning one who was solely a "private person." The Greeks considered an idiot as a person who was disconnected from the *polis* or city-state. What is blocking American men from using their public voice? Why do we have so few voices speaking out across America?

Hillman: Your question of why this historical role of men is not being fulfilled goes right to the heart of the matter. I see therapy as one of the reasons why men have not been engaged in the public domain. Psychotherapy emphasizes the private self. For the last 40 years the kind of men who are sensitive, intelligent, and educated have been developing their inner life. They have been engaged in inner work, a process of growth, and self-development, focusing on their feelings and memories. The ideology of therapy has led them away from the questions of public relationships.

Wingspan: Michael Lerner, a psychotherapist, has written a book, *Surplus Powerlessness* (Institute of Labor and Mental Health 1991), in which he puts forth the thesis that the true role of therapy is not only to heal the individual wound but to help the individual see the structural issues that led to his or her wounding.

Hillman: Yes, I think so. Men need the value of being together. They are discovering the benefits of taking part in recovery groups for such problems as overeating, alcohol addiction, going through a divorce, and so on. As we know, they get very bonded in these 12-step programs. They share a "polis feeling" as a group. A community feeling. Unfortunately, the focus is not on the polis or the world out there, or on the social and cultural factors that have brought about their wounding. Instead the focus is on "me" curing my problem and you curing your problem. Recovery groups, instead of turning only inward to explore their members' pasts, looking at their past and their childhoods, their

problems with mothers and fathers, and so on, could also look outward at the social, political, and economic reasons that make work and life unsatisfactory.

Wingspan: The 12-step traditions reflect a "privatization." The traditions strictly oppose endorsing any other groups, products, services, seminars, or books, and reject the idea of seeking promotion or media coverage.

Hillman: That's part of the trouble. These groups sanction and encourage reliance on a higher power, but reject the value of society or social forces.

Wingspan: In the 1960s I think women really helped us with their call to arms: The Personal Is the Political. Their insight is that your choices of how you spend your time, energy, and money, and who you affiliate with, make enormous symbolic statements to your family, your children, and all the people in your community.

Hillman: The women's movement from the 1960s onward made us much more aware that the personal and the political are the same, that *we are the culture!* The culture is *not* outside ourselves. And, therefore, we can't recover by focusing only on ourselves. Our entire culture has to "recover." To give just one example: A man who overeats does so not just because of what happened at the family dinner table years ago. He also overeats because of relentless cultural pressure from agribusiness, food advertising, fast foods, school lunches, salty greasy popcorn, and all the rest of it.

Wingspan: And now with television we have "infomercials," which fall in a gray zone between real programming and long-running advertisements.

Hillman: We are abused and intruded upon and invaded and mishandled not only by TV but by a hundred things in a single day. Our outrage against these abuses is stifled and turned totally and wholly on the child within ourselves so that we have displaced our sense of being victims from where we are *today actually victims*, to the victimization we experienced 30 or 40 years ago.

Wingspan: You have been attacked for saying that the "child within" is overemphasized in the recovery movement. But what I get from reading your books is that you are *not* against recovering and empowering the child within the self. Instead you are against the emasculation of social responsibility that comes if we stay too closely wedded *only* to the child and do not allow the adult self to speak up.

Hillman: According to traditional therapy which says the self must first be reconstituted, people must first have strong egos to handle the problems of their past. Only then, the theory goes, can they enter the political world. Without an intact ego, you are going to have half-baked,

neurotic, disturbed, dysfunctional people running around. And the world already has too much of that. Therefore it is much better that everybody go into therapy, come out of it, and *then* enter the political world. The prevailing notion is that first we have to do this consciousness-raising job with the self.

I challenge that idea. For centuries men have entered the political world without having been in therapy. They entered with their sense of social justice, their sense of wrong, their sense of morality and outrage, their sense of idealism toward the future. Those motives are deeply rooted in a man's soul. Even if you are neurotic, those motives are deep sensitivities in every man. That's one aspect of my challenge. Another aspect is that political awareness and sophistication are not things you learn in therapy at all. You learn that experience from being on committees and sitting in meetings, from the careful reading of propaganda, and from participating.

It is a specialist kind of work to become politically aware. The kind of consciousness you get in therapy is a consciousness of relationships and of differentiating internal feelings, memories, and projections. This perspective is very valuable, but it has nothing to do with politics and action in the world. So the fantasy that you can do therapy first, become conscious, and then enter the world does *not* mean you are going to enter the world any more *politically* conscious. You may be the same political dope you were when you first entered therapy.

Wingspan: I've been astounded over the years by the lack of affiliation and relationship between the great universities and the communities in which they reside geographically. There seems to be a widespread denial or negation of *polis* issues in the way we train our therapists, clergy, and other human service providers. For example, we have hundreds of Jewish, Christian, and other seminaries. But a Southern Methodist University study showed that less than 10 percent of these seminaries had any environmental curricula at all as recently as 1989. No courses equip men and women going into the ministries to deal with what has become the number one global problem, the ecological crisis. Do you see any steps being taken by elders in graduate schools to deal with this kind of shirking of the real-life issues of the *polis*?

Hillman: No, I don't see it at all in the training programs. I see individual therapists being active as citizens. But this has not become part of the theoretical framework of training at all. In fact, when interviewing or supervising trainees or reading patient case reports, I find that almost no questions are asked on the person's political life. Were their fathers red-wing socialists? Blue republicans? Were their mothers politically active? Did they have arguments about politics at the dinner table? What feelings did they have as teenagers about politics and political leaders? Did they vote? Whom did they vote for? None of that comes into the case reports even though there is great detail about patients' sexual lives and their relationships. Nothing indicates that the person is a citizen, a political entity. Nothing to show how the political culture affected the formation of this person's nature at all.

Wingspan: Some observers have noted a collapse of civic-mindedness among the well-educated, well-trained middle class—the very population most able to respond to such chronic problems as education, unemployment, environmental holocaust, racism, and so on. The

A North Carolina men's group serves its community by picking up litter along a one-mile stretch of highway.

HILLMAN,
CRAVER
MASCULINITY
AND SENSE OF
COMMUNITY

League of Women Voters has documented the dramatic slide in voting over the last 30 years. It's really quite alarming that less than 40 percent of eligible Americans voted in the last presidential election.

Hillman: In India there is over 60 percent voter participation. And yet we regard India as an undeveloped nation.

Wingspan: What can be done at the local level, other than moralizing and decrying the problem of *polis* apathy and numbness?

Hillman: I would suggest to men who are already doing men's work and reading *Wingspan* that each men's group or each man sit down and make a list of the five most critical areas that disturb his life. And then find groups or agencies active in those areas. Farm labor groups working on pesticide controls, for example. If it's racism, groups like the NAACP. I'm talking about major public issues affecting the entire nation, not just saving the dolphins. Then, within a group, pledge a certain amount of time, money, and energy to work on these issues. This will galvanize men to join in political action. I see no other way for men in groups to move from their compassionate support of each other unless they face outward.

Wingspan: This is a crucial point because we have various camps within men's work. There are the recovery groups, the mythopoetic groups. Still others view the men's council as a seedbed for social change allowing men to take off from that support base to affiliate locally and work on a social or community issue.

Hillman: I see no conflict at all between any of those three approaches. I think a man can be trapped in any one of them. But from this conversation today, the third aspect of men in the *polis* ought to be moved forward.

Men's role is to bring their feeling, their development in the group, their awareness and honesty into structures that already exist to support the areas of social justice and political vitality. We are limited; we can only focus on certain things. So political sophistication is an art of its own. Joseph Campbell knows about mythopoetic work, but that does not mean he knows anything about cities. Jung and Campbell are not political experts, nor would you study Lyndon Johnson for inner, emotional work. But Johnson was a master of the political craft. We have to realize there is a vast difference in the kind of consciousness that politics offers and the kind of consciousness that therapy and personal inner work offers.

Wingspan: But clearly there is an acute need to bring those two worlds together—the personal and the political.

Hillman: Certainly. And that's one of the things we begin to see in this West Virginia Intercultural Men's Conference that Michael Meade organized which integrates the gifts of European, American, and African

Masculine spirituality emphasizes action over theory, service to the human community over religious discussion, truth-speaking over social graces, and doing justice over looking nice. Without this masculine element, our spirituality in its inwardness will lack the vigor to carry out effective social change.
—Richard Rohr

men with their rich and varied backgrounds. The bringing together of the Jung-Campbell mythopoetic work and the inner city work is achieved in ritual through art, aesthetics, and passion. As Michael Meade says so well, "You can't have compassion unless you start with passion." There are ways of meeting and revitalization. There is no question about that.

Wingspan: So you see events like Earth Day as a way of overcoming our chronic isolation?

Hillman: Yes, but much more is needed. We need more rock stars and movie actors and people like Madonna to speak out and show, as she does, the importance of tolerance, liberty, and freedom of imagination. Outrage against social injustice is very important for leaders in all sectors to show. But the leaders of consciousness, keep in mind, are not necessarily the political leaders.

Wingspan: Yes, certainly many rock stars and movie actors have had enormous impact. Sting, for example, has taken on the rain forest issue. He has been credited even by many mainstream environmental groups with having enormous impact because of the strength of his public persona and the resources he can move into that battle quickly.

Hillman: The stars of the media are the capitalists of the information age. They are the ones who hold immense capital power. Because today capital has to do with influencing the media. It isn't all in the hands of Ted Turner or CBS. And the Japanese recognize that by their purchase of media groups. The media form public opinion. What broke down the Berlin Wall was the Walkman cassette player. Any public figure has the potential for being a leader of the *polis*. That doesn't mean such figures are politically sophisticated, nor does it mean they could actually run a bureaucratic institution.

Wingspan: And where then should we be looking for these leaders?

Hillman: Well, so far it has been in the arts, in the broadest sense of the term. The academics in our universities, with lots of knowledge, need to get out in the streets and take part much more in their communities. It is a pity how they are locked up in their universities. We need intellectuals in the city!

Wingspan: Robert Moore likes to remind us that the key catalyst to this work, Robert Bly, is standing in the lover-poet space. This enormous breaking-loose of men was activated by his kind of energy, not the corporate energy or the bureaucratic energy. Where is our hope as we move through the turbulent 1990s?

Hillman: It lies in the rekindling of men's imaginations, individually and in groups. This calls not only for support for their woundings, but for rekindling their fantasy and imagination and their eagerness to risk and to make a difference. To carry the past with them, to carry knowl-

Following your bliss just seems to me to be the clue to believing what might be called the mythologically inspired life. . . . Those who are fortunate enough to be artists and move into a field that is always involving the life of the imagination are the ones who have the easiest time, but that's not the only way to have your life of bliss.

—Joseph Campbell

HILLMAN, CRAVER
MASCULINITY AND SENSE OF COMMUNITY

edge with them and to be concerned with the future. This is not something new. It is about our doing the right things.

Wingspan: In the tradition of *Wingspan*, we ask you for the challenge you would give to the men of the world engaged in this work.

Hillman: The most important thing you can do as a man is to be loyal to your star. You felt a star as a boy or as a teenager. His wings. The star of the *puer* in your 20s. Be faithful to that. This does not mean being crazy or wild but being faithful to the extremes of your nature, because this will lead you into connections with other men. Respect that. Feel that. Live that. It may be part of your pathology, your freakishness and oddity, but it may also be your most valuable contribution to others and to the world.

BOOKS ON NON-JUNGIAN PSYCHOLOGY FOR MEN

Though the language and theoretical framework of the mythopoetic men's movement is largely derived from the work of Carl Jung and depth psychology, there are some books that use approaches and terminology more familiar to social workers, community therapists, and hospital workers. These educational works promote wider awareness of men's special needs in the counseling professions, which currently cater primarily to women.

Gerald I. Fogel, Frederick M. Lane, and Robert S. Liebert, *The Psychology of Men: New Psychoanalytic Perspectives.* New York: Basic Books, 1986. Thirteen essays, most by psychiatrists on various aspects of male sexuality/psychology. Among the contributions: "Men Who Struggle Against Sentimentality," "Homosexuality in Homosexual and Heterosexual Men" and "Reciprocal Effects of Fathering on Parent and Child."

Richard L. Meth and Robert S. Pasick, eds., *Men in Therapy: The Challenge of Change.* New York: Guilford, 1990. Using examples from popular culture and everyday case histories, this collection of articles by sociologists and therapists review such topics as men's friendships, men and their mothers, men and their fathers, and workaholism.

Dwight Moore and Fred Leafgren, eds., *Problem Solving Strategies and Interventions for Men in Conflict.* Alexandria, VA: American Association for Counseling and Development, 1990. This excellent collection of articles for therapists includes "Divorce: Are Men at Risk?", "Gay and Bisexual Men: Developing a Healthy Identity," "Exploring the Macho Mystique: Counseling Latino Men," and "Helping Men Become More Emotionally Expressive: A Ten Week Program." Extensive bibliography of articles on men's issues up until the mid-1980s.

VII
RESOURCES

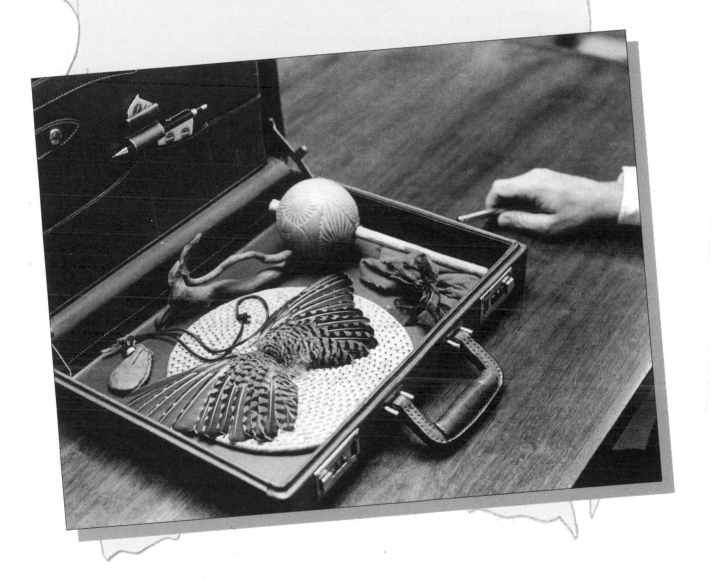

Now What?

●

THE PURPOSE of this book is to whet men's appetites. Reading between the lines of these stories, you doubtless sensed and perhaps envied the aliveness and settled masculinity of many of the contributors. You may be wondering, "How can I get me a piece of this?" The Resource Directory that follows should go a long way toward answering that question.

The ease with which you can slide into a "premade" men's group depends on geographical luck. Some areas, such as greater Washington, D.C., have more subgroups and spin-offs than they can keep track of. Other cities have no apparent activity. Check the list of Men's Councils and Centers in the Directory, or contact the North American Confederation of Men's Councils (202) 675-6325, because new councils are forming every week. Most guys, like the authors in section 2, are going to have to bite the bullet and organize something themselves. There's no sense in feeling forlorn. Even in men's-movement hotbeds, most existing support groups do not accept new members, and so recent "converts" in those areas have to start from scratch.

Talk about reinventing the wheel! Each little community of men finds itself having to reinvent the men's circle. There's no one right way, no set of franchise rules to follow. Each region has its own differing needs for safety and for challenge.

A wise first step in any venture is to research it as thoroughly as possible. The men's movement depends heavily on the study of books and audio- and videotapes. This renaissance of interest in literature, spirituality, and psychology signals that reading and writing are no longer thought of as "unmanly" pastimes. Advance copies of hot new books are passed around like girlie magazines in a boys' dorm.

One important contribution that individual men or men's groups can make is to see to it that the better men's books find their way into bookstores and public libraries. Gordon Clay of the National Men's Resource Center (P.O. Box 800-WS, San Anselmo, California 94979) has done a tremendous service by preparing a kit for bookstore owners, including a letter explaining the value of a Men's Studies section and a suggested list of titles.

It is also vital to subscribe to local and national men's movement periodicals. Consult the list of men's publications in the Resource Directory that follows. If there is a magazine or paper for your region, sign up; if one isn't listed, that doesn't necessarily mean that one doesn't exist in your area. There are scores of limited-scope irregular newsletters, published by the men's councils and centers, that we haven't listed under periodicals. They can be obtained by contacting virtually any of the councils and centers, which are listed in a separate section. These newsletters consist primarily of schedules of upcoming local men's events and the minutes of recent meetings, with a few poems.

The calendar pages of *Wingspan* (the paper) are generally agreed to provide the best overview of what is going on in the men's movement in North America. But even they are designed to "raise consciousness about the scope of men's work across the continent rather to be a comprehensive listing." Study current and back issues of *Wingspan* to locate some event that is scheduled to occur or has occurred in your state. Contact the organizer, and he will likely be able to put you in touch with other men's event organizers, perhaps closer to your home base.

The Resource Directory also lists book and tape retailers. Most of these companies offer free and very informative catalogs to help you decide whether you want a videotape to introduce you to drumming techniques or a collection of poems by Rumi. Buy books or tapes by the writers whose contributions to this book spoke to you most strongly. Split the expenses with other guys who are also mulling the idea of forming a men's group.

There soon comes a point when reading books and listening to tapes is not enough. You will most likely have to spend money and precious vacation time to travel by car pool or plane to some other part of the country to see what a men's retreat or gathering feels like. Men's periodicals routine-

ly run reports on their events, and *Wingspan* profiles workshops from two or three states in each issue. Get over any inhibitions about calling perfect strangers listed in these publications. That's what their phone numbers are in there for. Get a feel for any men's event that intrigues you by talking personally with someone who attended the event before or by calling the man who is running the show. Have the courage to ask those "stupid" questions.

Usually, it only takes one intense retreat like the New Warrior Training Adventure Weekend or a week among the redwoods in Mendocino, California, for a man to become passionate about the special kind of society that prevails at these gatherings. He will ache for it when he gets back home and will go to extraordinary lengths to recapture it and share it with his friends.

Fortunately, there's a lot of support for those who want to adapt or re-create an event they have experienced. There are two excellent handbooks for those who wish to assemble a small weekly or biweekly support group. Bill Kauth's *A Circle of Men* (St. Martin's Press, 1992) is the more comprehensive; Wayne Leibman's *Tending the Fire: The Ritual Men's Group* (Ally Press, 1991) has a

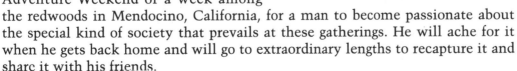

NOW WHAT?

stronger mythopoetic bent. Gordon Clay of the National Men's Resource Center (P.O. Box 800-WS, San Anselmo, CA 94979) offers a guide to books and pamphlets on men's support groups.

The organizers of seasonal retreats or annual gatherings are usually very willing to share schedules, menus, and organizational advice with those who wish to imitate the event. Some model men's retreat organizers, such as Mainely Men, go even further by lending seed money and by sending some of their seasoned staffers as on-site consultants to the first spin-off event. Other groups, such as the Mid-South Men's Council, have an impressive Mission Statement and packets of other materials which they are glad to share with men forming new councils.

Wingspan™ sponsors an annual retreat for men's group leaders from all over the world to exchange ideas on how to conduct men's events. It's a wonderful opportunity for men determined to start a men's community in their city to meet veteran organizers and consider whether they might want to bring these veterans in as consultants or as presenters to stir up interest back home.

Tom Daly, Ph.D., Keith Fairmount, and Jeffrey Duvall, who make up the Men's Council Project, headquartered in Boulder, Colorado, travel around North America helping men form men's councils, create male initiations, and transmit other rituals.

Some church officials look askance at the men's movement, equating its interest in Native American ceremonies and neoprimitivism with paganism and satanism. Other Christian leaders, however, are producing books and videotapes that link Jungian psychology and Native American traditions with mainstream Christianity. These materials are intended to be used by church-sponsored men's groups. (See the bibliography of books on men's spirituality on page 183.)

The increasing number of all-male 12-step programs fill many men's need to be in a men-only discussion group. Contact the national headquarters of Alcoholics Anonymous, Overeaters Anonymous, Gamblers Anonymous, Survivors of Incest Anonymous, and the rest for meeting times and places in your area.

The men's movement is capturing the interest of big business. Publishers are rushing manuscripts of books into print. Therapists are suddenly advertising that they specialize in treating men and opening clinics that cater to male clients. The cost of some retreats is climbing higher and higher. Men's councils are staggered by the high fees that big-name presenters command.

Many men are disappointed at what they see as the runaway commercialism and wish that this material could be made available to every man for free. Others look at the cost of, say, a tape deck, a new car, or six months of therapy, and decide that the experience of a pricey men's event is worth it. But just because something's on the market doesn't mean that you have to buy it. The movement can remain as pristine as it wants to.

Men's organizations are evolving by continuing the cycle of reading new authors, investigating new workshops and new presenters, and customizing their formats and rituals.

Study the Resource Directory and go to it! ✒

RESOURCE DIRECTORY

THE FOLLOWING list contains addresses and/or phone numbers of contact persons for a variety of men's councils and men's centers across the country. Because groups are forming and disbanding on a weekly basis, we cannot pretend that this list is currently accurate or comprehensive. Those listings marked by an asterisk (*) are for-profit, professionally run counseling centers. ✒

SELECTED MEN'S CENTERS AND COUNCILS

*Alachua Men's Center
3601 SW Second Avenue
Suite V
Gainesville, FL 32607
904-335-4004

Arlington Men's Council
3102 Viscount Court
Annandale, VA 22003
Flemming Behrand
703-971-9320
Newsletter: *The Seventh Direction*

*Austin Men's Center
1611 West 6th Street
Austin, TX 78703
512-477-9595
Newsletter: *Man!*

Baltimore Men's Council
612 Overbrook Road
Baltimore, MD 21212
Tom Casciero
301-377-0041

[Boulder] Men's Council
P.O. Box 385
Boulder, CO 80306

Dallas Men's Center
8111 L.B.J. Freeway Suite 665
Dallas, TX 75251
Richard Carter, Ph.D.
214-234-6136 or 214-644-3691

Fairfax Men's Council
1809 Baldwin Drive
McLean, VA 22101
Chuck Zelonis
703-471-0492
Newsletter: *The Menbrane*

Falls Church Men's Council
3132 Colchester Brook Lane
Fairfax, VA 22031
Randy Simmons
703-280-5066

Frederick Area Men's Council
Hillcrest Family Center
93 South McCain Drive
Frederick, MD 21701
Duane Voitel
301-831-0203
Newsletter: *The Talking Stick*

Gaithersburg Men's Council
12409 Keenland Place
Gaithersburg, MD 20878
Tom Golden
301-948-4692
Newsletter: *The Sage*

Gathering Place
1828 Mershon
Ann Arbor, MI 48105
Nick Meima
313-769-0268

Indiana Men's Council
5002 Central Avenue
Indianapolis, IN 46205
Tim Laughter
317-283-8701
Newsletter: *Gathering Information*

Inland Northwest
Men's Evolvement Network
P.O. Box 132
Spokane, WA 99210

*Los Angeles Men's Center
9012 Burton Way
Beverly Hills, CA 90212
Stephen Johnson, Ph.D.
213-276-9598

Mainely Men
P.O. Box 278
Stillwater, ME 04489–0278

Men Alive
P.O. Box 823
Burlington, VT 05402
802-658-2453

Men From the Heart
201 Westport Road
Kansas City, MO 64111
913-262-5032

*Men's Center Foundation
2931 Shattuck Avenue
Berkeley, CA 94705

Men's Center of Raleigh and Wake County
723 West Johnson Street
P.O. Box 6155
Raleigh, NC 27628
919-832-0509

Men's Center of San Diego
103 Highway 101, Suite 256
Encinitas, CA 92024
George Wolford

Men's Council of the Houston Area
P.O. Box 980818
Houston, TX 77098
David Spaw
713-862-3002

Men's Council of Washington
2114 Belvedere Boulevard, #6
Silver Springs, MD 20902
Doug Giauque
301-593-8182
Newsletter: *The Drum*

Men's Gathering Place
1208 Executive Drive West
Richardson, TX 75081
Larry Kevin
214-234-6136

Men's Resource Connection
24 South Prospect Street
Amherst, MA 01002
413-253-9887
Newsletter: *Valley Men's Newsletter*

Men's Resource—Project Phoenix
P.O. Box 331296
Corpus Christi, TX 78463
Marshall Hardy
512-887-8290

Men's Wisdom Council
14538 Warwick Street
Detroit, MI 48223
Dick Halloran
313-965-3860

Mid-South Men's Council
6001 Knight Arnold Road
Memphis, TN 38115
Bill Hedzel
901-795-7387
  or
3200 Medora Cove
Memphis, TN 38118
Ralph Chumbley
901-362-3941

Minnesota Men's Council
1901 SE University Avenue
(U of M YMCA)
Minneapolis, MN 55414
612-333-5857
Newsletter: *Man Alive!*

Northern Shenandoah Valley Men's Council
707 South Washington Street
Winchester, VA 22601
Jack Bellingham
703-667-6954

Oakland Men's Project
440 Grand Avenue, Suite 320
Oakland, CA 94610
Charles Jones
510-835-2433

Omaha Men's Council
5550 Mason
Omaha, NE 68106
Steve Abraham
402-553-5976

*Phoenix Center for Men
3620 Long Beach Boulevard
Suite C-1
Long Beach, CA 90807

Richmond Area Men's Council
P.O. Box 35613
Richmond, VA 23235
Dick Leatherman
804-320-2415
Newsletter: *Connections*

*Rocky Mountain Men's Center
P.O. Box 6274
Boulder, CO 80306

Santa Fe Men's Center
P.O. Box 653
Santa Fe, NM 87504
505-982-5654

Seattle Men's Evolving Network
602 West Howe Street
Seattle, WA 98119
206-285-4356
or, Robert Carlson 206-454-1787

*Texas Men's Institute
8012 Shinoak Drive
San Antonio, TX 78233
512-945-9112

Tidewater Men's Council
1465 Lake James Drive
Virginia Beach, VA 23464
David Grulke
804-623-1721
Newsletter: *Tidewater Men's Council Men's Center Newsletter*

Tulsa Brotherhood Lodges
701 South Cincinnati
Tulsa, OK 74103
Newsletter: *Brotherhood*

Twin Cities Men's Center
3255 Hennepin Avenue South
Suite 55
Minneapolis, MN 55408
612-822-5892
Newsletter: *Men Talk*

West Michigan Men's Enrichment Center
357 Covell Road Northwest
Grand Rapids, MI 49504
William B. Beidler
616-452-9926

West Palm Beach Men's Council
Jayson Trussel
443 Wilder Street
West Palm Beach, FL 33405
407-533-0987

MEN'S MOVEMENT PUBLICATIONS
Periodicals with At Least Some Mythopoetic Content

*(Subscription price often includes membership dues in an organization.
Many publications have back issues with special themes available for purchase.)*

Dragonsmoke
Ally Press Center
525 Orleans Street
St. Paul, MN 55107
800-729-3002

- Quarterly from Ally Press Center Book Club reviewing Ally Press books and other myth and poetry releases.

Icarus Review
McOne Press
P. O. Box 50174
Austin, TX 78763
$8/year; published
semiannually

- Fledgling men's literary magazine with emphasis on poetry and fiction.

Inroads: Men Creativity Soul
P. O. Box 14944
University Station
Minneapolis, MN 55414
$7.50/year

- Semiannual somewhat scholarly journal featuring interviews, poetry, art critiques from a strong mythic and male-positive perspective. Inspired by the work of Robert Bly, James Hillman, Michael Meade, and Joseph Campbell.

Journeymen
513 Chester Turnpike
Candia, NH 03034
603-483-8029
$18/quarterly

- Poetry, book reviews, interviews with national men's movement figures.
  (Not allied with any one branch of the movement.)

*Man!: Men's Issues,
    Relationships & Recovery*
Austin Men's Center
1611 West Sixth Street
Austin, TX 78703
$11/year
414-477-9595

- Glossy quarterly blends health, addiction, and recovery pieces with mythopoetic pieces. Has featured reprints of articles by big names in the movement. Texas-based periodical with national ambitions.

*Man, Alive!: New Mexico's
    Journal of Men's Wellness*
Network Press
P. O. Box 40300
Albuquerque, NM 87196
503-255-4944

- Quarterly "journal of sharing, of men talking openly and candidly with other men about the problems and joys of being male." Poetry, reflective essays and memoirs.

WINGSPAN
INSIDE THE MEN'S
MOVEMENT

Men's Council Journal
Box 385
Boulder, CO 80306

- Quarterly with descriptions of council ceremonies, personal accounts, photo and poetry layouts. Lively letters section. Strong mythopoetic content.

Men Talk
3255 South Hennepin Avenue
Suite #55
Minneapollis, MN 55408
612-822-5892
$14/year

- Official and informal quarterly of the Twin Cities Men's Center. Prints articles from diverse points of view. Local resource/events listings suggest Twin Cities area provides the healthiest environment for men's personal growth work.

MENTOR: The Oregon Resource for MEN
P. O. Box 10863
Portland, OR 97211
503-621-3612
Contribution
$20/year out-of-state

- Five times a year. Interviews, poetry, book reviews, but largely a calendar and resource list.

Redwood Men's Center Re-Source
705 College Avenue
Santa Rosa, CA 95404
$6/year

- Regional men's quarterly with absorbing, intelligent articles on archetypal psychology.

The Talking Stick: A Newsletter About Men
182 Thomas Jefferson Drive
#200
Frederick, MD 21701
301-829-2460
Contribution

- Quarterly with poetry, interviews, short tape and book reviews, essays. "Happy to print newcomers."

Thunder Stick
3392 West 34th Avenue
Vancouver, British Columbia
V6N 2K6
Canada
604-290-9988

- Organ of the Vancouver Men's Evolvement Network. Articles on mythology, ecomasculinity, traditional peoples. Calendar of Canadian men's events.

Wingspan: Journal of the Male Spirit
P.O. Box 23550
Brightmoor Station,
Detroit, MI 48223
313-273-4330

- Largest-circulation publication in the men's movement, with extensive national calendar of events, interviews with movement leaders, and a lively mix of articles.

Brother
1042 Greenfield Avenue #1
Los Angeles, CA 90025
Eds: Bob Baugher,
    Mike Dittmer

• Occasional newsletter of NOMAS, the National Organization of Men Against Sexism (formerly NOCM, National Organization for Changing Men), a profeminist, gay-affirmative group. Includes reports on task groups on homophobia, men's studies, fathers, pornography.

Changing Men
306 Brooks Street
Madison, WI 53715
$16 for 4 issues

• Appears twice a year. Slickest of men's magazines. Profeminist, gay affirmative. Sharply critical of the patriarchy, men's violence, etc. Poetry. Affiliated with NOMAS.

Inside Men's Lives
MAS Medium
P. O. Box 800-WS
San Anselmo, CA 94979-0882
$10/year
Ed: Gordon Clay

• In 250 words or less, "men share their personal stories of the hurt, sadness, and pain in their lives and how they dealt with it."

Journal of Men's Studies
P. O. Box 32
Harriman, TN 37748
Ed: Jim Doyle
615-369-3442
$30/year individuals
$45/year institutions

• Scholarly quarterly documenting research done in men's studies. Now publishing original articles and theme issues with guest editors. Issue themes: black men, men's spirituality. Academic book reviews, doctoral thesis abstracts, extensive bibliographies, etc. International in scope. New venture by former, longtime editor of *Men's Studies Review*.

The Liberator
Route 6
17854 Lyons Street
Forest Lake, MN 55025
Ed: Richard Doyle
$18/year

• Monthly newsletter on "commonsense male perspective on family and other gender issues." This men's/fathers' rights publication has succeeded the now-defunct *Legal Beagle*. Sometimes hot-temperedly critical of feminists.

Men's Advocate
12819 SE 38th Street #237
Bellevue, WA 98006
Ed: Eugene Hopp

• Newsletter of the Special Interest Group of MENSA. Men's rights orientation.

National Men's Resource Calendar
P. O. Box 800-WS
San Anselmo, CA 94979
415-453-2839
Ed: Gordon Clay

• "Working to End Men's Isolation Since 1985," calendar list of men's events, support groups, and services in the San Francisco Bay area. Editorial page, mini–book reviews, national men's publications directory.

NetWORK
223 15th Street, SE
Washington, DC 20003
202-FATHERS
$35/year

- Quarterly newsletter of the National Congress of Men, an umbrella group for fathers' and men's rights. Responsible, careful about statistics. Also NCM annual directory of fathers'/men's rights groups across the United States. $8 from 1241 E. Chestnut #D, Santa Ana, CA 92701.

RFD: A Country Journal for Gay Men Everywhere
P. O. Box 68
Liberty, TN 37095
615-536-5176
Ed: Short Mountain Collective
$18/year ($25/first class)

- Quarterly whose premise is that gay men have a special spiritual connection with the earth. Poetry, fiction, gardening, cooking, "Brothers behind Bars."

Transitions
P. O. Box 129
Manhasset, NY 11030
516-482-6378
Eds: Francis Baumli,
    Tom Preston
$30/year

- Bimonthly publication of the (National) Coalition of Free Men. Promotes "awareness of how gender-based roles limit men legally, socially, psychologically, and emotionally." Refutes feminists' blaming of males for society's woes.

Among those men's periodicals that have ceased publication are *Axis* (formerly *Sun/Father*), *Men's Journal*, *Men's News*, *m/r report*, and *Nurturing News*. Fathers' publications seem to have particularly short publication histories. Someone makes a superhuman effort to get the first issue out and then there is not enough support or money to keep the periodical going.

Related Publications of Interest

Parabola: Myth and the Quest for Meaning
656 Broadway
New York, NY 10012-9824
$20/year

- High-quality magazine published by the Society for the Study of Myth and Tradition with articles by top names in the study of myth and faith. Each issue centers on a theme. Back issues available for $7 each include the Hero (1:1); Initiation (1:3); Rites of Passage (1:4); the Trickster (4:2); Animals (8:2); the Knight and the Hermit (12:1); Addiction (12:3).

Shaman's Drum
Cross-Cultural Shamanism
271500 Schow Road
Willis, CA 95490
$15/year

- Glossy quarterly "journal of experiential shamanism," native medicineways, transpersonal healing, ecstatic spirituality, and caretaking of Earth. Includes regional calendars, resource directory, information on drums.

BIBLIOGRAPHIES

Men's Issues: A Bibliography (1987)
American Association of Counseling and Development Committee on Men.

- Hundreds of citations of articles from psychological and counseling journals, dissertation abstracts, books. Chapters include: Changing Roles of Men; Burnout and Stress; Fathering; Men's Groups; Mentoring Younger Males; Mother/Son Relationships; Working; Intimacy and Friendship; Counseling and Sex Roles; Stereotypes; Divorce; Homosexuality; Power; Self-nurturance. Most easily available in the appendix to *Problem Solving Strategies and Interventions for Men in Conflict*, edited by Dwight Moore and Fred Leafgren. AACD, 5999 Stevenson Avenue, Alexandria, VA 22304.

Men's Studies (1985)
Eugene August
Libraries Unlimited
P. O. Box 263
Littleton, CO 80160

- Some 591 fully annotated entries arranged in topical chapters: Bibliographies; Anthologies; Men's Liberation; Men's Rights; Divorce and Custody; Military/Draft; Health; Violence by and against Men; Prisons; Women and Men; Gender and Sex Roles; Psychology; Sexuality; Homosexuality; Expectant, Divorced, and Single Fathers; Single Men; Midlife Transitions; Men in Literature; Images of Men; Minorities; Religion; and Humor. Fully indexed and cross-referenced. Hardback.

Note: August is updating *Men's Studies* for a second edition, which will be twice the size of the original and will be published in 1993. Unfortunately, the first edition is officially out of print. Look for copies in secondhand bookstores. Get individuals who have a copy to donate it to the local council or library.

BOOK AND TAPE SOURCES

Ally Press Center
525 Orleans Street
St. Paul, MN 55107
800-729-3002

- Mail order service for books and cassettes of Robert Bly's poetry, translations, essays, lectures. Also anthologies of other poetry, videotapes. Ally's catalog-newsletter *Dragonsmoke* contains international speaking schedule for Bly, Meade, Hillman, Moore, etc. The proper pronunciation of Ally is not as in bowling alley, but as friend-ally.

Bioenergetics Press
P. O. Box 9141
Madison, WI 53715
608-255-4028

- Mail order service for hard to find books on men's rights.

EarthMen Resources
P.O. Box 1034
Evanston, IL 60204

- Source of information about books, audio- and video-tapes, and appearances by Robert Moore and Douglas Gillette.

Interworld Music
482 Hickory Street
San Francisco, CA 94102
415-864-5675

- Free catalog "The Essence of Percussion." Videos, books, recordings, etc. on drumming

Limbus
Jim Alkire
P. O. Box 364
Vashon, WA 98070
206-463-9387

- Cofounded by Michael Meade. Source of tapes, books, and Meade's appearance schedule.

Sounds True
1825 Pearl Street
Dept CM91
Boulder, CO 80302
800-333-8185, ext. 275

- Free catalog of audiotapes related to the men's movement and drumming plus interviews.

Spring Publications
P.O. Box 222069
Dallas, TX 75222
214-943-4093

- Publisher of works by James Hillman and other archetypal psychologists.

Other Resources

American Men's Studies
    Association
Sam Femiano
22 East Street
Northampton, MA 01060
413-584-8903

- Coordination of men's studies and gender studies programs in universities. Interdisciplinary organization devoted to promoting feminist scholarship and understanding of men's issues.

Archon Institute
3700 Massachusetts Avenue,
    Suite 121
Washington, DC 20016
Joseph Palmour
202-342-7710

- Consulting around mentoring, leadership, and the rhetoric of the men's movement.
  Annual membership fee is $25/individual and $15/student.

Center for Men's Studies
Sam Julty
2490 Channing Way
Berkeley, CA 94704
510-549-0537

- Among other projects, publishes a directory of men's organizations and periodicals.

Changing Men Collection
Peter Berg
Head of Special Collections
Michigan State University
East Lansing , MI 48824-1048
517-355-3770

- Research collection focusing largely on the National Organization for Changing Men and its annual Men and Masculinity conferences. Also contains 300 individual files with newsletters and reports on active and defunct men's organizations from all over the country.

Circumcision Resource Center
P.O. Box 232
Boston, MA 02133
617-523-0088

- Information on hazards of circumcision and on foreskin restoration.

Coalition of Free Men
P. O. Box 129
Manhassett, NY 11030

- National men's rights organization.

Men's Resources Northeast
Barrie Petersen
New Views Educational
   Services
P.O. Box 137
Little Ferry, NJ 07643
201-848-9134

- Semiannual guide to greater New York men's group contacts and events. Fraternity Project seeks past and active fraternity men to work on bringing principles of the men's movement into Greek life.

Menswork Center
1950 Sawtelle Boulevard
Suite 34
Los Angeles, CA 90025
James Sniechowski
213-479-2749

- Resources for tapes, male and female gender reconciliation speakers, media.

Men's Council Project
P. O. Box 17341
Boulder, CO 80301
Tom Daly, Ph.D.
303-444-7797

- Consulting service supporting individual men and men's councils. Leadership training, creating male initiations, forming men's groups. Jeffrey Duvall, associate director (303-444-3473).

MR, Inc. (Men's Rights, Inc.)
Frederic Hayward
P. O. Box 163180
Sacramento, CA 95816
916-484-7333

- "Concerned with sexism and men's problems." Sponsors MR. Mediawatch to protest negative images of men in the media and applaud positive ones. Quick to point out instances of sexism that discriminate against men.

National Organization for Men
   Against Sexism (NOMAS)
54 Mint Street, #300
San Francisco, CA 94103

- Long-standing profeminist, gay-affirmative organization that sponsors yearly Men and Masculinity conferences. Formerly known as the National Organization for Changing Men (NOCM).

NO CIRC
P. O. Box 2512
San Anselmo, CA 94960
818-710-9465

- Anticircumcision information center. Newsletter available for a donation.

North American Confederation of Men's Councils
1921 N. Utah Street
Arlington, VA 22207
Forrest Craver
202-675-6325

- Information clearinghouse and support system/service agency for men's councils all over North America.

O.A.S.I.S. Collective
15 Willoughby Street
Brighton, MA 02135
617-782-7769

- Videotape for rent or purchase. "Stale Roles and Tight Buns," about the stereotyping of men in the media, particularly advertising. "Men and Masculinity: Changing Roles, Changing Lives," a lively documentary of the pro-feminist men's movement.

On the Common Ground
John Guarnaschelli
250 West 57th Street
Suite 1527
New York, NY 10107
212-265-0584

- Monthly drop-in drumming, events with nationally known figures and formation of small men's support groups.

Pangaea Institute for Gender Studies
Box 862
Sebastopol, CA 95473

- Source for articles and male and female leaders for workshops concerning the art of partnership between men and women. Speaking schedule for Aaron Kipnis.

P.L.E.A.
356 W. Zia Road
Sante Fe, NM 87505
505-982-9184

- Combating the widespread problem of male sexual, physical, emotional abuse and neglect. Referrals, resource materials, and speakers.

The Tracking Project
Box 266
Corrales, NM 87048
505-898-6967

- Tracker John Stokes leads workshops for boys and men including "Bringing the Pieces Together: A Native People's Approach to Men's Work." Hawkeye Training is a skills-based summer camp for boys 12–18.

Canadian Men's Contacts

Island Men's Network
35 Cambridge Street
Victoria, British Columbia V8V 4A7
604-383-7664

Toronto Men's Clearinghouse
104 Spencer Avenue
Toronto, Ontario M6K 2J6
416-233-0025

Vancouver Men's Evolvement Network
3392 West 34th Avenue
Vancouver, British Columbia V6N 2K6

PHOTO CREDITS

Bill Abranowicz: 132
Cass Adams: 103, 147, 174, 193, 212
Bud Clarke: (illustrations) 220, 221
Bonita Cohn: 215
Albert Noyes Cook: xvii, 1, 24, 231
Robert Cornett: 140
Dante: 251
Peggy Darnell: 3, 27, 235, 238
B.D. Drums: 210, 211
Gurudarshan: 93
Bohdan Hrynewych: 224, 225
Mark Judelson: 19
Roger Kose: ii, xviii, xxi, 6, 12, 15 (top), 32, 37, 66, 75, 77, 78, 82, 85, 88, 91, 97, 106, 113, 119, 124, 149, 151, 153, 158-159, 162, 164, 181, 190, 194, 195, 196 (both), 197, 198 (both), 199, 201, 204, 205, 229, 249
Doug Lester: 245
Courtesy of Peter Narbonne: 73, 116
William Parker: 170
Courtesy of the United States Government: 187
Courtesy of Yale University Sports Information Department: 40 (both)
Dan Zola: 15 (bottom)

ABOUT THE EDITOR

Bill Tonra

CHRISTOPHER HARDING received his Ph.D. in English from Harvard University in 1976 and has taught college for 10 years. He has been active in the men's movement since 1984 and has led men's workshops and organized conferences and retreats in New England and the Midwest. Since 1987 he has edited *Wingspan™: Journal of the Male Spirit*, the most widely circulated men's movement publication in the world. He is also a video and print journalist, and has written two books, *A Cop's Cop* and *Yale Trivia*.

Wingspan™ welcomes comments from readers about what they found helpful, confusing, or lacking in this book and will use them to improve future editions of this work. Questions, ideas, and suggested contributions may be directed to:

Christopher Harding/*Wingspan*
St. Martin's Press, Inc., Box JTK
175 Fifth Avenue
New York, NY 10010

Readers who would like to receive a free sample issue of *Wingspan*™ should send their request to:

Wingspan
P.O. Box 23550
Brightmoor Station
Detroit, MI 48223